DEVS NOBIS HÆC OTIA FECIT

CITY OF LIVERPOOL
PUBLIC LIBRARIES

NATURAL HISTORY

OF THE LAKE DISTRICT

Natural History of the Lake District

EDITED BY
Canon G. A. K. Hervey
and
J. A. G. Barnes

WITH 8 PLATES IN COLOUR
24 IN BLACK AND WHITE
AND LINE DRAWINGS
IN THE TEXT

FREDERICK WARNE & CO LTD · LONDON
FREDERICK WARNE & CO LTD · NEW YORK

ISBNO 0 7232 1127 2

LIBRARY OF CONGRESS CATALOG CARD NO. 77–114789

Printed in Great Britain by
W & J Mackay & Co Ltd
1501 · 969

CONTENTS

CONTENTS

LIST OF PLATES

FOREWORD

It is a matter of the deepest regret to everyone concerned with the production of this book that its originator and editor, Canon G. A. K. Hervey, did not live to see it in print. He was working on a revision of the text only a few days before his death at Penrith in June, 1967.

The publication of a book on the natural history of the Lake District was a natural outcome of Canon Hervey's lifelong love of this region and his profound concern for the safeguarding of its beauty and the conservation of its wild life. It was his driving energy and persuasive charm that led to the formation of the Lake District Naturalists' Trust in 1962, and as its first chairman he was largely responsible for framing its policy. From the first he emphasised that it was not enough for the Trust to acquire nature reserves and oppose immediate threats to the plant and animal life of the district; he urged that it should also play an active part in education, in its widest sense, so as to develop among residents and visitors to the Lake District a fuller appreciation of the meaning and value of nature conservation. The writing of this book was very closely linked with this wider aim.

No one could be better qualified than he was to produce such a volume. From boyhood he had walked the fells and studied the plants, insects and birds of the Lake District, and he had an exceptional gift for lucid exposition as a lecturer or party-leader in the field. It was characteristic of his modesty that when he planned the outline of the book in collaboration with Mr John Clegg he invited others to write specific sections of it, in spite of the inevitable difficulties of combining the work of different authors into an acceptable unity. But whatever the shortcomings of the book as a whole, Canon Hervey's personal contribution will convey to every reader something of his wide knowledge and infectious enthusiasm for his subject, and for his many friends and acquaintances it will refresh affectionate memories of a fine field naturalist and an outstanding Lakeland personality.

J. A. G. BARNES

ACKNOWLEDGMENTS

The publishers are extremely grateful to the following people for their kind assistance and permission to use material in this book: Mr R. Walker for information on mosses incorporated in Section Two; Mrs G. D. Caldwell for compiling the index; Dr W. E. Frost for information on fish incorporated in Section Three; Mr R. B. Davis for drawings in Figs. 5–16; Mrs B. Finlow for Fig. 19; Dr O. L. Gilbert for Fig. 18; Mrs A. G. Lunn for Map 1 (based on Crown Copyright Geological Survey Map and reproduced by permission of the Controller of H.M. Stationery Office) and Map 2 (based on the Ordance Survey Map with the sanction of the Controller of H.M. Stationery Office, Crown Copyright reserved); Mr. J. R. Parker for Fig. 20; Dr T. T. Macan for Fig. 17; Mr G. V. Berry for photographs reproduced on Plates 3, 5, 11 (*below*) and 12; Mr and Mrs J. B. Bottomley for Plates 22, 23, 26, 27 and 28 (*below*); Mr W. R. Cairns for Plate 29; Mr and Mrs G. D. Caldwell for Plate 9 (*above*), 13 (*below*) and 16; Mr John Clegg for Plates 2 (*above*), 7 (*below*), 10, 13 (*above*), 14, 15, 18, 19 and 20; Mr W. F. Davidson for Plates 1, 8 and 17; Dr Peter Delap for Plates 30 and 31; Mr N. Duerden for Plates 25 (*below*) and 32 (*below*); the Freshwater Biological Association for Plate 2 (*below*); Mr Stanley Jeeves for Plates 4, 6, 7 (*above*), 9 (*below*) and 11 (*above*); Mr H. Kinloch for Plate 25 (*above*); Mr G. Kinns for Plate 32 (*above*); Mr John Markham for Plate 28 (*above*); and Mr G. S. Woods and the Natural History Photographic Agency for Plates 21 and 24.

INTRODUCTION

The Purpose and Plan of This Book

Of the thousands of tourists who every year walk along the summit ridge of Helvellyn only a very small proportion are likely to realise that they are walking within a few hundred yards of magnificent natural rock gardens as great a delight to the eye as they are of interest to the botanist. Few visitors wandering through the woods of the Lake District are aware of the deer, the badgers, the red squirrels and other wild life which may be within a few feet, watching them. The deer of Scotland are far more numerous and more readily seen. The Lake District possesses no wild cat, no ptarmigan; it has far fewer specifically mountain insects. Nowhere in its borders is there anything comparable to the Breadalbane range either in the quantity or variety of its mountain flora; on Ben Lawers if one climbs high enough one can hardly fail to see its richness on all sides. In the Lake District one has to look for special gullies and ledges; but wherever the right conditions occur there is a feast of colour—red, yellow, purple, golden and white—for those who have reasonably good lungs and sureness of foot to reach them.

The fact that its treasures have to be searched for is the attraction of the Lake District. It is very small in area and its mountains are low even by British standards; there are no glaciers, no permanent snow; but it is in its very compactness and the illusion of height given by its steep slopes and precipitous crags that so much of its charm and interest lies. So many different habitats lie in such close proximity to each other, producing a wide variety of flora and fauna, that it is a delight to the naturalist and the observant walker.

It adds enormously to the interest of a walk to know something about the nature and origin of what one is looking at, the steps by which, as far as we can find out, it reached its present state, and where its more interesting features are to be found. That is the reason for writing this book. In no sense is it a comprehensive natural history. Its purpose is to help the interested walker to appreciate the better what he is likely to see in the Lake District and to help him to understand some of the underlying factors which contributed to its formation. Why is it, for example, that when travelling from north to south across the Lake District one notices a sudden change from mountains which in the main have smooth slopes to the rugged crags and precipices in the central area; or why, if one is approaching from the east, one passes across an area of red sandstone and then of limestone before reaching the slate mountains in the centre, and the same again in reverse order as one emerges on the western side? Why do most valleys appear to radiate, like the spokes of a wheel, from a centre in the neighbourhood of Sca Fell? Why is it that seashore plants occur also on the high mountains but not in the area between? And why is there so much similarity between plants of the Lake District mountains and those of the Alps, Wales, Scotland, and the tundra of the Arctic?

We do not know the full answers to these and many similar questions, but in the sections which follow an attempt is made to give a picture of how the rocks came to be laid in the first instance, how they were folded and contorted and finally sculptured by ice and snow and wind into the Lake District we know, with its crags and slopes, torrents and streams, tarns and lakes; how soil formed and the Lake District became clothed with vegetation which has constantly changed and goes on changing today; how it came to be inhabited by animals large and small, including man, and how much man in particular has altered the face of the Lake District and goes on altering it.

Clearly in trying to map out such a process, which has been going on for at least 500 million years, numbers of questions must arise to which no certain answer can possibly be given, and the further back one delves into the past the greater the difficulties. In spite of greatly improved techniques which have developed in recent years and widened our knowledge of what must have happened in the past (the development of pollen analysis is a case in point), we can still at best only make inferences from data which leave vast gaps in the chain of evidence. Nevertheless, despite these inevitable limitations, a definite pattern does emerge in which we can see the present structure of the Lake District and its present inhabitants, including ourselves, as part of a great process of development which is still going on.

The formidable task of presenting the natural history of the Lake District in such a framework has been entrusted to a team of naturalists who share a common love of the Lake District, have tramped its fells and describe what they are familiar with at first hand, and each of whom has made a special study of some section of its life and development. Each individual writer is free in respect of his own subject, but we have discussed each other's drafts and made suggestions, so that in the general presentation the whole team has contributed. We have tried to ensure that each contribution, having been read by other members of the team, is readily understandable by the non-specialist in that subject.

To follow a strictly chronological order in the evolutionary process was not found to be practicable. Quite frequently a particular line of development is pursued, and then we retrace our steps in order to pursue another. The general plan of the book is as follows: we begin in Section I with a consideration of the rocks of which the Lake District is built and how they may have reached their present state through heat and pressure and in particular by the tremendous influence of ice. Section II gives a description of the plant life of the Lake District as a whole, habitat by habitat, from mountain top to the seashore. This includes a probable account of how the pioneers first obtained a footing on the bare rocks and slopes of the mountains, to be replaced in due course by others; of the adaptations that were developed to cope with the severities of life on a mountain top; and of problems of distribution. Section III describes plant and animal life in the lakes, tarns and streams of the Lake District. The following section, dealing with the terrestrial invertebrates, is subdivided under the headings of molluscs, insects and Arachnida, and the final section on vertebrates is similarly divided into three parts, covering the reptiles and amphibians, the birds and the mammals of our region.

It will be recognised that in most cases only a very small selection of all the species inhabiting the Lake District can be mentioned, and some groups have been omitted altogether. In the main we have picked out species either because they are likely to be noticed by the ordinary walker, or because they are of special interest.

We decided that the best definition of 'Lake District' for our purpose was that area lying within the boundaries of the Lake District National Park. To this we have adhered strictly except where some feature of adjacent areas contributes to a better understanding of the Park itself.

The natural history of the Lake District is in a constant state of change, both geologically and biologically, partly as a result of natural causes and also from the action of man. Gradually we are acquiring knowledge about the significance and probable result of these changes. It is important that we should apply this knowledge to the changes being proposed to satisfy the ever-increasing needs and whims of man. The Lake District with its wild life is a great national heritage; it is the duty and privilege of all those who come to the Lake District for enjoyment to obtain a fuller understanding of its nature, and to use their influence to ensure that it is handed on to our descendants in a form which they too can appreciate.

Habitats and Communities

Probably the greatest difference between the field naturalist of today and his predecessor of a hundred years ago is that today he has a much greater interest in plant and animal communities and in how they are related to their physical environment and to each other. Thus the emphasis has shifted from the individual, and this wider approach is known as ecology —the science of living together. (The word is derived from the Greek for household. It occurs again in ecumenical, the practice of living together as one household, and in economy, the law of the household.) One of the field naturalist's aims, therefore, is to find out what factors govern the composition and distribution of the various communities, and so understand more of their inter-relationships—in fact, to study how they live together as a 'household' and what are the laws governing it.

As might be expected in an area which ranges from mountain tops to sea level there are a great number of different kinds of habitat in the Lake District, but the most exciting vegetation of the area for most people is that which occurs on the mountains themselves. With the exception of the Pennines and Cheviots, which are of different formation, this is the only truly mountainous area in England. Consequently the mountain plants are of particular interest, and more space is given here to these than to the lowland communities which have more in common with the rest of the country.

The nature of a community is determined very largely by three factors: soil; climate (in which altitude plays a considerable part); and the interaction between the plants and animals within the community. The habitat together with the community of plants and animals which it supports form a biological unit known as an ecosystem. It used to be thought that such communities had sharply defined boundaries, but now many people consider that they are merging and may overlap.

PLATE 1 Buttermere and Crummock Water from below Haystacks *Valley as left after severe erosion by its glacier. Unproductive ribbon lakes occupy part of valley floor*

Wastwater and Great Gable   *Borrowdale Volcanic scenery. Trough-like glaciated valley with unproductive lake*

PLATE 2   Windermere, middle reach   *Showing The Ferry House in foreground and houses along lake shore. Shallows marked by islands which are the tops of roches moutonnées*

les Tarn and
rp Edge,
dleback
*rie with tarn
ounded by
aine; arête
the right*

ATE 3

Head of Ullswater   *Delta of late- and post-glacial Glenridding Beck in foreground
and of Goldrill Beck beyond*

PLATE 4   Dore Head Screes, Mosedale   *Screes produced by frost-shattering of crags*

Soil The composition of the soil naturally depends largely on the nature of the rock which underlies it, but it can be influenced by materials, especially lime, carried in by water from elsewhere.

One important process concerned in the development of the soil in an area of heavy rainfall such as the Lake District is leaching. This consists of the removal from the surface soil, by water soaking through it, of nutrients in solution together with fine particles. In this way the soil becomes largely depleted of plant foods, including lime (calcium carbonate). In consequence the soil becomes acid (i.e. lime-deficient), and suitable for only a small number of rather specialised plants.

From a naturalist's point of view one of the most important factors in the composition of the soil is, in fact, whether or not it is rich in lime. Where it is rich, as on limestone, it tends to support a very varied and attractive flora. But apart from the ring of Carboniferous limestone referred to in Geology and Terrain (page 15), the narrow strip of Coniston limestone which cuts across the Lake District roughly ENE.–WSW. and the alluvium of the valleys, by far the greater part of the Lake District is covered by acid soils which provide but poor nourishment for the majority of plants. This is a major factor in the predominance of coarse grass and heather moorlands and peat bogs, and in general of plants of a hardy type capable of existing on a poor diet. Cotton-grass, sedges, heaths etc, cover large areas of the Lake District, in strong contrast to the luxuriance and varied dominants of the limestone areas to the south and east. The plant and animal life associated with these extensive areas of poor soil are described in their appropriate place in the sections which follow.

But there are exceptions within the Lake District to these conditions. Where the central Borrowdale Volcanic rocks are exposed there occur locally lime-rich soils (see also page 41). It is here, high up on rock ledges, in crevices, and especially on the steep, eroding sides of gills that the rich mountain flora is to be found. Furthermore the lime gets washed down the slopes or issues in springs, and fans out into rich flushes where again the lime-dependent plants occur, often in abundance.

Where the National Park impinges on the coast, soils occur which are rich in salt. These carry a specialised flora tolerant of a high salt content. The most extensive saline soils are to be found on the fore dunes and estuarine salt-marshes which are only sparsely represented within the boundaries of the Park.

Climate The chief factors which influence the building up of a community of plants and animals are rain, temperature and wind. The average rainfall, especially in the mountain areas, is very high, but it rapidly decreases as the distance from the mountains increases. For instance, the average annual rainfall in the Eden Valley is about thirty inches (76 centimetres). Keswick, twenty-five miles (40 kilometres) to the west, has an annual rainfall of about sixty inches (152 centimetres). Seathwaite nine miles (14 kilometres) away at the head of Borrowdale, has an average of 120 inches (305 centimetres). Over 200 inches (508 centimetres) is recorded not far from the summit of Helvellyn. All these figures vary greatly from year to year.

The temperature of the area as a whole is generally equable, but this is combined with very severe conditions on the mountains in winter. The Lake District rarely has a complete snow cover for long, but on the other hand its summers are rarely very hot. As no growth can take place below a certain critical temperature, and severe conditions may begin in the autumn and continue well into the spring, the growing period for plants is very restricted. Only hardy plants and animals can survive under these conditions and a high degree of specialisation is required.

The force of the wind, like the rainfall, increases with altitude. The altitude even of the central area is not very great by Alpine standards but it is quite high enough to produce severe conditions, including considerable blizzards, in winter. A special wind condition of the north-west is the bitingly cold Helm wind. This is much less conspicuous in the Lake District than in, say, the Eden Valley, but it is still significant. It is due to the combination of a strong, persistent east wind with the north–south lie of the Pennines. The spectacular cloud formation which gives it its name is not infrequently seen from Keswick through the gap between Helvellyn and Blencathra (Saddleback).

How these factors affect the development of a community is described in Section II (page 37).

Competition and Interaction A community will usually arise wherever there is a bare space suitable for colonisation. Originally, after the melting of the ice of the last glaciation, the whole area of the Lake District was in this state. Today on a small scale bare patches may occur from a variety of happenings. There may be a landslide laying bare many square yards of soil; or a torrent in spate may cut a new channel. Such events occur most readily on the unstable glaciated slopes of the high mountains, as described on page 30. Apart, however, from any physical disturbance the community once formed will change according to a regular sequence related to soil and climate, and, if left to itself, will establish a more or less stable equilibrium or 'climax'.

In the first place the plants and animals alter the soil itself, particularly by accelerating the disintegration of the solid rock and by the creation of humus, and, in the case of the animals, by producing manure. Secondly, competitors arrive from outside the original community. Seeds may be brought in by wind, or in bird droppings, or clinging to the coats of mammals. These begin to compete with the earlier inhabitants for the necessities of life. Sometimes the invader is quickly crowded out, but sometimes it proves as well adapted to the now altered conditions as the original pioneers, or even better. In this case the newcomer will establish itself.

Sometimes these newcomers are aliens. In the Lake District in recent years the little New Zealand Willow-herb (*Epilobium nerterioides*), whose seeds, like those of its larger relatives, are wind-borne, has established itself up most of the becks and is rapidly spreading beyond them to damp places generally. Another colonist, in this case from the Himalayas, the large purple and white balsam known as Policeman's Helmet (*Impatiens glandulifera*) has also in recent years spread along many of our rivers and canals, completely altering their appearance. It was established in a few restricted sites in the Lake District in the late 1930s—a small colony near Glenridding, another at Rydal and a more extensive colony along the river Kent—but only in the sixties has it begun to spread rapidly and it is already a menace to other riverside plants. Its method of seed dispersal, like all balsams, of hurling its seeds some distance when the ripe seed-pod is touched, helps it to spread, but the reason for the sudden impetus is not clear. Another example on the outskirts of the Lake District is the hybrid cordgrass, *Spartina townsendii,* which is now well established in Morecambe Bay. It appeared first in Britain in Southampton Water and was later specially cultivated at Littlehampton in Sussex for the purpose of reclaiming mudflats and silted creeks.

This process is going on all the time. Once an invader gains a foothold acute competition with the earlier settlers begins. Ultimately, however, a climax is reached, after which little further change is likely to occur in the absence of any drastic outside influence, such as by man. We shall return to this in Section II, page 41.

All members of a community react on each other to a greater or lesser degree. Sometimes this takes the form of competition, but in a well-balanced community a satisfactory adjustment can be reached. A good illustration of how the members of a plant community can accommodate themselves to each other's needs is a typical woodland where all the members need sunlight, but not all to the same degree, and in the main at different times of year. As a result the woodland is built up, as it were, into four storeys. At the highest level is the canopy of the forest trees, oaks, ashes etc., which come into full foliage in the summer; beneath are small trees and shrubs which are either evergreen or flower earlier, such as holly, rowan and hazel; then come the tall herbs such as foxgloves and Spurge Laurel; and finally the ground level where snowdrops, primroses, wood anemones and bluebells develop and flower well before the full canopy overhead has developed sufficiently to cut off the sunshine, and where mosses find the sheltered, humid conditions which satisfy their needs. The boundaries are far from being clear cut, but definite accommodation has been reached between species.

In the process of accommodation certain plants tend to predominate in each habitat. These are called dominants and to a large extent they determine the conditions of life for the other plants and animals in the community. Sometimes there is only one dominant, sometimes two or even more, in which case they are called co-dominants.

As we shall see, left to themselves the lower slopes of the Lake District become covered with woodland, but as soon as man, perhaps 5000 years ago, began to make clearances in the forest for habitation (called 'thwaites' by the Norse who arrived about the tenth century A.D.), and later introduced sheep in a large way to graze the uplands, and drained the valley bottoms for cultivation, the whole face of the countryside was changed and a new equilibrium had to be sought. In the process of readjustment many of the earlier plants perished or became extremely rare. Equally the loss of the woodlands made a vast difference to the animal inhabitants. In much more recent times man has planted alien conifers which not only alter the appearance of the countryside, but owing to the deep shade they create make any development of undergrowth impossible. We shall return to this also in Section II.

Man, however, is not the only creature that upsets the delicately balanced equilibrium and alters the vegetative cover of the land. A change in the invertebrate population can have profound influence; the depredations that can be caused by the larvae of certain insects are described in Section IV page 125. Rabbits have had a tremendous effect on the ground vegetation, and their near-elimination by myxomatosis has set in motion a new set of checks and balances.

Any community we examine today is therefore not likely to be static, but is probably in a state of constant change, working towards an equilibrium which is rarely reached, and liable to be upset at any moment by some further influence from outside. The effect of these various influences on the extremely varied habitats and communities in the Lake District as we see them today is described in the following pages.

G. A. K. Hervey

SECTION ONE

GEOLOGY
AND TERRAIN

MAP 1

GEOLOGY OF THE LAKE DISTRICT

Recent

 New Red Sandstone

 Coal Measures

 Carboniferous Limestone
and
Millstone Grit

 Silurian

 Coniston Limestone

 Borrowdale Volcanic Series

 B Barrow

C Cockermouth

 Skiddaw Slates

K Kendal

M Maryport

 Intrusives

P Penrith

U Ulverston

 Outer boundary of Lower Palaeozoic rocks

Wh Whitehaven

W Workington

 Outcrop of high-quality slate

J.L.

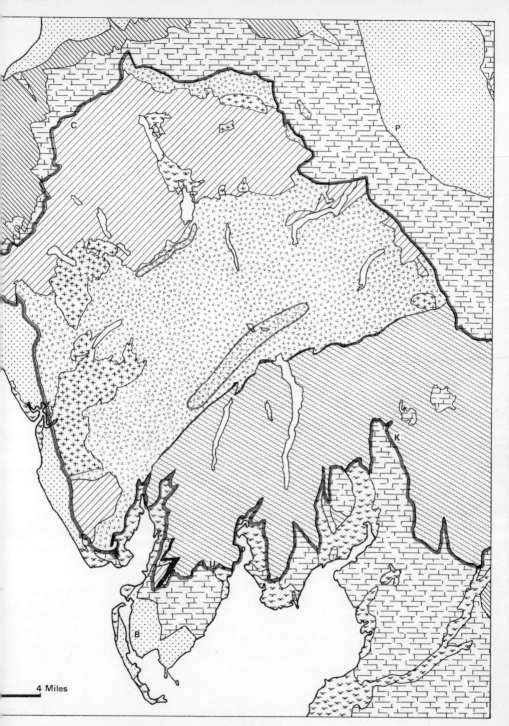

Geology of the Lake District

GEOLOGY AND TERRAIN

by A. G. Lunn

'Who ever travelled along the banks of Loch Lomond,' wrote Wordsworth in his *Guide to the English Lakes*, 'without feeling that a speedier
termination of the long vista of blank water would be acceptable?' No one
would make such a complaint in the Lake District. Within this small area
—just thirty miles (48 kilometres) in diameter, and with its highest mountain reaching only 3210 feet (978 metres)—is concentrated an astonishing
diversity of landscape, where every slope displays individual and intricate
patterns of colour and of relief. It is the purpose of this chapter to show how
geological processes have brought about such a varied landscape—a variety
expressed equally in the diversity of habitat and of wild life.

Packed with variety though the landscape may be, there are patterns to
be discerned. The rocks, the valleys, the lakes, the waterfalls have an
arrangement which is ordered and therefore, presumably, capable of explanation. Map 1, of the distribution of solid rock as it would appear if
loose and recent deposits were stripped away, shows such patterns (between
pages 28 and 29). The map indicates how the rocks inside the blue line—in
fact in the Lake District itself—are arranged in belts running ENE.-WSW.
Around the Lake District the rocks are arranged in a different pattern, this
time in concentric rings one outside the other.

This apparent simplicity of rock distribution belies the great complexity
of local geology. Parts of the Borrowdale Volcanic area have yet to be
mapped in detail, so difficult is it to make sense of the many lava flows and
ash deposits; and even more difficult to sort out are the tightly folded and
contorted strata of the Skiddaw Slates in the north. These central Lake
District rocks are up to 500 million years old and even the youngest of the
solid rocks were formed some 200 million years ago, so that any account of
what was happening in the area between then and the recent glaciations is
based largely on guesswork—there are no rocks to afford direct evidence
of what the Lake District was like during this long period. Unfortunately
it was during the latter part of these 200 million years that rivers, the sea,
the wind and the weather were shaping the present landscape out of the

solid rocks, so that of this long and important phase little is known. For this reason, and because it is the consequences of glaciation and of post-glacial events which have played such an important part in determining the nature and distribution of wildlife habitats, this chapter will concentrate on these very latest episodes in local geological history. Also, for reasons of space and because the information is readily available elsewhere, no description will be given of even earlier geological history—the sequence of formation of the rocks themselves, and the successive disturbances whereby the rocks came to be disposed in the patterns of outcrop shown on Map 1. It is necessary, however, to describe the rock types characteristic of each of the main outcrop zones.

The Lake District

As mentioned on page 13, the rocks inside the blue line of Map 1 belong to groups of strata, the outcrop area of each group being a belt which trends ENE.–WSW. These rocks are geologically old (lower Palaeozoic). Within each belt individual beds of rock, not separately shown on the map, also trend broadly ENE.–WSW. at outcrop.

The Skiddaw Slates occupy the northern Lake District. They consist of alternating beds of dark-coloured slates, shales, mudstones, siltstones and sandstones to a total thickness of at least 6000 feet (1800 metres). Such rocks are formed as a result of the compaction and cementing of debris—mud, silt and sand—swept by rivers into a sea, in this case one which formerly covered the area of the Lake District. Shales are laminated mudstones. Slates are the consequence of pressure exerted on fine-grained rocks such as shales and mudstones due to movements in the earth's crust. Pressure caused all the flaky mineral particles in the rock to lie parallel to one another so that the altered rock now readily splits, or cleaves, between the planes so formed (which need not coincide with that of the original bedding of the rock) and in no other direction. The Skiddaw Slate slates however are not normally suitable for roofing. The strata of this group have been broken and rucked up into tight folds.

The Borrowdale Volcanic Series occupies the central Lake District and is a pile, some 12,000 feet (3600 metres) thick, of volcanic lavas (individual flows reach 100 feet (30 metres) in thickness), tuffs (strata of volcanic ash,

now compacted and hardened) and agglomerates (where the ejected fragments are larger, more than about half an inch (13 millimetres) in diameter).
Some of the finer tuffs have been altered to slate; such is the origin of the
famous green roofing slates which outcrop in limited patches within the
two zones shown on Map 1. Among the lavas are some which are 'flow-
breccias'—they formed solid crusts when still molten below, and then the
crust broke up into angular fragments on further flow, so that the rock,
when it finally solidified, came to resemble a coarse agglomerate. Some
tuffs and agglomerates are 'welded tuffs'—streaky rocks where the fragments were still hot and plastic enough on landing to be compressed into
discs, which on broken edges of rock appear as thin streaks. Like the
Skiddaw Slates these volcanic rocks have been broken (faulted) and warped
by disturbances, but being more rigid have taken up much less folding;
rather have they been thrown into broad arches and sags.

The Coniston Limestone Group, cropping out in a narrow band as
shown on Map 1, is made up of volcanic material, shales and some rather
muddy limestones, the latter consisting largely of the compacted remains
of marine shells.

The Silurian rocks (the name denotes their age) of the southern Lake
District are similar to those of the Skiddaw Slates, but with relatively more
sandstones. The sandstones have suffered less folding than the yielding
Silurian slates, shales and mudstones.

Granite and other 'intrusive' rocks have locally been intruded from below,
as molten magma, into the groups just described. Outcrops of granite are
at Skiddaw, Eskdale and (a variety) Shap. The Skiddaw granite, when it
was emplaced, baked hard the surrounding rocks of the Skiddaw Slates.

The area surrounding the Lake District

Here the very different pattern, of concentric rings of outcrop, is made up,
working from the inside, of the **Carboniferous Limestone** (the term
Carboniferous refers to the geological period when these rocks were
formed) consisting mainly of thick, pure, white limestone beds; the **Millstone Grit** and **Coal Measures** (also of Carboniferous age), made up of
alternating sandstones, shales and coal seams (worked in the west Cumberland coalfield); and the **New Red Sandstone**, a group of red-coloured

conglomerates (compacted pebbles), sandstones and shales. These rocks were not affected by the disturbances which so deranged by folding and faulting the rocks of the central Lake District, but have been lightly warped and tilted, and also faulted, by less intense disturbances.

By the time that the New Red Sandstone rocks were formed, shortly after 200 million years ago, the events—folding, faulting and partial denudation—which were to determine present patterns of rock outcrop, were largely completed. Topographically, however, the Lake District of that time bore no resemblance to that of the present. Final uplift of the land to present altitudes, the erosion of valleys, the sculpturing by erosion of scenic detail—all of this had yet to happen. The main lineaments of present topography were blocked out later during the long period of denudation which preceded the recent glaciations. As already suggested, however, little is known about the processes involved. It was then that the thick, folded and faulted pile of slates, shales, sandstones, limestones, tuffs, lavas and the rest were dissected into isolated uplands, which are now the individual mountain masses. The modern mountains are the remnants of a once more continuous upland. Dissection was accomplished by river erosion; downward incision by rivers, accompanied by down-slope movement into the rivers of loose soil and rock material, produced valleys.

We now come to the pattern that has long exercised the imaginations of geologists and geographers: the radial arrangement of valleys in the Lake District (and of the lakes in the valley floors) about a centre in the vicinity of High Raise, one mile north of Stickle Tarn. If we accept that valleys are carved out by the rivers which flow in them, then what we have is a radial pattern of drainage. There is a difficulty in explaining this pattern, however, which lies in the disharmony between a radial drainage and the prevailing ENE.–WSW. pattern of rock outcrop. Rivers after all seek out soft rocks in which to cut their valleys, and the less resistant rocks outcrop mainly in ENE.–WSW. belts, not radially.

For over one hundred years, in fact, the drainage of the Lake District has been regarded as a typical example of 'superimposition'. It is postulated that the present drainage originated not on the rocks which now form the central Lake District, but on a fairly smooth and uniform cover of younger rocks which no longer exists. If this cover, dating quite likely from the time when chalk was formed elsewhere in England—about 140 million years ago—had been gently domed about a centre where High Raise now is, it can readily be imagined that a radial pattern of valleys would thus be initiated by rivers coursing on its surface, and would then be cut down through the smooth cover rocks to become impressed on to the older rocks below which were of disparate structure and trend. In this way the pattern would be 'superimposed', while in the process the cover rocks would be eroded away.

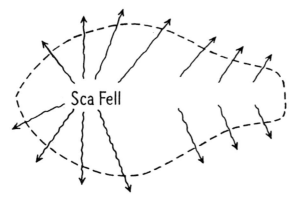

Fig. 1 The 'caddy spoon' pattern of uplift and drainage as envisaged by Marr

There is no evidence as to how much and when the cover was arched up to initiate the modern river system. But probably there were several more intermittent uplifts, followed by complete or partial denudation, without disrupting the main lines of stream flow. It was these more recent movements which left the area with a surface substantially at the present level.

While most, although not all, workers accept the superimposition theory, versions of it do vary. Professor Marr, more than half a century ago, pointed out that the drainage pattern more nearly resembled that to be expected from a 'caddy-spoon'-shaped uplift rather than from a dome (Fig. 1). Another version, suggesting an initial northward and southward drainage system from an east–west watershed through Dunmail Raise and the Kirkstone Pass, is referred to on page 26.

In any case there has been ample time for partial adjustment of the drainage to the complex ENE.–WSW. trend of the earlier rocks, as tributaries of the original rivers cut into belts of readily erodable rock.

Not all of the valleys trend radially or ENE.–WSW.; much faulting occurred at various times, particularly evident in the hard Borrowdale

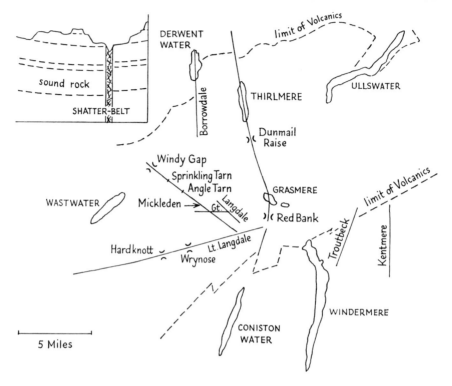

Fig.2 The unbroken lines indicate some important shatter-belts

Volcanic rocks which tended to relieve stress by sharp breaks as well as by folds. Relative movement of rocks on either side of one of these breaks or fault-planes could generate friction so that the rocks crumbled into a belt of rubble several yards wide. The outcrop of one of these features at the surface today is known as a 'shatter-belt', along which the broken rock is easily gullied by streams or evacuated by soil avalanches (Plate 8). Some major valleys seem to have developed along lines of weakness presented by shatter-belts, and other shatter-belts can be traced for many miles through the hard lavas and tuffs by means of valleys, gills, skyline notches and tarns which are in alignment. Fig. 2 shows some of them and the features caused by them. Some shatter-belts have consolidated the original drainage pattern (whether this was radial or north and south). Others, such as those responsible for Great Langdale, have modified it. Apart from the fractures depicted there are innumerable other shatter-belts and faults which have been picked out by erosion as chimneys and gills.

Rocks and scenery

The patterns of rock outcrop and their structures produce corresponding patterns of scenery. The New Red Sandstone country is low, because not recently uplifted. The soil is red, so is the building stone, and so are rock outcrops as at St Bees Head, where the bedding and jointing of the sandstone cause it to be eroded in such a way as to provide numerous ledge nesting-sites for birds.

The Carboniferous Limestone country is higher, framing the uplifted old rocks of the central Lake District. Fields have white limestone walls; quarries, old kilns and modern lime-works abound. In the southern Lake District thick, hard, pure, easterly tilted slabs of limestone, broken on the west by steep scars, form sloping plateaux; Whitbarrow is an example (Plate 16). They are dry, with patches of limestone pavement and scree among the turf. Locally the limestone is reached by the Morecambe Bay estuaries to produce the only substantial limestone cliffs on the west coast between North Wales and Sutherland. The much thinner and impure beds of limestone in the Coniston Limestone Group carry a sliver of limestone natural history through the Lake District proper.

The high mountains are of Skiddaw Slate and Borrowdale Volcanic rocks, but, whereas those of Skiddaw Slate in the north are in the main smooth and conical (Plate 8), the Volcanic mountains are often rugged, knobby, rocky, craggy and spiky. The Skiddaw Slates are soft and fairly uniform in durability throughout their outcrop; the rock readily weathers down to rock waste and soil. There are exceptions: hard sandstones make craggy slopes on Grasmoor End above Crummock Water, on either side of Bassenthwaite Lake and elsewhere; and the rocks around the Skiddaw granite outcrops north of Saddleback, baked hard and altered by heat from the granite as it was intruded, resemble in durability the Borrowdale Volcanic rocks. These last are predominantly hard and able to make precipitous crags, but some of the tuffs are relatively unresistant. This variety among the Volcanic rocks, compared with the soft uniformity of the Skiddaw Slates, ensures contrasting scenery on valley sides. This is well seen from Castle Head, near Keswick. As one looks southwards into

Borrowdale the long horizontal crags on the left (east) consist of resistant lavas and agglomerates, the less resistant tuffs between having been worn back to reveal as a bench the surface of whichever hard stratum lies immediately beneath. There is a striking contrast over the valley on the right, where the Skiddaw Slates have weathered back uniformly into smooth slopes which make sharp skyline ridges where the sides of neighbouring valleys impinge—as for example on Cat Bells. A couple of miles further east the Borrowdale Volcanic strata dip fairly steeply towards the south, and from the Vale of St John one can see the more resistant strata standing out prominently as oblique ribs down the fellside of High Rigg.

But in addition the two groups differ in their joint pattern. Most rocks are criss-crossed with cracks or joints, which are the result of past stress. The joints of Borrowdale Volcanics are often far apart; when blocks fell off along these joint planes of weakness, or were dragged off by glaciers, sheer joint faces were left as crags, large and small, with clean-cut slabs and buttresses. Hard, angular blocks were left lying around. The joint and bedding spacing in the Skiddaw Slates however, is often minute, even in many of the sandstones; the rock breaks down into chips and splinters and the sockets from which these tiny fragments are removed are smothered by rock waste creeping down-slope, as are any small crags. In this way the smoothness of Skiddaw Slate slopes is enhanced. Where Borrowdale Volcanic tuffs are slaty, the cleavage planes act as joints, and these rocks also readily break up into slaty scree. In the Volcanics, shatter-belts and soft dykes (a dyke is a vertical sheet of rock, intruded in the molten state) make crenellations where they cross the skyline.

Mickledore, between Sca Fell and Scafell Pike, is on the line of a dyke and fault. It is worth noting that long crags or scars like those below Bleaberry Fell, or those caused by the hard, pale tuffs of the Sca Fell area, are not common in the Borrowdale Volcanic area. This is so cut up by criss-crossing faults and shatter-belts that hard, crag-forming rock is soon interrupted by soft or rotten rock along the length of an outcrop.

The Silurian country in the south is lower, being at the edge of the area affected by the most recent uplifts. But rock hardness has something to do with the contrast; the Borrowdale Volcanic country rises like a wall at the junction, as at Coniston village. The sandstones in the Silurian form ridges, the slates and mudstones lower country.

Roche moutonnée, Borrowdale

PLATE 5

Easedale Tarn   *With hummocky moraine of a late corrie glacier*

PLATE 6   Royal Fern (*Osmunda regalis*)

Parsley Fern   (*Cryptogramma crispa*)

PLATE 7

Common Spleenwort   (*Asplenium trichomanes*)

Sprinkling Tarn and the Gables *Rugged Borrowdale Volcanic mountains. The tarn and Aaron Slack (gully back centre) mark the outcrop of a shatter-belt*

PLATE 8

Causey Pike (right) from Catbells *Skiddaw Slate mountains with upper zone of heather moor*

The granites and related rocks are well jointed but uniform in durability, and so form irregular undulating hills.

Rocks and natural history

Their complex geological history has ensured that the mountains of the Lake District are made of rocks varying considerably in their chemical and physical properties within short distances. They vary particularly in the ease with which they break down to form rock waste and then soil, and in the texture of the resulting soil, which affects drainage and soil nutrient status, and therefore vegetation. The remarkable variety of colouring on Lakeland slopes depends upon this geological diversity, expressed through the soils and vegetation.

Apart from the limestones of the Carboniferous Limestone Series and Coniston Limestone Group the rocks do not readily yield to the soil large quantities of calcium. This mineral, through its abundance in the soil, is of considerable direct and indirect importance to plants and, probably more than any other soil chemical factor, influences the nature of local vegetation. Soils which are rich in calcium are loosely stated to be 'lime-rich'. The lavas, tuffs and agglomerates contain minerals which are compounds of calcium, but which weather so slowly as to contribute negligible quantities. However, some of these calcium compounds have in many strata been altered at some stage in their history to calcite (crystalline calcium carbonate) which is a more available source of calcium. Sometimes the calcite fills small cavities (often steam bubble-holes in lava) and fissures, and locally may be of significance to plants. But the rate of release of calcium from such calcite either in cavities or dispersed through the body of the rock is determined by the overall rate of rock-weathering, which is often negligible. The volcanic rocks when ground into powder by ice would, however, yield a soil at first relatively rich in calcium. More important are the veins of calcite impregnating fault-planes and shatter-belts. Not only are the crumbling walls of the deep gills associated with shatter-belts often calcium-rich, but water soaking through calcite veins inside the mountain contributes calcium where it issues as a spring or seepage.

Glaciation

Even the New Red Sandstone is 200 million years old. The ice of the last glaciation probably culminated about 20,000 years ago and finally melted away only 10,000 years ago, and its effects are still fresh in the landscape. Without ice there would be no lakes or tarns, crags or screes. That the lakes are still with us indicates that they cannot have been in existence long, because lakes soon fill up with sediment or are drained by outlet streams cutting down their beds. Glaciers converted hills to mountains; without glaciers there would have been no Lake District as we know it.

It is of course impossible to know in any detail what the landscape must have looked like before glaciers began to form, anything between three and a half million years ago (the dating is insecure). By running the film backwards and eliminating the known effects of glaciation and of the very cold climates of near-glacial conditions we are left with a subdued upland countryside with few rock exposures. Rivers flowed in shallow valleys, the floors of which were high above modern valley floors; the valleys were narrower in the hard Borrowdale Volcanic rocks than in the Skiddaw Slates. The ridges separating the valleys were not high, and perhaps showed the ribbing of hard lavas and sandstones through the forest. Soils were deep, and smothered all but the strongest of bed-rock features.

Information is lacking on the number of separate glaciations in northern England, and on most minor readvances and retreats of glaciers within each episode. The effects of later glaciations would in any event be to refurbish and sharpen up the land-forms of earlier ones. During each glaciation a phase when ice was confined to high mountain corries was succeeded by a phase when tongues of ice advanced down the valleys, as do glaciers in the high Alps today. At the glacial maximum, ice filled the valleys and brimmed over the mountains to form a more or less continuous ice sheet, although it is uncertain whether the highest ridges were covered. Ice gave the Lake District a very severe drubbing indeed; its effects were largely erosional among the mountains, and depositional on the margins.

The corrie phase of glaciation At the onset of glacial conditions the subdued land-surface provided sheltered hollows which had been cut by the headwaters of pre-glacial streams. The hollows were on the flanks of low ridges, which were precursors of the present mountains, and many of which trended north–south, as the Helvellyn and Coniston Old Man ranges now do. Because the prevailing south-westerly winds whipped snow from the smooth western and southern slopes and summits, it was the

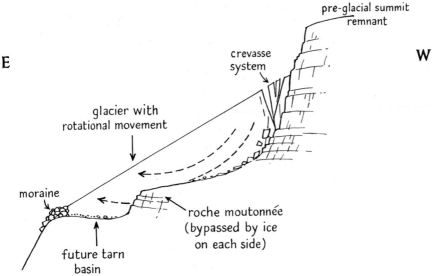

Fig. 3 Section through a corrie glacier

hollows on eastern and northern slopes which were favoured locations for snow accumulation and it was here that basal layers of deep snow became compacted into ice.

In this way small glaciers were formed, usually on east- or north-facing slopes, and each began to move downhill within its hollow, gouging it, scouring it, deepening it, enlarging it, in fact, into a corrie—this is the name given to the mountain basins with precipitous back and side walls, open only to the front. However, the exact processes of corrie enlargement are by no means fully understood. Grinding and scratching by ice shod with angular rock fragments could lower the corrie floor. The corrie ice is believed sometimes to have had a wholesale rotational movement (Fig. 3), allowing the glacier to scoop out a basin in solid rock. Blea Water, 207 feet (63 metres) deep, occupies such a basin in the floor of its corrie below High Street. Frequently the modern corrie tarns are deeper than if impounded by a rock barrier alone, for rubble, which the ice carried out of the corries, was deposited on the solid rock thresholds, raising their effective level. Such loose, ice-deposited debris is called moraine.

But to increase the area of a corrie, as opposed to its depth, different processes were involved. A possible sequence of events is that crevasses developed in the ice as it pulled away from the back and sides of the corrie. These crevasses were either at the junction of rock and ice, or, quite commonly, a few yards on to the ice (Fig. 3). These last may have descended to meet solid rock, and in either case water from melt, and rain descending into the crevasses, seeped into the joints in the rock at their base and, by freezing, so rived and loosened the joint-bounded blocks that they could be plucked away easily by becoming frozen to the glacier ice. The corrie walls were thus undermined at the base of the crevasse system by a process of basal sapping, and collapsed. They retreated backwards, while maintaining their steepness. The removed rock fragments, frozen into the base of the glacier, abraded the corrie floor and were carried through to the moraine. And so the sequence of events was repeated.

By this time an original north–south ridge had been scalloped on its eastern side into a row of neighbouring corries. The remnants of the divides between adjacent corries became narrower and sharper as steep corrie side-walls retreated towards each other, leaving eventually knife-edged 'arêtes', of which Striding Edge and Swirral Edge on Helvellyn are magnificent examples. The cleavage planes of the slates just here are almost vertical and happen to run parallel to the lengths of the arêtes. Frost, working at these division planes of weakness, caused slabs to leaf off, increasing the knife-edge effect. In some cases the original, smoothly rounded, north–south ridge crests have persisted, not quite destroyed by the growing corries, and now form broad, gently rolling, summit plateaux. These may therefore be more or less unmodified remnants of the pre-glacial landscape.

In some such way was produced the pattern of land-forms so often encountered on Lake District mountains, particularly well developed on the Helvellyn, Fairfield, High Street and Coniston Old Man ranges. Each has its array of deep, east-facing corries, its tarns, arêtes, and broad, flat summits. The whole high mountain landscape of the Lake District can be interpreted in terms of a loose, interlocking mesh of corries. One finds also that almost all of the corries open eastwards and northwards, with a consequent asymmetry of the mountains.

The valley phase of glaciation   As the climate became colder and the snow line descended, not only the corries but also the valley heads (which are really corries at valley-floor level) and the broader upland plateaux and slopes acted as gathering grounds which poured their ice as tongues into the valleys below to form valley glaciers. The thickness of the ice about the valley heads in the central Lake District was sufficient, because of heavy snow-fall, to maintain a flow of ice fast enough to perform severe erosion as the glaciers ground and quarried their way along the old river valleys. An important exception is the area north of a line through the Whinlatter

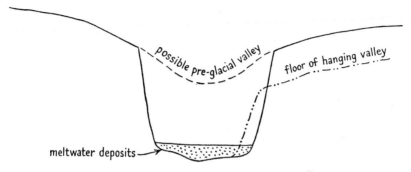

Fig. 4 Cross-section through a glaciated valley

Pass and Keswick, then passing north of Saddleback. Here ice flow was so impeded by congestion due to the confrontation between ice from the Lake District and ice from south-west Scotland that much more of the pre-glacial landscape has survived intact, and the scarcity of clear glacial features enhances the smoothness of the Skiddaw Slate hills in this area.

Everywhere else abrasion—marked by smooth, rounded, polished and scratched rock surfaces—and the plucking (tearing away) of joint-bounded blocks, altered the shallow, smoothly swinging river valleys to deep, very steep-sided troughs—the present valleys. All have their array of features bespeaking a common glacial origin. The ice, unable to accommodate itself to the bends in the old valleys, planed off obstructions, demolishing the old spurs to produce the great triangular gable-end faces such as those of Saddleback above the Keswick–Penrith road, and a great number of smaller truncated spurs which appear on the sides of every glaciated valley. Hundreds of feet above the valley floors the steep, often craggy, valley sides suddenly open out to gentler slopes; this break marks the angle where valley glaciers cut into the old pre-glacial valley slopes (Fig. 4). Tributary glaciers, in tributary valleys, had less ice and eroded their beds much less than the main glaciers, so that when the ice melted, their floors were left suspended high above those of the severely deepened main valleys—they join the main valleys high up in the walls of the latter (Fig. 4). Every main Lakeland valley has its series of waterfalls where streams cascade from these hanging valleys, or from corries which hang for the same reason. Borrowdale has its Taylor Gill Force, Sourmilk Gill, the cascades down from Honister, Lodore Falls and Barrow Falls. The smaller streams simply pour themselves over the side; larger ones, as at Lodore, have cut gorges in the rock lip, the shaded, moist climate of which offers a distinctive habitat. Even major valleys can hang: Little Langdale hangs with respect to Great Langdale to form Colwith Force.

Variations in resistance to ice erosion on the part of the rocks of the valley floors led to the scouring out of basins in the solid rock. Many of the lakes occupy these. The rock barrier closing the basin is often less well jointed than the rocks beneath the basin, indicating that the plucking of jointed, or well-cleaved, rocks was a potent erosive process. Equally the thickness of valley ice may have influenced the amount of erosion; for instance it contributed to the formation of hanging valleys. Dr Gresswell has shown how the presence of two separate rock basins containing Lake Windermere, separated by shallow water off Bowness (Plate 2), may be explained at least in part by the overspill of ice eastwards across a col at Windermere Town towards the Kent valley and south-eastwards past Bowness towards the Winster valley. A smaller amount of ice was thus available to perform erosion in the area south of this loss, and indeed Windermere would be two separate lakes if its level were only twelve feet (3.7 metres) lower, and the shallows north of the ferry, which affect freshwater and bird life (see page 166), would be dry land. Receipt of valley ice from Esthwaite allowed the main Windermere glacier to scour out the south basin. Wastwater (Plate 2) is the deepest lake—its 258 feet (78.6 metres) take it fifty-eight feet (17.7 metres) below sea-level.

Ice not only deepened valleys, it created new ones. As the ice thickness augmented, it increasingly spilled over low points in the dividing ridges, as just described at Windermere, scouring out steep-sided glacial troughs. An example is the ice spill-way past Blea Tarn, from Great to Little Langdale, but towards the glacial maximum such occurrences were widespread. On a broader scale the tendency for radial dispersal of ice from the centre of accumulation in the Scafell–Langdale Pikes area may, according to Professor Linton, have modified what he considered to be an original north–south pattern of valleys, with a main east–west watershed through

Dunmail Raise, so as to produce the familiar radial pattern (see page 16). The ice dispersal may have been powerful enough to cut through pre-glacial watersheds and to integrate favourably trending segments of old valleys into a more or less radial system. The congestion in the northern Lake District, which has been mentioned, caused some of the surface ice from the Thirlmere and Brothers Water glaciers to flow back over the cols at Dunmail Raise and the Kirkstone Pass respectively, imparting to each the form of a glaciated valley. Everywhere the effect of actively moving valley ice was to deepen, steepen and sharpen the old landscape.

Where active valley glaciers maintained their snouts in more or less the same position for some time—ice movement being balanced by melt—debris in the ice was delivered to form terminal moraines across the valley floors. Such morainic ridges, possibly representing the furthermost push of late readvances of valley glaciers, hold back the surface waters of Windermere and Coniston Water. Bassenthwaite Lake on the other hand is prevented from escaping westwards towards Embleton by a plug of boulder clay in its pre-glacial valley. Boulder clay is the general name for moraine deposited under the ice, consisting often of sheets of stiff clay, mixed with boulders. It has locally been moulded by ice flow into oval hills known as drumlins. The islands of Derwentwater are the summits of drumlins, and the rounded peninsulas of Esthwaite Water (Plate 16), which occupies a hollow in boulder clay, are also half-drowned examples. Often the upper limit of enclosed fields corresponds with the edge of boulder clay sheets lodged in the valley bottoms.

The phase of sheet ice   As ice filled valleys and corries to the brim it slewed over the old pre-glacial valley slopes and intervening plateaux. Only the highest summit ridges may have remained above actively moving ice. Ice removed the deep soil which had weathered out of the rocks over the preceding millions of years. It probably wiped out any surviving plant or animal life—in fact, biologically, the slate was wiped clean and the present fauna and flora must have re-entered the area since the last maximum of glaciation. For this reason the end of the last glaciation is a convenient point of departure for the discussions, in the sections which follow, on the history of plant and animal life in the Lake District. Ice picked out the variations in rock resistance to erosion, grooving the high surfaces, pocking them with basins later to become tarns or peat-filled hollows, and leaving rocky knolls and hummocks—generally in fact producing a scraped, scratched, rough, knobby upland landscape. It laid down innumerable patches of boulder clay between the rocky outcrops, and carried boulders considerable distances so that they are now foreign to the rock upon which they lie. Some large boulders were let down by the melting ice so slowly as to have remained perched on a narrow base. The Bowder Stone in Borrowdale is probably such a perched block.

Most of the rocky hummocks just mentioned are 'roches moutonnées'. They have the shape of the mound in Plate 5, their backs smoothed and rounded by the passage of the ice and their craggy fronts quarried by plucking along joint-planes as the ice pulled away. Everywhere in the Lake District rock has been moulded into the streamlined moutonnée form, in the valleys as well as high on the fells (see Fig. 3). It is the most widespread and convincing indication of glaciation. The roche moutonnée crags always face in the direction in which the ice was moving, and the features vary from a few feet in height to hill masses the size of The How at Rosthwaite (Borrowdale). Whole fell-sides are smoothed and polished, with innumerable small moutonnée crags, as is Grange Fell in Borrowdale. If, on the other hand, the rock was poorly divided by joints it resisted plucking and formed smoothly symmetrical knobs. Many lake islands, as those towards the head of Ullswater, or in the central Windermere shallows, are roches moutonnées (Plate 2).

Sheet ice, as well as valley ice, also glaciated the lower-lying Silurian country of the south. Much of the area between Coniston Water and Windermere has alternating outcrops of soft slate or mudstone and hard sandstone which favoured roche moutonnée development by the southerly streaming ice. This is therefore a country of countless low crags, with drumlins in the valleys.

Ice sharpened up the landscape. Glacial erosion created instability of slope by leaving the corrie walls, valley-side slopes and moutonnée crags precarious and liable to disintegrate, and it caused soils on these steep slopes to be themselves unstable, ever likely to creep or slip downhill. Ice made sheer corrie cliffs and their ledge habitats. It disorganised the drainage and made lakes, tarns and marshes. It deeply dissected the strata to lay bare the solid rock in all its variety. It caused waterfalls and their gorges. And the immediate after-effects of the last ice age were hardly less important.

MAP 2

THE LAKE DISTRICT

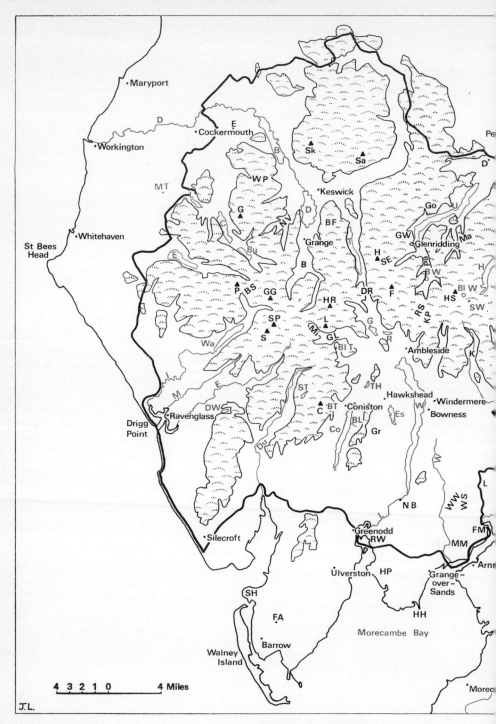

The Lake District

RIVERS

BL	Beckleven
D	Derwent
Du	Duddon
Ed	Eden
E	Esk
I	Irt
K	Kent
L	Leven
Lu	Lune
M	Mite
W	Winster

MOUNTAINS

C	Coniston Old Man
F	Fairfield
G	Grasmoor
GG	Great Gable
H	Helvellyn
HR	High Raise
HS	High Street
L	Langdale Pikes
P	Pillar
Sa	Saddleback
S	Sca Fell
SP	Scafell Pike
Sk	Skiddaw

LAKES AND TARNS

B	Bassenthwaite Lake
BlT	Blea Tarn
BlW	Blea Water
BT	Boo Tarn
BW	Brothers Water
Bu	Buttermere
Co	Coniston Water
C	Crummock Water
D	Derwentwater
DW	Devoke Water
E	Ennerdale Water
Es	Esthwaite Water
G	Grasmere
H	Haweswater
L	Loweswater
MT	Mockerkin Tarn
R	Rydal Water
ST	Seathwaite Tarn
SW	Small Water
TH	Tarn Hows
T	Thirlmere
Wa	Wastwater
W	Windermere
U	Ullswater

AREAS AND SETTLEMENTS

BS	Black Sail Pass
BF	Bleaberry Fell
B	Borrowdale
CS	Cunswick Scar / Scout Scar / Underbarrow Scar
D	Dalemain
DR	Dunmail Raise
E	Embleton
FM	Foulshaw Moss
FA	Furness Abbey
GW	Glencoyne Wood
Go	Gowbarrow
GL	Great Langdale
Gr	Grizedale
HP	Holker Park
HH	Humphrey Head
K	Kentmere
KP	Kirkstone Pass
L	Lyth
Ma	Martindale
MM	Meathop Moss
Mi	Mickleden
M	Mosedale
NF	Naddle Forest
NB	Newby Bridge
NV	Newlands Valley
Pa	Patterdale
RS	Red Screes
RW	Roudsea Wood
SH	Sandscale Haws
SE	Striding Edge
WP	Whinlatter Pass
WS	Whitbarrow Scar
WW	Witherslack Woods

Land over 800 feet

Boundary of National Park

Late-glacial time

During the period before 12,000 years ago the ice melted, although with interposed phases of renewed cold and glacial advance. Ideas on the way in which deglaciation occurred, and on the correct interpretation of land-forms associated with deglaciation, have changed recently in favour of rapid thinning through general melt of stagnant ice rather than back-melting of the snouts of actively moving glaciers (although renewed cold certainly caused readvances of valley and corrie glaciers after partial or complete deglaciation). In any event copious meltwater cut many of the gorges and ravines now occupied by modern rivers and streams, as well as numerous shallow valleys on hillsides now dry and quite unrelated to the present drainage system. Abundant debris was released from the rapidly melting ice, being material eroded by the ice and incorporated as blocks or comminuted powder, or which had fallen from above on to the surfaces of corrie or valley glaciers. Some of this was dropped in a jumbled mass under, or at the edge of, the ice as moraine. (In the case of some types of boulder clay, or of the terminal moraines of corrie or valley glaciers, moraine deposition was by active, not stagnant, ice.) When dead, stagnant corrie or valley glaciers wasted away, irregular mounds of rubble were left behind.

The rest of the material was carried away by meltwater to be laid down on stream floors as stratified layers of sand and gravel, or in the newly formed lakes. This glacial outwash material accumulated in valley bottoms often to considerable thicknesses. The meltwater floods not only brought in debris just released from the wasting ice, but also redistributed recently formed moraine over which they happened to flow, or which, being saturated and unstable, moved *en masse* down valley-side slopes into the meltwater streams. In this way were built up the level and now often marshy valley bottoms. It was at this time too that deltas advanced rapidly into the lakes, as the swollen rivers carried in their abundant loads of sediment. Some small and shallow lakes would be rapidly infilled, or alternatively lost by natural draining as outlet streams cut down through morainic dams, but it is difficult from the surface evidence alone to know whether a flat valley floor represents a deltaic lake fill, or the result of valley-floor alluviation by rivers. Certainly many corrie tarns and innumerable smaller tarns and pools have been filled in post-glacial times by silt, mud and peat.

Of larger lakes Kentmere had been considerably reduced by late- and post-glacial delta growth and, in this special case, by deposition of workable diatomite deposits formed from the skeletons of minute plants (diatoms) before being artificially drained in the nineteenth century.

All the lakes have had their areas reduced by delta growth. Derwent-water and Bassenthwaite, and Buttermere and Crummock (Plate 1), were probably single lakes each divided into two by delta growth in shallow water. Important marshy habitats were thus formed on the level, ill-drained delta surfaces. Where mountain torrents debouched on to flatter ground, their velocity, and therefore capacity to carry debris, were much reduced and fan-shaped masses of alluvium—large stones, gravel, sand and silt—were deposited. The edges of valley floors are often lined by rows of these fans, brought down by small streams, and in one case a tarn has been held back. At the foot of Coniston Old Man, alongside the Walna Scar road, Boo Tarn occupies part of an elongated depression developed in some soft Silurian shales, and is impounded between two adjacent fans built across the depression by streams from the Old Man.

The late-glacial period was punctuated by episodes of severe cold which, as well as bringing about readvances of corrie and valley glaciers, caused rock waste and boulder clay to sludge off the mountain slopes, choking the smaller valleys. This type of mass down-slope movement of unconsolidated material—the process of solifluction—is characteristic of cold climates. It is favoured by super-saturation of the surface soil layers, due to water being held above an impermeable layer of still-frozen ground (melting in summer proceeds from the surface downwards). It is also favoured by disturbance and loosening of the soil through alternating freeze and thaw, and by absence of a continuous vegetation cover to anchor the soil. Solifluction, by masking rock outcrops under a layer of rubble, has probably been very important in the production of smooth slopes in the Lake District, especially at higher altitudes and particularly in the area of the Skiddaw Slates, which readily yield loose, rotten rock material. In addition rock fragments were split off crags at all altitudes to collect below as scree; this was due to repeated exertion of stresses brought about by freezing of water in the joints. The famous Wastwater Screes descend over 1000 feet (300 metres) to lake level and a further 200 feet (60 metres) below water.

A final short-lived cold episode of perhaps 500 years, from which recovery was only about 10,300 years ago, caused many corries and some valley heads again to be occupied by their glaciers. The really fresh-looking hummocky moraines, which are so plentiful at the heads of some valleys—irregularly scattered piles of angular rock rubble up to forty feet (12 metres) high—date from this period. Also at this time of renewed cold active solifluction operated even at low elevations, and contributed to valley-floor and lake infill.

During the late-glacial period plants and animals were able to re-enter the Lake District. Successful plants among the early arrivals were those able to take advantage of the new and bare soil not yet leached of its calcium by thousands of years of rain. These included the arctic, alpine and arctic-alpine species, now mainly confined in the Lake District to high altitudes.

Post-glacial time

During the last 10,000 years the land surface has changed little. The erosional processes associated with our present climate are innocuous compared with those of glacial and near-glacial conditions. It is as if ice had melted from the corries only yesterday. The exceptions to this statement are these:

(*a*)   High on the mountains there is still a near-glacial climate. Freeze-thaw is active in making scree out of crag;[1] solifluction is smoothing over the smaller crags and distorting the turf into small terraces. Rock, particularly if closely jointed, is rapidly being broken up by frost into soil, which is therefore deep but easily ravined by run-off from torrential downpours.

(*b*)   On the lake shores waves are winnowing the boulder clay, carrying out into calmer, deeper water the clay, sand and gravel, and leaving coarse shingle on the shore. Every river and every little stream is still pushing out its delta to indent the shore lines. Mud, derived in part from the remains of freshwater organisms, and in part from the finer material brought down by the rivers, slowly settles over the lake bottoms so that the water becomes shallower.

(*c*)   Streams are still eroding their beds in their steep mountain sections. Of the material loosened from their beds or falling in from the valley sides

---

[1] Little is known about rates of scree accumulation: many low-altitude screes are partly vegetated—page 41—and this fact, with the scarcity of freshly exposed rock surfaces in the parent crags, suggest that these screes are relics of former colder climates.

the finer particles are swept away immediately to the lakes, while the shingle and gravel remain longer on the stream bed.

(d) When sea-level rose again in the Morecambe Bay estuaries, as, all over the world, water was released from melting ice, the sea at one stage penetrated further inland than it now does. This was about 4000 B.C. and the tides brought in silt and mud to build up salt-marsh, just as they do around the Bay today. Since then the land has risen a little out of the sea and the old salt-marsh deposits have become raised above the tides by a few feet, forming just the sort of flat, badly drained surface upon which peat accumulates (Plate 16). The raised peat bogs around Morecambe Bay developed on such surfaces.

It remains to draw attention again to the close-textured colour patterns on valley sides and mountain slopes in the Lake District, and to their equally variegated micro-relief (Plate 9). The former depends upon intimate intermixture of rock, scree, bracken, grass, heather, bilberry and juniper; the latter upon juxtaposition of moutonnée crags, gills which pick out fault-lines, gullies which scar moraine and solifluction debris, lava terraces, ice-transported boulders, landslips and sheep-tracks. Vegetation diversity on this scale is due to rock diversity and its effect upon soil; topographic diversity, to the glacial and more recent erosional processes already discussed.

Both colour and relief were submerged beneath the natural post-glacial forest of the Lake District and it was man who, by causing deforestation, bared the soil surface and often, because of consequent soil erosion on these steep slopes, the solid rock. Ice had dissected the strata to expose their variety; man laid the resulting diversity of soil and vegetation open to view. It was man who thereby created the characteristic landscape beauty of the Lake District, and who in so doing contributed to the notable scale illusions which are so much part of the area. Intricate colour and relief patterns mislead the eye as to scale, and together with atmospheric effects, and the presence of glacial landforms proper to the Alps, can cause 3000-feet (900 metres) hills to assume the aspect of high mountains.

The beauty of the Lake District is an artifact, and it is fragile. It is not difficult to imagine developments which could destroy the colour-texturing and submerge the broken relief. The scale illusions likewise can easily be shattered by obtrusive developments which give away true scale, and by loss of the variegated colour and relief patterns which promote the illusions. If it is indeed our desire to conserve the present beauty of the Lake District then it is our need to understand a little of its geological and ecological history.

The quantity of literature on Lake District geology is considerable; that on geomorphology less so. Only recent review papers on geology, recent popular accounts and the more important geomorphological papers can be listed in the Bibliography at the end of the book. This means, regrettably, that a number of papers upon which the author has drawn are unacknowledged. Recently published one inch geological map coverage exists only for the western fringe of the Lake District; the largest-scale published map for a large part of the area is the Geological Survey ¼ inch series sheet 3, covering the Lake District north of Coniston village—Bowness-on-Windermere (the adjacent southern sheet 5–6 is out of print).

THE PLANTS

FLOWERING PLANTS, FERNS AND MOSSES

by G. A. K. Hervey

The Lake District, like all other districts, is something much more than a build-up of rocks, however remarkably chiselled, containing large and small sheets of water. Without its vegetative cover most of its charm and beauty would be gone, as well as its indigenous animal life. As in all other chapters, any attempt to give an exhaustive account of species and habitats would be out of the question. The aim is, by careful selection from the most typical and most interesting plants, to give an over-all picture of this vegetative cover; and to indicate, so far as is known, how it got there in the first instance after the Ice Age had obliterated all previous vegetation, and how it maintains itself in the more inhospitable places today.

Summits, High Crags and Gills

Adaptation   It will readily be appreciated that to live permanently high on a mountain requires a marked degree of adaptation and specialisation. Even in summer, conditions can be severe; in winter they can be arctic. It is not surprising, therefore, that many of the mountain plants are specially adapted to meet the rigours of their environment.

A primary need of all plants is water, but surprisingly this may be a problem on mountains. Although the rainfall is abundant, it quickly runs off the exposed rock faces. It may be for this reason that plants so often establish themselves in crevices down which water is seeping, or on the sides of gills, or they develop apparent means of reaching or conserving water. Some plants, such as the Sea Campion (*Silene maritima*) develop very elaborate root systems. Others, such as Rose-root (*Sedum rosea*) develop very fleshy leaves, resembling desert plants (Fig. 5). Others again, such as the alpine hawkweeds and chickweeds, are covered with long hairs, which hold the water in droplets just like a tweed coat in a mist.

A second hazard is wind, which at times can be terrific. This exposes plants to a risk of excessive drying, as well as of being uprooted altogether.

It can be met by strong, deeply penetrating roots such as those of the willows or bilberry; or the whole plant may form a closely packed cushion so that the wind blows over it. The very lovely Moss Campion (*Silene acaulis*) is an example of the latter. The same result can be achieved by a very low stature which offers little resistance to the wind. The smallest of all British shrubs, the Least Willow (*Salix herbacea*), is a good example of this. On the summits it reaches about one inch in height (rather more on the sheltered crags) and bears catkins one-twelfth of an inch long (2 millimetres).

Fig. 5 Rose-root

No Lake District hills have a permanent snow cover, and it is not even usual for them to remain under snow throughout the winter; yet there is a risk of snow at any time from mid September to the end of May or even early June. Because of this and the short growing season caused by low temperatures it is essential that the processes of growth and reproduction should be accelerated and completed in about three months. It is possible that the relatively large flowers of some of the plants compared with their leaves and stature may serve to attract insects quickly and to secure pollination. The Purple Saxifrage (*Saxifraga oppositifolia*), one of the earliest mountain plants to bloom, has flowers many times larger than its leaves; so has the Alpine Mouse-ear Chickweed (*Cerastium alpinum*). Both these are pollinated by insects. It is also interesting that the former has leaves with a special device, in common with certain other saxifrages, by which excessive loss of water is checked. At the apex of each leaf is a pore surrounded by tissue capable of secreting chalk. When evaporation is rapid chalk accumulates quickly and closes the pore, preventing any further loss of water; when evaporation is less the escaping water dissolves some of the chalk and allows the flow to continue.

Many mountain plants abandon fertilisation in whole or in part and develop various means of vegetative reproduction. Many species double-bank, as it were, and employ both methods. The Alpine Bistort (*Polygonum viviparum*), a small edition of the Snake-root or Easter Ledges (*Polygonum bistorta*) of the lowland meadows, which is fairly common on the Helvellyn crags, produces a spike of small white flowers at the top, which are fertile and visited by insects, with red bulbils beneath, which readily fall off and produce new plants. The advantage of this method is that it eliminates the lengthy period between the opening of the flower and the setting of the seed, and is therefore particularly valuable in late seasons. The process has gone further in the rare and very beautiful Drooping Saxifrage (*Saxifraga cernua*), which is confined in Britain to a few Scottish mountains. This regularly produces bulbils in the same way, but it only flowers in suitable years and has never been known, in Britain, to produce fruit. It is, however, visited by insects and no doubt was once fertile. Its reliance on vegetative reproduction has probably weakened the species and could account for its increasing rarity. The Alpine Bistort may go the same way.

Some of the grasses, instead of producing a seed, usually have in place of the floret a complete new plant, giving them a curiously shaggy appearance. These drop off and grow. The Viviparous Fescue (*Festuca vivipara*) is a very common example in the Lake District; the Alpine Poa (*Poa alpina*) a much rarer one. In Teesdale the latter is not viviparous but produces flowers and seeds in the ordinary way.

Methods of vegetative reproduction found commonly among lowland plants also occur on the high tops and are clearly an advantage. Plants with runners and underground stems are obvious examples. Another common short-cut device known as apomixis is that of the dandelions and hawkweeds where the seeds set without fertilisation and there is no mingling of strains. The result is that any variety can become stable and perpetuated indefinitely, and in consequence there is a vast number of sub-species. Between two and three hundred hawkweeds, many of them mountain species, have been named, though for non-specialists it is usually considered adequate to recognise the main groups. Dandelions occur frequently on the high tops, and other groups well represented on mountains which reproduce in this way are the lady's-mantles and the eyebrights.

Colonisation We have seen the kind of adaptations plants must make in order to survive in such a highly specialised situation as a high mountain, and we may well wonder how plants ever got a foothold in such an inhospitable area in the first instance.

It would seem that the earliest pioneers on the bare rock were the lichens. These strange plants, part alga, part fungus, adhere so closely to the rock face that they cannot easily be removed. They are abundant on the rocks and their yellows and greys add much to the beauty of the scenery. They take an immense time to grow, gradually increasing their circumference over the years. They extract their nourishment from the rock and help in a small way to disintegrate it so that other pioneers such as mosses and ferns can find a foothold.

It has seemed best to treat both lichens and fungi separately at the end of this chapter, rather than integrate them with the rest of the flora.

The disintegrating rocks and thin soil, unstable through frost, only support a few colonising species of mosses. Of these the Woolly Hair-moss (*Rhacomitrium lanuginosum*) is by far the most conspicuous, and often covers the rough boulders of the summits. Bare rock faces, from 300 feet (90 metres) up to over 3000 feet (900 metres) are often covered with small reddish-black cushions of mosses of the genus *Andreaea*. When moist after rain these patches will appear purplish; when dry in summer they become black and crisp, and may be ground to powder between one's fingers. It seems incredible that they can survive such desiccation. In the moister crevices of the crags and in the gills other mosses, liverworts and ferns can establish themselves, and as they die and decay form humus, thereby preparing the way for successors.

As fragments, and often great boulders, split off the crag face under the influence of frost (as explained on page 30) they form a long apron of scree down the mountainside in which the large boulders frequently come to rest and are embedded among the smaller fragments (Plate 4). Just below these boulders the Parsley Fern (*Cryptogramma crispa*) (Plate 7) with its tough root system, so abundant on the Lake District mountains but very local elsewhere in Great Britain, finds shelter from further falls of scree.

Gradually humus forms; other plants, especially those with wind-borne seeds are able to get a footing; they in turn make more humus and still more plants come in, often ousting the original pioneers. In this way lines of vegetation tend to form down the scree, spreading from the original boulder in the form of an inverted V. Gradually these coalesce, and the whole scree is covered and stabilised. In early post-glacial times many of the late-glacial screes became covered with vegetation and stabilised in this way; but the process can still be seen going on today on more recent screes. At the higher levels the climax vegetation would be largely grass, heather or bilberry cover; at the lower levels woodland.

Had the Lake District been left to itself the probability is that the summit plateaux would have produced largely tundra conditions with Woolly Hair-moss, Rigid Sedge (*Carex bigelowii*), Viviparous Fescue, Least Willow, and a wealth of flowers such as occur on the tundra of the American Rockies. The high slopes, like the 'alps' of Switzerland, would have been in the main rich Agrostis-Festuca grassland with abundant flowers, such as the Alpine Lady's-mantle (*Alchemilla alpina*), growing especially in the patches made bare by frost disruption of the turf. The intensive selective grazing of sheep, however, has enormously impoverished these high grassy slopes and the summit plateaux, and the rich mountain flora is now largely confined to inaccessible crags, ledges and gullies.

This is how it comes about that the very lovely mountain flora of the Lake District, with only a few exceptions, is limited to those comparatively few areas in the high crags of the Borrowdale Volcanic rocks which are both inaccessible and sufficiently rich in calcium. These are to be found principally on the eastern face of Helvellyn (Plate 9) and Fairfield, the northern face of Pillar, a small area on the north-east face of High Street, some areas in the Sca Fell massif especially in the gills, the gills at the head of the Langdale Valley, and some very restricted areas on the Furness Fells, which are in the main lacking in calcium. Each locality covers only a very small area, though there may be several such areas on the same mountain, but they need searching for. All are among the precipitous crags and no one should adventure there without some previous experience of mountain scrambling unless in the company of someone who knows the way. A good indication that one is approaching lime-rich rocks is the presence of the conspicuous Rose-root which shows up on the crags from a considerable distance.

This mountain flora, and similar floras on the Scottish and Welsh mountains and in Upper Teesdale, have much in common with that of the tundra in the far north ('arctics') and the mountains of Switzerland ('alpines'), or both ('arctic-alpines'). These plants are relicts of a previous widespread cold-climate flora which covered most of Britain in late glacial

Fig. 6 Globe Flower

times. As the temperature rose the plants disappeared from the lower slopes and retreated up the mountains. As our Lake District mountains are comparatively low, many retreated off them altogether and are to be found only on the higher mountains of Wales or Scotland, on the mountains of Central Europe or on the tundras of the arctic regions. This is partly the reason why the Lake District cannot compete with Scotland either in the richness or variety of its mountain flora; the other reason is that the lime-rich areas, where they occur, are of much greater extent in Scotland.

The natural rock gardens of the high fells are not, however, by any means limited to arctic/alpine plants; many of the lowland plants have also found their way there and flourish, owing to the moist rich soil and the absence of grazing; and they contribute in no small degree to the spectacular colour scheme. The Globe Flower (*Trollius europaeus*) supplies splashes of gold along the ledges (Fig. 6), the Wood Cranesbill (*Geranium sylvaticum*) large patches of purple in the hollows; Red Campion (*Silene dioica*) supplements the pink of the Moss Campion; and the large umbels

of Angelica (*Angelica sylvestris*) and Hogweed (*Heracleum sphondylium*) add
to the white display of Alpine Scurvy-grass (*Cochlearia pyrenaica*), Vernal
Sandwort (*Minuartia verna*), and Mossy Saxifrage (*Saxifaga hypnoides*).
Both Common Wintergreen (*Pyrola minor*) and the curious Moonwort
(*Botrychium lunaria*), which belongs to the Adder's Tongue Family, are
found locally on rock ledges (Plate 17). Some of the smaller spring flowers
are also up there in plenty, but flowering six to eight weeks later than in
the valleys—Wood Anemone (*Anemone nemorosa*), Wood Sorrel (*Oxalis
acetosella*), violets and Early Purple Orchis (*Orchis mascula*). The time of
flowering varies from year to year, but June and early July is usually the
peak period for the rock gardens, though the Purple Saxifrage which
festoons the crags in April will probably be over, and the hawkweeds and
Alpine Saw-wort (*Saussuria alpina*), which are a blaze of colour in the late
summer, will not be out.

Certain other inhabitants of these alpine gardens are mainly found elsewhere in Britain as maritime plants—Thrift (*Armeria maritima*), Sea
Campion and Sea Plantain (*Plantago maritima*). Although they are so
different in many ways, certain conditions in common, in particular the
reduced competition due to the unstable soil, enabled these plants to find a
niche in both situations when forests or bogs spread across the rest of the
countryside, and successful competitors were able to establish themselves
as the climate became warmer.

There are other much rarer plants which also have curious distributions.
The Shrubby Potentilla (*Potentilla fruticosa*) flourishes on the high crags of
the Pillar Mountain and the Wastwater Screes; its nearest station is along
the Tees not far from Middleton. The Alpine Catchfly (*Lychnis alpina*),
which in favourable years turns a gill on the Grasmoor range into a cascade
of rosy-red, is found elsewhere in Britain only on the flat muddy top of
Meickle Kilrannoch in Angus—a very different habitat, but probably with
some nutritive factor in common. The inaccessibility of the Lake District
site may well be the reason for its preservation. (It has also been reported
in the past from the Lancashire Fells, but if it is still there it is kept a very
close secret.)

Many of the mountain plants which once flourished in the Lake District
are now extremely rare and limited to the more inaccessible spots, owing,
to a large extent, to the depredations of botanists and alpine gardeners.
Examples of this are the Mountain Avens (*Dryas octopetala*) and ferns such

as Woodsia (*Woodsia ilvensis*) and the Holly Fern (*Polystichum lonchitis*). One cherished clump of Holly Fern known to the author was, alas, buried under three feet (1 metre) of scree and rubble in a landslide down a gill on Helvellyn a few winters ago. Fortunately the Oak Fern (*Thelypteris dryopteris*) and Beech Fern (*T. phegopteris*) still flourish on the wet ledges and among the boulders of the moister slopes.

The most spectacular of these natural rock-gardens are to be found among the eastern crags of Helvellyn at the head of the corries (Plate 9). One consists of a nearly vertical rock face, dripping with water, and broken up by chimneys and crevices and also by horizontal ledges, some of which are wide enough to traverse. The whole is covered with plants and ablaze with colour at the appropriate times of year. It is here that some of the rarest of the alpines are to be found mixed up with commoner ones. The Downy Willow (*Salix lapponum*) clings to a spur of rock overhanging a cascade of Alpine Scurvy-grass and Rose-root. On a ledge among Wood Cranesbill, Water Avens (*Geum urbanum*), Smooth Lady's-mantle (*Alchemilla glabra*), Lesser Meadow Rue (*Thalictrum minus*), Angelica and tufts of Greater Woodrush (*Luzula sylvatica*), grows the Black Sedge (*Carex atrata*) with its nodding heads, and the Alpine Poa which is stouter than the Viviparous Fescue but similarly shaggy and viviparous. Festooning the crag face itself creeps the Purple Saxifrage together with cushions of pink Moss Campion (not always in bloom together), the white Vernal Sandwort, clumps of Mountain Sorrel (*Oxyria digyna*) and Starry Saxifrage (*Saxifraga stellaris*). Right in the crevices is the delicate Brittle Bladder Fern (*Cystopteris fragilis*); the upper ledges are golden at the right time of year with Globe Flower; and lower down, where the ledges are wider, there are beds of Mossy Saxifrage with its large creamy flowers.

Not far away on a different system of more precipitous crags at the head of another corrie is a very remarkable saucer among the rocks which requires some scrambling to get into. This corrie comes into its glory in the late summer when the purple Alpine Saw-wort which fills it is in bloom, and the knife-like rocks which bound it are decorated with the golden flowers of the Alpine Hawkweed (*Hieracium holosericeum*). Here too is to be found Alpine Bistort in some quantity, large clumps of pink Thrift, and the mountain variety of the delicate blue Thyme-leaved Speedwell (*Veronica serpyllifolia*) known as sub-species *humifusa*. On the very wet ground below the saucer the inconspicuous Alpine Meadow Rue (*Thalic-*

trum alpinum) flourishes, and here and there where it is muddy, with little else growing, is the tiny rush *Juncus triglumis*. The cracks of the rock above are filled with the Least Willow, growing far more luxuriantly than on the more exposed sheep-nibbled summit.

Among these high crags, and especially where running water is coming down the crevices or over the face of the rock, mosses of many species grow in abundance and add much to the beauty of the scene. The deep gills, in particular, provide shelter from high winds and create the per-petually mild, humid micro-climate in which they flourish best.

Below the crags, and especially on the floors of the corries, are wet lime-rich flushes where the botanist finds some of his most rewarding plants. Where the water gets held up in a basin very wet conditions prevail and the vegetation more or less floats; it quakes if walked on and easily gives way. It is characterised by bright green mosses, especially *Philonotis fontana* and *Dicranella squarrosa*, Alpine Scurvy-grass growing very close to the ground, Starry Saxifrage, Golden Saxifrage (*Chrysos-plenium oppositifolium*), and Blinks (*Montia fontana*). In one such flush just below the summit crags of Helvellyn the Lesser Kingcup (*Caltha palustris minor*) is found rather sparsely and may be easily passed over as Lesser Celandine (*Ranunculus ficaria*).

Coming out of these flushes, and often running through them, is usually a stream, along the banks of which may be found the very lovely pale blue smallish flowers of the Short-leaved Mountain Forget-me-not (*Myosotis stolonifera*). As the angle of the slope lessens, the lime-rich conditions tend to fan out into a wide flush. It is in these lower flushes that the Grass of Parnassus (*Parnassia palustris*) with its delicately veined white petals occurs —not nearly as plentiful, alas, on the Lake District fells as it used to be, though still abundant in certain damp localities near the coast.

However, by far the greater number of the streams, or becks, which come hurtling over the boulders down the fellside are lime-deficient. Beside these grow large patches of Yellow Mountain Saxifrage (*Saxifraga aizoides*) (Plate 17), a rather late-flowering plant, together with the Starry Saxifrage, both of which are fairly tolerant of acid conditions. Also by these streams among the boulders grows the Mountain Fern (*Thelypteris limbosperma*) with yellow glands under the fronds which, when crushed, give out a strong scent of lemon. This plant is intolerant of lime so is absent from the lime-rich areas.

The Lower Slopes

So far we have been considering the high-altitude habitats, which are the most distinctive of the Lake District, and the streams which issue from them. We must now turn to the lower slopes, below about 2000 feet (600 metres), which have more in common with other parts of England. These are in the main the steep glaciated valley sides and the ice-scarred plateaux above them.

Fig. 7 Juniper

A few thousand years ago these slopes, at least below about 1500 feet (450 metres), were covered with woodland, the drier slopes with oak (*Quercus*), the wetter and higher areas with birch (*Betula*), lime-rich areas with Ash (*Fraxinus excelsior*), and the more swampy areas towards the valley bottoms with Alder (*Alnus glutinosa*). Mixed woods, especially on the richer sites, would also have occurred, and there would have been a widespread sprinkling of Scots Pine (*Pinus sylvestris*), Juniper (*Juniperus communis*) (Fig. 7) and Yew (*Taxus baccata*). The level valley floors carried a tangled scrub of willow and alder, some of which remains to this day. These were the conditions which met the first human settlers in the area.

The disappearance of these extensive woodlands is partly due to the fact that, since the coming of the Vikings at least, they have been steadily cut down and, until recent times, not replanted, But the principal reason has been the intensive grazing by sheep. Sheep were probably used by the first settlers, but it was the Cistercian monks particularly of Furness Abbey who in the twelfth century first introduced sheep farming in a big way. The bulk of the woodlands disappeared as the replacement seedlings were regularly cropped and regeneration became impossible.

Probable relics of these primeval woodlands can still be found; for example, Naddle Forest by Haweswater, and two areas of stunted oak-wood on the north side of Newlands Valley at Keskadale and Rigg Beck (Plate 8). A large alder wood, also possibly natural, still survives in upper Martindale. Apart from these, probably all the existing woodlands have been coppiced or otherwise altered by man. The main markets for the timber have been for firewood, boat-building, charcoal burning and various wood-working industries.

A further effect of the intensive grazing by sheep has been the very considerable replacement of Heather (*Calluna vulgaris*) and Bilberry (*Vaccinium myrtillus*) by Bracken (*Pteridium aquilinum*), and of the sweet Festuca Grass by the coarse Matgrass (*Nardus stricta*). Sheep will not normally eat either bracken or Matgrass which rapidly encroach as the heather and Festuca are cropped. There is far less heather in the Lake District today than there was fifty years ago and fully covered heather slopes are becoming markedly fewer. For the same reason, apart from the more craggy areas, bilberry is sparse and mainly stunted, with little fruit. Where, however, the Forestry Commission has protected the growing trees, both from sheep and rabbits, by fencing, the heather and the bilberry once more grow luxuriantly. It can only be temporary, for as the trees grow the shade will become too great.

From the scenic point of view neither the loss of woodlands nor of heather is altogether bad. Forests mask many contours and interesting features of the landscape. The Lake District mountains are far more varied than the forest-clad ones of Vermont, U.S.A., which are of comparable height. Similarly bracken is beautiful at all times of the year, especially in winter, whereas heather is only a glory for some six weeks. Even the erosion caused by the trampling of sheep across slopes which have become unstable owing to the removal of the forests adds considerable charm and variety to the scene.

These lower slopes have predominantly acid soils, as described on page 5, with correspondingly coarse vegetation, but where lime-rich slopes occur either on the Carboniferous limestone or locally in the central Lake District through flushing, a rich grassland develops. On the drier sites this is dominated by Sheep's Fescue (*Festuca ovina*) and other fescues. Beside lime-rich rills and springs are to be found several of the mountain plants from higher levels, such as Alpine Scurvy-grass, Starry Saxifrage and Short-leaved Mountain Forget-me-not growing amongst large patches of the bright green moss *Philonotis fontana*. Another moss, *Mnium punctatum*, growing by the sides of these streams, is conspicuous because of the trapped water droplets in its leaves, which sparkle in the sunshine.

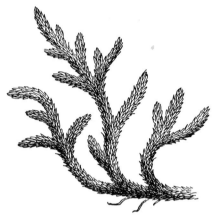

Fig. 8 Stag's-horn Club Moss

On the other hand, the more acid slopes are dominated by the coarse Matgrass and the Wavy Hair-grass (*Deschampsia flexuosa*) and at the lower levels by Purple Moor-grass (*Molinia caerulea*) which frequently grows in great tufts. As it completely loses its leaves in winter it is quite useless for winter grazing. It is on the grassy slopes that the sheep mainly graze. A further effect of their presence is that owing to their close cropping the flora is very restricted. Tormentil (*Potentilla erecta*) and Heath Bedstraw (*Galium saxatile*) are frequently the only two abundant herbs. With them on a few fellsides, but only very sparsely distributed, is the small white crucifer *Teesdalia nudicaulis*. A number of alpine plants descend well into this zone, including Alpine Lady's-mantle. All five club mosses which occur in the Lake District are to be found here, the diminutive descendants of the giant trees of the Carboniferous Age: the Fir Club Moss (*Lycopodium selago*), abundant on the upper slopes; the Lesser Club Moss (*Selaginella selaginoides*), inconspicuous but not uncommon where it is wet; the Stag's-horn Club Moss (*Lycopodium clavatum*), very much less common than it used to be (Fig. 8); the Alpine Club Moss (*L. alpinum*), now much the commoner of the two, and the Interrupted Club Moss (*L. annotinum*), rare and very local. Below a certain altitude, which is not constant, the bracken in places takes over almost entirely and, like the Matgrass, is spreading. This is not only due to its rejection by the sheep, but to the facts that there are now fewer cattle to trample and bruise it and lack of labour to cut it.

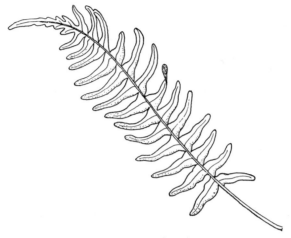

Fig. 9 Common Polypody

No one who has visited the Lake District could fail to be impressed by the miles of walls, running in all directions from summit ridge to valley bottom. These are of particular interest for the mosses and ferns which grow on them. This wall flora naturally varies according to the type of rock from which the walls are built. The dry stone walls of Lakeland are mainly siliceous in character, and their tops are frequently covered with the Woolly Hair-moss which we have already noticed on the bare mountain tops. Towards the valleys vast clumps of Polypody (*Polypodium vulgare*) (Fig. 9), Common Spleenwort (*Asplenium trichomanes*) (Plate 7) and the delicate Wall-rue (*A. ruta-muraria*) are always prominent. Among the mosses of these siliceous walls the silky yellow-green foliage of *Brachythecium populeum* is conspicuous.

Limestone walls in the Carboniferous limestone areas within the National Park, as at Whitbarrow and Underbarrow Scars, look completely different. They are clothed with feathery growths of the mosses *Campto-thecium sericeum*, curling gracefully when dry, and long stems of dark green *Anomodon viticulosus*, hanging down from the lower parts of the walls. Both Male-fern (*Dryopteris filix-mas*) and Lady-fern (*Athyrium filix-femina*) grow abundantly at the base of the walls bordering the lanes and—wherever lime is present—the lanceolate fronds of the Hart's-tongue Fern (*Phyllitis scolopendrium*).

Bogs (Mosses)

As anyone who has tramped the Lake District fells knows, a considerable area of their total surface is covered by wet, boggy ground into which one can easily sink over the ankle. Except where there is flushing from lime-rich rocks these wet places are strongly acid and nutrient-deficient, and are composed of peat deposits. The waterlogging which causes this peat formation may be due either to poor drainage or, in the case of the high fells, to heavy rainfall, or to a combination of both.

At any altitude wherever a depression in the underlying rock, or a flat-bottomed valley, can hold stagnating water, bog conditions tend to occur and peat to be formed. Most of the bogs in the Lake District are those which depend upon a heavy rainfall for the maintenance of the water-logged conditions. Of these there are two main types, the 'blanket bog' and 'raised bog'. They are not, however, always readily separable, and grade into each other.

A blanket bog normally develops on an elevated, relatively flat surface, poorly drained and often intersected by gullies. The most characteristic plants are the two common species of cotton-grass, *Eriophorum vaginatum* and *angustifolium*, whose waving, silky plumes when in seed are a common but spectacular sight often covering many acres. Both plants have long white silky hairs closely packed among the seeds as they develop—the former has a single, upright head, the latter several nodding heads which wave in the wind (Fig. 10). Another common plant is the Deer Grass (*Trichophorum cespitosum*) which grows in tightly packed tufts and whose yellow stamens make a good show in early summer. All these plants are in fact sedges, not grasses. It is thought probable that much bog was once dominated by Sphagnum Moss, and that the present vegetation has come about as a result of man's disturbance of the original conditions.

Many raised bogs in fact still retain their carpet of *Sphagnum* which is of several species not easy to separate. These contribute a very beautiful variety of reds, greens, browns and yellows to the scenery. To understand the part which *Sphagnum* plays in the building up of these raised bogs, or 'mosses' as they are called in the Lake District, it will be convenient to begin at lake level.

Fig. 10 Cotton-grasses   (left) *Eriophorum angustifolium*   (right) *E. vaginatum*

As we have explained in Section I, the shallow margins of lakes and tarns tend to become filled with deposits of silt and peat, producing eventually marsh conditions where the deposit is mainly inorganic, and fen where it is peat. Later, the advent of sallow and alder produces the fen-like terrain known as carr. In some parts of Britain oakwood would ultimately replace the carr, but in the Lake District, because of the heavy rainfall, the normal succession is to raised bog.

The first stage in this process is colonisation of the carr by the Purple Moor-grass in large tufts, the sweet-smelling Bog Myrtle (*Myrica gale*), growing compactly and often covering large areas, and the Cross-leaved Heath (*Erica tetralix*) (Plate 17). These all tend to raise the surface above the level of the lake water so that the natural acidity of the peat formed by the decay of the tussocks is not neutralised by the less acid water.

The next important colonist is *Sphagnum*. This moss has a very specialised structure consisting of large empty perforated cells interspersed with the living cells. These empty cells absorb water like a sponge, a fact that can be easily tested by plucking a handful and squeezing it out. Consequently the moss in wet areas is able to carry its own water with it as it grows upwards and outwards, and a slightly convex cushion saturated with water forms on the surface; the leaves die from the bottom as the living plant pushes upwards, and a continuous sheet tends to form over a wide area, submerging and killing the earlier vegetation, and forming a layer of peat below, which gets deeper and deeper. This peat, because the *Sphagnum* depends on nutrient-deficient rain-water, is itself nutrient-deficient and acid, contrasting therefore with the carr and fen peat below, which was provided with nutrients by the lake water in which it accumulated. In this way a raised bog is formed which in ideal conditions slopes gently on all sides from the centre and is terminated by a relatively steep bank.

Although many raised bogs occupy the sites of former tarns or shallow lake margins, as just described, any very flat surface can provide the necessary waterlogged conditions if the rainfall is sufficient. For example, the fine raised bogs around Morecambe Bay have developed on top of the flat raised beaches described in Section I, page 32. Raised bogs at various stages of development are widespread. Where draining is taking place or where peat-cutting has occurred the bog tends to dry out and pine and birch quickly take over, as in the Nature Reserve of the Lake District Naturalists' Trust at Meathop on the Morecambe Bay raised beach.

Quite considerable areas of the Lake District are covered by blanket and raised bogs, and though they lack the variety of the lime-rich areas, these are by no means without botanical interest. It is here that are found the insectivorous plants which supplement a poor diet by their adaptations to digest animal proteins. We cannot produce anything as spectacular as the Pitcher Plant (*Sarracinea purpurea*) in the Lake District, but three separate genera of partially carnivorous plants occur, and some of the species are abundant. On the wet acid peat the commonest is the Round-leaved Sundew (*Drosera rotundifolia*) with sticky circular leaves and red gland-tipped tentacles which close in over the victim. In some of the very wet bogs the Great Sundew (*D. anglica*) with its long strap-shaped leaves occurs. The third British sundew, the Long-leaved (*D. intermedia*) occurs very rarely in one or two places, though this is the commonest on the south-country peat bogs. Not confined to peaty places but occurring in abun-

White Fork Moss (*Leuco-bryum glaucum*)

PLATE 10

Dog Lichen
(*Peltigera canina*)

Tree Tops
Observation
Tower *Erected
in Grizedale
Forest by the
Forestry Com-
mission to
facilitate
observation of
deer and other
wildlife*

PLATE 11

Track in
Grizedale
Forest *Inte-
grated land use,
with spruce and
larch plantations,
old hardwoods
and pasture*

PLATE 12

Dale Beck, Caldbeck *The stream has cleared away from the valley floor all glacial debris except the boulders which form its bed*

Confluence of Wren Gill and River Sprint, Longsleddale *Waterfalls due to hard strata outcropping across the course of a hill stream*

dance along streams and among wet boulders is the Common Butterwort (*Pinguicula vulgaris*) with its violet flowers. This has oval-shaped leaves which are also sticky and curl in on its victims. The third genus contains the bladderworts, two of which occur rather locally in the open pools among the peat where there is a slight current. Their leaves are submerged and are provided with open-necked little bladders full of air into which small invertebrates are swept by the current.

Even the casual walker cannot fail to notice in the bog areas the tall, dark green stems of the moss *Polytrichum commune*. The plants are often eighteen inches (45 centimetres) tall, and, when fruiting, the capsules borne on stems up to four inches (10 centimetres) long are a conspicuous feature, particularly when they are still covered by the shaggy golden-brown calyptra, or caps, which remain until the four-cornered capsule ripens. The male plants are shorter and end in a conspicuous star of leaves not unlike a small flower.

One bog plant confined to higher altitudes is the Cloudberry (*Rubus chamaemorus*), which is very common on most blanket bogs but, curiously, only occurs very sparsely in the Lake District. There is a considerable patch on the Langdale plateau, otherwise only a few isolated plants, probably bird-sown, appear from time to time. Lower down, the peat bogs are gay with the yellow flowers of the Bog Asphodel (*Narthecium ossifragum*) (Plate 17) in the summer and its brilliant orange seed-cases in the autumn. On the surface of the bog the Cranberry (*Vaccinium oxycoccus*) creeps with its curled-back pink petals in summer and red fruit in the autumn. Locally plentiful are the bell-shaped pink flowers of the Bog Rosemary (*Andromeda polifolia*). If one is very persevering and fortunate one may find half-buried in the *Sphagnum* and over-topped by sedges a few single spikes of the Bog Orchid (*Hammarbya paludosa*) in the late summer. There are certainly two localities in the Lake District where it occurs. Equally local and in similar sites is the Few-flowered Sedge (*Carex pauciflora*). The handsome Royal Fern (*Osmunda regalis*) (Plate 6) is still to be found very locally on peaty soils, especially among trees.

Other types of wet peaty areas depend for their water upon inflow from the surrounding slopes or upon ground water seepage. Usually this inflowing water contains some nutrients so that the vegetation may be anything from sphagnum bog, with perhaps a few indicators of less acid conditions, to extremely rich flushes and fens usually dominated by dense areas of rushes and sedges (especially *Carex rostrata*). These may occur quite high on the mountainside.

A common species which is found in more acid conditions is the Bog Bean (*Menyanthes trifoliata*) growing in peaty pools with its large trefoil leaves, slightly raised above the surface, and its feathery pink and white flowers. Where conditions are somewhat drier, sometimes where a pool has dried out, the leaves of the Marsh Pennywort (*Hydrocotyle vulgaris*) may be found closely appressed to the ground with its minute flowers close to the roots and none too easy to find. In similar areas the Marsh Violet (*Viola palustris*) may be found in considerable quantities, and the Bog Pimpernel (*Anagallis tenella*) trails its delicate shell-pink flowers. Among the sedges, the Star-sedge (*Carex echinata*) is abundant, the Flea Sedge (*C. pulicaris*) plentiful and the Dioecious (*C. dioica*) less common.

Trees and Woodlands

Woodlands of the acid soils We have already seen that left to itself the natural climax in the clothing of the mountainsides with vegetation would have been woodland, and many of the woods of the Lake District are found on stabilised scree, sometimes with very little depth of soil. In Glencoyne Wood by Ullswater one has only to kick the surface to find the underlying scree. But very few of these woods today are truly natural. Either they have been coppiced at some time, especially in the southern Lake District, or they have been altered by man in some other way.

Most of the existing woods are mixed oak and birch woods, with occasional pine, Larch (*Larix*), Sycamore (*Acer pseudoplatanus*) and Ash; and with Rowan (*Sorbus aucuparia*) (Fig. 11), Holly (*Ilex aquifolium*), Hazel (*Corylus avellana*), Hawthorn (*Crataegus monogyna*) and Juniper as under-trees. Of these last, Rowan and Holly occur frequently as isolated trees high up the mountainside; small bushes of Hawthorn not infrequently are spread widely over a hillside at intervals of a few yards from each other; and in a few places there are fairly dense areas of Juniper bushes. In the woods the juniper forms considerable shrubs up to fifteen feet (4.5 metres) high; on the higher hillsides they rarely exceed three feet (0.9 metres); and on the crags a sub-species (*Juniperus communis* ssp. *nana*) grows tightly appressed to the rock. Another widespread tree of the Lake District, but rarely growing in any density in the National Park, is the Yew. Most of these trees are very old and no vegetation can grow under them. The Borrowdale Yews are famous.

The glory of these Lake District woods and perhaps their most distinctive feature, whether they be mixed woodlands or oakwoods, are the mosses, a great variety of which grow on the woodland floor, on rocky outcrops within the woods, or on the trees themselves.

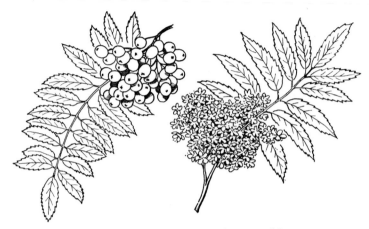

Fig. 11 Rowan, showing berries, flowers and leaves

The mossy carpet is composed in the main of species from seven genera. There are two species of *Dicranum* (*D. scoparium* and *D. majus*), both easily recognisable by their sickle-shaped leaves; two species of *Polytrichum* (*P. formosum* and *P. piliferum*) which catch the most casual eye with their tall little-branched stems, stiff leaves and prominent capsules when in fruit; *Plagiothecium undulatum,* conspicuous with long, flattened, pale green branches of tightly packed leaves, almost white when dry; *Mnium hornum,* a dull dark green moss often forming extensive patches; the red-stemmed *Rhytidiadelphus loreus,* uncommon in Britain outside the north-west; the easily recognisable White Fork Moss (*Leucobryum glaucum*) (Plate 10) which forms large rounded yellowish-green cushions which become almost white in dry weather; and in the damper woods conspicuous patches of the bright green *Thuidium tamariscinum* which, owing to its frond-like manner of branching, looks not unlike a mass of little ferns.

Prominent on the lower parts of tree trunks are *Hypnum cupressiforme* which adheres close to the trunks; and the paler, more loosely packed

Isothecium myosuroides. In the damp conditions of these woodlands, cushions of the *Leucobryum* often spread upwards from the ground carpet several feet up the trunks. Higher up on the branches of oak trees the neat round cushions of the epiphytic *Ulota crispa* frequently occur, often bristling with fruiting capsules. On the undersides of fallen and rotten logs the small yellow-green *Tetraphis pellucida* is often abundant. It rarely bears fruiting capsules but reproduces itself vegetatively by minute green 'buds' situated in conspicuous cup-like structures at the endings of the sterile shoots.

Among the rarer mosses of the woodland are *Hylocomium umbratum* and the magnificent Ostrich Plume Moss (*Ptilium crista-castrensis*) to be found in Glencoyne Wood, Naddle Forest, Longsleddale and Borrowdale.

In some woods where grassy patches appear between the oak trees, as at Holme Wood near Loweswater, *Rhytidiadelphus squarrosus,* with strongly reflexed leaves, is often very plentiful among the grass. Two red-stemmed mosses are often plentiful in similar situations, the frond-like *Hylocomium splendens* and *Pleurozium schreberi.* Where banks of broken soil occur the lovely bright green tufts of *Bartramia pomiformis* may be found, often bearing in profusion green apple-like capsules which eventually turn a beautiful bright orange. Patches of the common moss *Dicranella heteromalla*, again usually with fruit, are to be found in similar situations. It grows in close silky tufts from half to three-quarters of an inch (12–18 millimetres) high, and the pale brown capsules are borne on a pale yellow bristle-like stalk (seta) making the plant very conspicuous when it is fruiting in the early months of the year. Another moss of similar situations and habits where there is a clay soil is *Polytrichum aloides.* The plants look like green stars against the clay, but it is most conspicuous in spring when the ring (peristome) surrounding the fruiting capsule becomes white and attracts attention.

Where rocky outcrops occur in the woodland the Woolly Hair-moss and the somewhat similar *Rhacomitrium heterostichum* frequently gain a footing; and where the outcrops become larger in extent other invaders from the fellside also come in.

So far we have been considering woodlands of predominantly acid soil. But just as lime-rich areas occur higher up on the mountain slopes interspersed among the predominantly lime-deficient surroundings, so it is in the woodlands. There are several rich flushes into Troutdale Wood in

Borrowdale, and Glencoyne Wood as well as being very rich in mosses contains Alpine Enchanter's Nightshade (*Circaea alpina*) on its slopes and Wilson's Filmy Fern (*Hymenophyllum wilsonii*) where a beck runs through it. The lower part of the wood is mainly planted but it contains some fine conifers and beeches as well as some exotic plants escaped from neighbouring gardens.

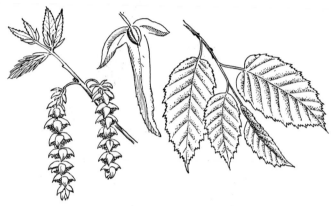

Fig. 12 Hornbeam, showing flowers, fruit and leaves

A tree of some interest is the Small-leaved Lime (*Tilia cordata*) which occurs in Roudsea Wood and also for some distance along the north side of Beckleven on the eastern side of Coniston Water. How it got to Coniston in such numbers is something of a mystery. There is a saying that wherever there were charcoal pits there were lime trees. There are certainly plenty of charcoal pits in the east Coniston woods, but the connection does not seem obvious. Another unexpected tree of the same woods is the Hornbeam (*Carpinus betulus*) (Fig. 12).

Many of the lower woods are very wet, especially at their margins, and it is here that considerable colonies of Yellow Balsam are to be found. This is the only balsam that has any claim to be native in Britain, and that only in the Lake District and North Wales. It maintains itself like the other balsams by a device by which the seed-pods when ripe burst open at a touch, scattering the seeds in all directions—hence the name *Impatiens noli-tangere*. It is of considerable entomological importance as the exclusive food-plant of the Netted Carpet, whose caterpillar feeds on its flowers and seeds (see page 127).

Wetter conditions still are to be found in the fen woodlands or carrs at the edges of sheltered bays alongside some of the lakes, especially Esthwaite and Derwentwater. There is, however, one such fen-woodland not far from Penrith which without doubt occupies the site of a former tarn. It is an unusually lime-rich peat site, situated as it is upon the Carboniferous

Fig. 13 Sedges (left) *Cladium mariscus* (right) *Schoenus nigricans*

limestone. It is just outside the National Park, but the boundary lies within two miles of it, and because of its special interest it deserves a brief description here. It is in the main a tangle of birch and alder interspersed with a good many shrubs of the Northern Sallow (*Salix phylicifolio*). There is a stream running along the edge and within are areas of quaking vegetation. Here grow the rare Great Spearwort (*Ranunculus lingua*), the Great Reed Mace (*Typha latifolia*), and many interesting sedges such as *Cladium mariscus* and *Schoenus nigricans* (Fig. 13). There was not long ago a considerable patch of Marsh Helleborine (*Epipactis palustris*), but this unfortunately seems to have disappeared as a result of dumping.

Woodlands of the limestone areas As one would expect, there is a great difference between the woods of the mainly acid soils of the Lake District and those of the Carboniferous limestone to the south of the district. Here Ash has become the dominant tree and the richer soil carries such woodland plants as Lily-of-the-valley (*Convallaria majalis*), Green Hellebore (*Helleborus viridis*) (Fig. 14), Herb Paris (*Paris quadrifolia*), Dark Red Helleborine (*Epipactis atrorubens*), Spurge Laurel (*Daphne laureola*) and Deadly Nightshade (*Atropa belladonna*); and the hedges at the edges of the wood are festooned with Old Man's Beard (*Clematis vitalba*), and White Bryony (*Bryonia dioica*).

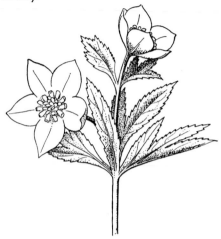

Fig. 14 Green Hellebore

Most of the larger woodlands situated on limestone within the National Park are in its southern area roughly between Kendal and the Greenodd estuary. An extensive area on the eastern side of Whitbarrow (Plate 16) is at the moment being partly reafforested by the Forestry Commission. Higher up, however, there is an extremely interesting flora. The Rigid Buckler Fern (*Dryopteris villarii*) and the Limestone Polypody (*Thelypteris robertiana*) grow in the fissures ('grikes') of the limestone pavement, and in the open spaces at the top of the wood where the limestone is exposed the Bird's-foot Sedge (*Carex ornithopoda*) is not uncommon. Lower down the much larger but very similar Fingered Sedge (*C. digitata*) grows plentifully. The boulders below the scree, which extend into the woodlands, are predominantly covered with a limestone-loving moss, the curly, golden-yellow *Ctenidium molluscum*. On the damp, calcareous clay between the loose stones, the most conspicuous and common moss is the large feathery *Thuidium tamariscinum*. There are a considerable number of yews in the upper part of the woodland, and Lilies-of-the-valley and Wild Daffodils (*Narcissus pseudonarcissus*) in abundance carpet its floor. Dense cushions of the moss *Tortella tortuosa* are frequent on rocky outcrops.

On the other side of Whitbarrow on its steep western slopes there are many whitebeams (Fig. 15) including the local *Sorbus lancastriensis*. In the

Fig. 15 Whitebeam

valley below lie the Witherslack Woods of considerable entomological interest and the home of many uncommon moths. The considerable areas of ash provide food for the very local Barred Tooth-striped (*Nothopteryx polycommata*) which in southern England is a privet feeder, but in the north has a strong preference for ash. Further west still on the eastern side of the Greenodd estuary is perhaps the most interesting wood of all, Roudsea Wood, which is a National Nature Reserve (page 204). Here woods of the limestone and woods of the Silurian slate join together forming one wood, with a wet marshy area included and a salt-marsh at the margin. The difference between the flora of the lime-rich and the acid woodland is obvious even to the casual eye. In this wood the very local Large Yellow Sedge (*Carex flava*) flourishes (Fig. 16). The conservation policy of the Nature Conservancy clearly agrees with it for it is spreading rapidly along the rides. The warden will gladly show it to visitors but no picking is allowed in a National Nature Reserve.

Conifer forests and afforestation   During the last half-century vast changes in the vegetative cover have been taking place over a considerable area of the Lake District, once again brought about by man, but this time as a piece of deliberate policy and with the effect of producing new woodlands, not destroying old ones.

Fig. 16 Large Yellow Sedge

Considerable replanting of woodlands had been carried out by big landowners in the eighteenth and nineteenth centuries, and it was during this period that the European Larch was introduced; but the first large-scale afforestation was undertaken by Manchester Corporation around their Thirlmere reservoir just before World War I. In 1919 the Forestry Commission was formed and it began its afforestation programme with woods around the Keswick area.

Naturally the object of forestry is to grow timber for profit and to produce saleable timber as quickly as possible. As coniferous species such as larch and spruce grow far more vigorously and more quickly on the thin soils of the Lake District than the native oak, it is not surprising that the first plantings were almost wholly of conifers. It came to be realised, however, that the planting of the hillsides with conifers in serried lines produces a very formal effect, and nowadays the purely economic objective is usually tempered by the desire to blend the forests into the traditional landscape by softening the outlines, and some hardwood plantings are being carried out on suitable sites. These are chiefly Beech (*Fagus sylvatica*), which, though only doubtfully native, has certainly been in the Lake District for a long time, and Sycamore which was introduced into Britain in the fifteenth and sixteenth centuries. Both are more high-volume timber producers than oak, which they are gradually superseding.

The principal conifers used are larches, Scots Pine usually on heather, and the hardy high-volume timber producer Sitka Spruce (*Picea sitchensis*), usually on the higher hillsides where *Molinia* is often the dominant grass. Whatever may be thought of the scenic effect of conifer forests, certainly they bring economic improvements from the point of view of land use. In the first place the bracken-covered hillsides, with little feed even for sheep, are put to economic use, and the new tree cover slows down the run-off of the heavy rainfall and assists in preventing flooding in the valleys.

We have already seen that the exclusion of sheep and rabbits from young conifer plantations has encouraged a luxuriant undergrowth of heather and bilberry, and other plants normally associated with this type of cover would be expected to appear, as in the native forests of Scotland, were it not for the fact that the opportunity is short-lived owing to the density of planting—as the trees grow the shade becomes so intense that most under-growth is impossible, and what has developed quickly disappears. How-ever, some mosses such as *Polytrichum formosum* and some species of *Sphagnum* often flourish in the low-light conditions. When the trees reach a size to be thinned out after fifteen or twenty years the Wavy Hair-grass (*Deschampsia flexuosa*) and some species of *Festuca* become established and provide winter grazing for the sheep. Also relics of the old plant communi-ties remain in the clearings, rides and knolls, ready to re-invade the wood-land to some extent as it is thinned out. This is particularly true of heather.

With the change in cover provided by a conifer forest, naturally there are also changes in population. Many insects feed on conifers and the recesses of the forest provide day-time resting places for various moths. As the forest grows up many birds, including game birds, will leave, but they are to some extent replaced by tits, and several mammals will find welcome shelter—deer, Fox, Rabbit, vole and Pine Marten. (See Sections IV and V.) So that in these ways formal forestry though it has changed populations, has helped to maintain and in some ways to increase the holding capacity of the land for the native fauna of the area.

Limestone cliffs and scars

The maritime cliffs and the inland escarpments ('scars') of the Carboniferous limestone hills surrounding the Lake District provide habitats in
some ways similar to those of the high crags in the centre of the area. Here
are to be found some of the rarest and at the same time some of the most
colourful flowers of the area. On the narrow ledges typical of this formation, out of reach of both sheep and humans, with abundant nourishment
and little competition from other species, plants which find it difficult to
get a foothold elsewhere flourish in profusion and provide brilliant patches
of colour in their flowering season.

Most of these cliffs and scars are outside the National Park, but two
escarpments running north and south to the west of Kendal fall within it.
We have already mentioned Whitbarrow (Plate 16) in the woodland
section. Nearer to Kendal is a long escarpment consisting of Cunswick,
Underbarrow and Scout Scars which is richer in the more spectacular
flowering plants. Bloody Cranesbill (*Geranium sanguineum*) provides
patches of crimson-purple; Horseshoe Vetch (*Hippocrepis comosa*), Hoary
Rock-rose (*Helianthemum canum*) and Common Rock-rose (*H. chamaecistus*) patches of brilliant yellow. Less conspicuous are the Mountain
Everlasting (*Antennaria dioica*), the Fragrant Orchid (*Gymnadenia conopsea*),
the Lesser Butterfly Orchid (*Platanthera bifolia*) and the Wild Columbine
(*Aquilegia vulgaris*).

There are many mosses growing on these limestone uplands, which are
absent from the areas of acid rocks and soils. Various lime-loving mosses
hang down in cascades over the rock faces, principally belonging to the
genera *Neckera* and *Anomodon*. Peculiar to the limestone top is *Funaria
muehlenbergii*, half an inch (13 millimetres) tall, in loose tufts, bearing a
slightly curved capsule with a swelling on one side. It is a close relative of
the familiar Fire Moss (*Funaria hygrometrica*), which is found wherever
brushwood has been burned, irrespective of the nature of the soil, and is
particularly conspicuous when its fruit turns the sites of fires into patches of
bright orange.

Among the rarities of the limestone within the National Park are the
delicate Maidenhair Fern (*Adiantum capillus-veneris*) flourishing within the
crevices of a limestone cliff, its exact locality a closely guarded secret; the
naturalised *Potentilla norvegica* on a limestone floor and the Dark-red

Helleborine among the rocks and screes. Not very far away, but outside the boundaries of the National Park, the cliff ledges are gay with the magnificent purple-blue spikes of the extremely local Spiked Speedwell (*Veronica spicata hybrida*), and, in a much more restricted area and flowering very late in the year, the yellow of the Goldilocks (*Aster linosyris*), both preserved no doubt by their inaccessibility.

Plants of the fresh water and waterside

In Section III the succession of plant communities according to the depth of water and the nature of the in-filling process are mentioned: the under-water plants growing in deposits on the lake bottom, those with floating leaves, the emergent plants, and the fen plants. Earlier in this Section we traced the succession further to carr and bog (page 51). It still remains to describe in more detail some of the plants themselves.

Growing in the sediment, completely submerged, at the bottom of certain lakes and tarns may be found two cryptogamic (i.e. spore-bearing) plants. One is Quill-wort (*Isoetes lacustris*) (Fig. 17). This bears its spores at the base of the quill-like pointed leaves where they clasp the plant, and it is rather distantly related to the club mosses (page 48). It is locally abundant where conditions are suitable, and as it is only lightly rooted, in stormy weather the lake margins are often strewn with it. The other plant, which is rare and very local, is Pillwort (*Pilularia globulifera*). It is related to the ferns and bears its spores in a hairy globular 'sporocarp' which gives it its name. It is not always submerged but may be found creeping along the muddy margin.

Another plant which is usually submerged but can also grow along the margins is the curious member of the Crucifer family, Awlwort (*Subularia aquatica*), with very sharp-pointed leaves and a white flower only 2.5 millimetres in diameter. It is very local, but not uncommon where it occurs. In similar situations but not normally submerged is the much commoner Shore-weed (*Littorella uniflora*) (Fig. 17), a member of the plantain family. Until comparatively recently along a short stretch of shingly foreshore on Ullswater the rare *Ranunculus reptans* crept in a series of loops, with a small yellow flower springing from each rooting node. Almost certainly in the last few years this has been trampled out of existence by the crowds of visitors who now frequent the site, with no knowledge, of course, of what they are treading on. It may possibly occur in other places round the lake and it has been reported from the shore of Windermere. Its other station in Britain is Loch Leven in Scotland.

A plant which has its leaves wholly underwater in a rosette on the bottom but sends up a tall spike of flowers well above the surface is the

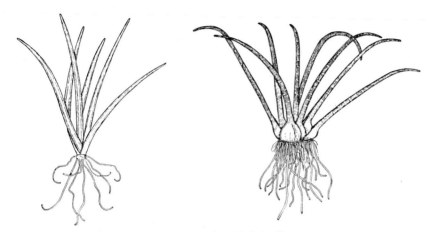

Fig. 17 (left) Shore-weed   (right) Quill-wort

Water Lobelia (*Lobelia dortmanna*). This is common in shallow water at the edge of many lakes and tarns and its delicate pale blue flowers make a great contribution to the scene. Often growing in streams but with its leaves and flowers above water is the Yellow Monkey-flower (*Mimulus guttatus*) and less commonly the Blood-drop Emlets (*M. luteus*), the petals of which are spotted deep red.

Of the plants with floating leaves by far the most spectacular are water-lilies. Both Yellow (*Nuphar lutea*) and White (*Nymphaea alba*) occur throughout the Lake District but they seem to be less plentiful than they were. Several species of water crowfoot occur, the commoner ones in profusion. Some as well as having more or less circular floating leaves have long submerged linear leaves. Not infrequently streams get almost choked with them. The white flowers of the larger-flowered species are often so closely packed that they give the appearance of a continuous white patch on the water. The commonest plant with floating leaves is the Broad-leaved Pond-weed (*Potamogeton natans*). Ponds everywhere get covered with it; in sluggish rills high on the fells it is often replaced by *P. polygoni-folius*. The flowers are inconspicuous. Several other species occur, many with submerged leaves often on very long thin stalks. These are usually in deeper water and, like the Quill-wort, are easily uprooted in stormy weather when the margins become littered with a tangled mass of long streamers.

On a few of the smaller tarns and ponds, often at a considerable altitude, the long narrow leaves of the Floating Bur-reed (*Sparganium angustifolium*) may be seen on the surface of the water with a spike containing stamens and ovaries on separate spikelets raised above the surface. One beautiful little rock tarn, Hard Tarn, not fifty yards (45 metres) across, lies immediately under the Helvellyn Crags and only about 700 feet (210 metres) below the summit ridge. Here the common Water Starwort (*Callitriche stagnalis*) grows, but instead of forming a green mass of leaves floating on the surface of the water as it does in lowland streams, each plant has one single stem which grows upright and never breaks surface but flowers and fruits under water. The stems are separated from each other by an inch or more, and as one looks down into the crystal-clear water, provided it is not ruffled by the wind, it looks for all the world like a miniature underwater forest.

A handsome moss, growing on wet ground along the margins of lakes and tarns, is *Climacium dendroides*. The conspicuous secondary growths shooting up at intervals from the long, creeping main stems are like miniature green trees, up to three inches (76 millimetres) tall. Its tree-like appearance readily identifies it. The long, trailing dark green stems of another moss, *Fontinalis antipyretica*, may be found growing submerged in rivers, becks and tarns up to over 2000 feet (600 metres). The keeled leaves are arranged on the stems in three rows, giving the plant a triangular cross-section.

Along the margins of lakes and streams the vegetation is often rank. The yellow flowers of the Common Loosestrife (*Lysimachia vulgaris*) make dense clumps in many places. A colony of the smaller, much less common, and very interesting *L. terrestris* used to flourish near Bowness, but has unfortunately been built over. This colony produced flowers in abundance and also red bulbils in the axils of the leaves. Another colony at the southern end of Lake Windermere, which is taller in stature, also produces flowers plentifully, and large elongated brown bulbils after the flowering is over. The more normal condition elsewhere is to produce bulbils and only rarely flowers (Clapham, Tutin and Warburg, page 633). It is a native of North America.

We have already mentioned the rapid spread of Policeman's Helmet (*Impatiens glandulifera*) along our streams and rivers (page 7). There is a colony of another of the balsams, the Small Balsam (*Impatiens parviflora*), a native of Siberia, on the shore of Lake Windermere, but this has not spread beyond its immediate surroundings. Both are closely related to the native Yellow Balsam of our wet woods already referred to (page 57).

A showy riverside plant which has also spread in recent years is the Broad-leaved Ragwort (*Senecio fluviatilis*) mostly along the River Eden, but also in some places within the National Park. Other smaller plants of the riverside are the deep blue Skull-cap (*Scutellaria galericulata*), the figworts (*Scrophularia spp.*) and Large Bittercress (*Cardamine amara*); and where the streams pass through deep gorges, such as those described in Section I, the variety of the Prickly Shield-fern (*Polystichum aculeatum* var. *lonchitidoides*) which is often mistaken for the Holly Fern.

As the Lake District valleys widen typical plants of the damp fields bordering the streams are Large Burnet (*Sanguisorba officinalis*), Bistort (*Polygonum bistorta*), known locally as Easter Ledges, whose leaves are eaten in a herb pudding, and, abundant everywhere, the purple Betony (*Betonica officinalis*).

Coastal habitats

Owing to its geographical situation between two great estuaries, the Solway to the north and Morecambe Bay to the south, with a long bow-shaped coastline between them on the west, the Lake District is surrounded on three sides by an exceptionally long coastal area. But only a very small part of this, and by no means the most interesting botanically, is included in the National Park.

The longest stretch in the Park is from Drigg to Silecroft, measuring direct about a dozen miles (20 kilometres). This includes the dune-covered spit at Drigg which partly separates from the sea the estuary of the Irt, Mite and Esk at Ravenglass; the salt-marshes which fringe its eastern margin facing the mainland and the shingle beach southwards. The only other coastal areas within the Park are the head of the Leven estuary near Greenodd, which includes the salt-marsh bordering Roudsea Wood and the head of the Kent estuary near Arnside (Plate 16). These, though important botanically, are only of very small extent. Consequently, although the main types of coastal habitat are to some degree represented in the Park, they are not of sufficient extent to justify more than a brief reference to each.

Flats and salt-marsh The estuarine flats of silt and fine sand for some distance below high-water mark are being colonised by vegetation which will in due course turn them into salt-marsh. The principal pioneer is Glasswort (*Salicornia spp.*), whose spikes stick up through the wet sand at some distance from each other like a miniature pine forest. We have already mentioned the hybrid cordgrass, *Spartina townsendii*, which has invaded Morecambe Bay, but has not yet been reported from within the Park (page 7).

Beyond the risk of regular total submergence other plants which thrive on a salt solution in the soil around their roots begin to consolidate the vegetation. Herbaceous Sea Blite (*Suaeda maritima*), Sea Aster (*Aster tripolium*), Sea Arrow-grass (*Triglochin maritima*), Sea Plantain (*Plantago maritima*), Sea Spurry (*Spergularia media*) and the grass Sea Poa (*Puccinellia maritima*) all contribute. Most spectacular of these is the Sea Aster, which covers considerable areas and looks like a very fleshy Michaelmas Daisy. As the salt-marsh builds up (described in Section I, page 32) other plants appear—the mealy-leaved Sea Purslane (*Halimione portulacoides*), Sea Rush (*Juncus maritimus*), the pink Thrift, the white Scurvy-grass (*Cochlearia officinalis*) and the blue-purple sea lavenders. Two species of the latter occur side by side in the National Park, the Common Sea Lavender (*Limonium vulgare*) and the Lax-flowered (*L. humile*). Out of reach of all but the highest spring tides a compact turf develops, to which the Red Fescue (*Festuca rubra*) largely contributes, mixed with Sea Milkwort (*Glaux maritima*) and Sea Sandwort (*Honkenya peploides*), as well as several of the other plants already mentioned, especially round the pools of brackish water and along the winding channels up which the tide flows. This periodically sea-washed turf is extensively grazed by sheep and is of considerable commercial value for high-grade lawns and bowling greens.

Beyond the salt-marsh but still within the influence of the sea are clumps of the umbelliferous Wild Celery (*Apium graveolens*) and Parsley Water Dropwort (*Oenanthe lachenalii*); the creeping Rest Harrow (*Ononis spinosa*) often bearing spines; and in one part of the National Park three species of

North Fen, Esthwaite *A National Nature Reserve showing reed-swamp and carr. Drumlins beyond*

PLATE 13

Oakwood, Little Langdale *Typical breeding habitat of Pied Flycatcher, Redstart and Tree Pipit*

PLATE 14 Some typical animals from the stony substratum of a lake
1 Flat mayfly nymph, *Ecdyonurus*   2 Freshwater Shrimp (*Gammarus pulex*)
3 Large stonefly nymph, *Perla*   4 Water hog-louse, *Asellus*
                                                     5 Flatworm, *Polycelis*

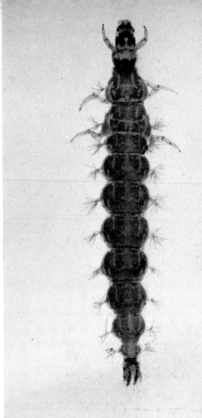

PLATE 15 Some typical animals from a swift stony stream
1 Mayfly nymph, *Baetis*   2 Free-living caddis larva, *Rhyacophila*
3 Caddis larva, *Odontocerum*   4 Larva of buffalo   5 Bottom-living
  albicorne, in a case of stones   gnat, *Simulium*   beetle, *Helmis*

Whitbarro
Scar over F
Estuary *A*
block of Ca
ferous Limes
Salt-marsh
foreground a
raised beach
beyond estu

PLATE 1

Esthwaite
Water *A*
productive l
among drum
in Silurian
country

centaury grow within a stone's-throw of each other—the Common (*Centaurium erythraea*), the narrow-leaved large-flowered *C. littorale* with its deeper pink petals, and the more spreading *C. pulchellum*.

The only moss tolerant of salt-marsh conditions is *Pottia heimii*, a small moss up to half an inch (12 millimetres) high, which is one of the few strictly maritime mosses.

The shingle beach   The north-west produces no extensive shingle spits comparable with Chesil or Blakeney on the south and east coasts, but considerable stretches of shingle do occur fringing the coast line and one of these is in the National Park.

These beaches are formed of water-worn pebbles of varying sizes, probably derived in most cases from boulder clay deposits just off the coast. An interesting feature of the foreshore near Drigg is that offshore there is a considerable deposit of peat, containing large portions of trees, which must at one time have been an area of forest during the period of lower sea-level (page 32). In stormy weather large blocks of peat are thrown up and form a continuous line parallel to the shore.

Plants can rarely establish themselves on shingle that is within the reach of frequent storm-waves, but above this zone where the shingle is more or less stable and mixed with a little sand a sparse vegetation grows up. The most spectacular plants are the Yellow Horned Poppy (*Glaucium flavum*) with its large flowers and long seed-pods, and the mauve Sea Rocket (*Cakile maritima*). Other plants are the Sea Campion which also grows on the mountains (page 37); various species of orache (*Atriplex*); and here and there the yellow Isle of Man Cabbage (*Rhynchosinapis monensis*). For the rich blue flowers of the rare Oyster-plant (*Mertensia maritima*) one must extend one's search of the shingle some few miles beyond the limits of the National Park.

Dunes and slacks   Wherever a wide sandy beach is laid bare at low tides, sand grains as they dry are driven landwards by on-shore winds. Any small obstacle will cause a slowing down of the wind speed, and in the sheltered lee of the obstacle sand will be deposited, starting to build up a small mound. If the obstacle is a plant such as Marram Grass (*Ammophila arenaria*) which is capable of growing up through the sand, an embryo dune will start to be formed. In time Marram is joined by other plants and large and lofty systems of dunes are built up. Frequently a new series of dunes may arise on the seaward side of the original system, more or less protecting it from the wind so that the supply of sand is cut off and the older dunes cease to grow.

As the vegetation develops the dunes become stabilised and there is a succession of plant communities from the embryo dunes on the seaward side to the fully stabilised dunes to the landward. The principal stabilising plants all have extensive underground parts. Most frequent is the Marram Grass which covers vast areas, but with it are the Sea Couch-grass (*Agropyron pungens*) and here and there the very beautiful Lyme Grass (*Elymus arenarius*) with its wide glaucous leaves. On the lower part of the dunes the Sand Sedge (*Carex arenaria*) sends its runners in almost dead straight lines which produce upright tufts at more or less regular intervals and give them an artificial appearance as if they had been planted in rows. A moss, *Tortula ruraliformis*, also helps to fix the dunes. It is hoary and has white points to its leaves.

On the more stable flats may be found large patches of another moss, *Ceratodon purpureus*, which is very conspicuous in spring when it is covered with the profusion of purplish-red cylindrical fruit. Several other mosses also occur. In bare patches among the Marram, and often on the shore below the dunes, are clumps of the misty blue Sea Holly (*Eryngium maritimum*), both Sea and Portland Spurges (*Euphorbia paralias* and *E. portlandica*), and the Dune Pansy (*Viola tricolor* ssp. *curtisii*).

The hollows between parallel systems of dunes are called 'slacks'. These produce a highly specialised flora, its variety depending very largely on the degree of moisture. Among our local dune systems there are slacks second only to Ainsdale, near Southport, in the variety and interest of their vegetation and the rare plants to be found in them, but there is nothing comparable to this at Drigg, the only part of the system which is in the National Park.

Sea cliffs Both the New Red Sandstone and the Carboniferous Limestone which encircle the Lake District produce cliffs at the coast, St Bees on the one hand and Humphrey Head on the other. Each has a highly specialsed and interesting flora, but neither is included in the National Park and they are, therefore, out of the scope of this book. It is, however, of interest that the three shore plants which also occur on the mountains (page 43) all occur on St Bees Head. There is one rock-loving moss, *Grimnia maritima*, which is tolerant of sea spray and occurs on the very small strip of coastal cliff in the National Park; it grows in dense, rigid, dark green cushions.

In this chapter we have tried to give some picture of the different habitats in the Lake District and the variety and attractiveness of their plant life. It will be the purpose of subsequent chapters to show how these habitats have become the homes of vast hordes of animals from the microscopic dwellers in the soil to the Red Stag standing four and a half feet (1.4 metres) at the shoulder.

LICHENS

by O. L. Gilbert

The high humidity, pure air and diversity of natural habitats help to make the Lake District one of the best parts of the country for studying lichens. Everywhere they cover rocks, trees and stone walls, seeming to increase in abundance with the barrenness of the habitat. These curious plants—a symbiotic association between an alga and a fungus—are physiologically suited for surviving in such places. Most can dry out completely without suffering permanent damage; then when it rains they become wet immediately and resume photosynthesis. This is combined with a remarkable power for concentrating the minute traces of nutrients which come down in the rain, an ability which has led to a considerable build-up of radioactivity in their thalli.

Summits

As one ascends the hills lichens become increasingly important in the vegetation. At lower levels competition from higher plants restricts them to the more extreme habitats, but above 2000 feet (600 metres) the alpine grassland and dwarf shrub communities become increasingly lichen-rich until on some of the summits, together with various bryophytes such as the Woolly Hair-moss (*Rhacomitrium languinosum*) and *Andreaea* spp., they form the leading and often the only vegetation type. Around the cairn on Scafell Pike five flowering plants, six bryophytes and twenty species of lichen can be found. Many of them are insignificant-looking grey or black species which form an inseparable crust on the surface of the rocks, but *Lecidea dicksonii* is a rather striking rusty red. It must be admitted that many of the most celebrated of our alpine lichens seem to be absent from the Lake District.

Crags and middle slopes

Where heather and other dwarf shrubs start to form an open, windswept community, *Cetraria islandica*, a lichen confusingly called Iceland Moss, can often be found. This is one of the few edible lichens. Its forked, chestnut-brown, strap-like thallus up to three inches (76 millimetres) long and edged with short black spines must be boiled to get rid of the poisonous lichen acids before it is ready to eat. The best-known cliff lichen is probably *Umbilicaria crustulosa*. Its large, grey, leaf-like thallus is confined to sheltered crevices in Langdale, its only British station.

Lower slopes and walls

Here the typical lichens of fine-grained siliceous rocks can be studied. Most conspicuous is the Map Lichen (*Rhizocarpon geographicum*) shown on the boulder in the foreground of Plate 8. It forms large smooth patches of a bright yellow-green colour intersected by fine black lines so the whole somewhat resembles a map with boundaries drawn in. A lichen which sometimes grows with it is *Haematomma ventosum*; it has a thick grey warted thallus and large dark blood-red fruiting bodies.

Flat leafy lichens are very conspicuous on walls in the valleys. The most prominent genus is *Parmelia*, several species of which were once in great demand for dyeing. One of the commonest Lake District species *P. saxatilis* is grey, with a pattern of fine white lines on the younger lobes, the older parts becoming roughened. It produces a rich rusty-red dye which does not need a mordant. There is at present a revival of lichen-dyeing and details can be found in several books.

Lichens of the genus *Peltigera* can often be found in grassy places and among mosses on trees or wall bases. The species illustrated in Plate 10 is known as the Dog Lichen and was once thought to be a cure for rabies. Around farms the well-known *Xanthoria parietina* forms orange patches on walls, roofs and trees. Its growth seems to be enhanced by bird droppings.

Bogs

In bogs where there is much *Sphagnum* and eroding peat the lichen genus *Cladonia* comes into its own. The cladonias are the hawkweeds and brambles of the lichen world, an extremely difficult group of about sixty British species, all of which show plasticity. Some have a very intricately branched, sponge-like appearance and form small grey hummocky lawns among heather. This freely branching type is loosely called reindeer moss (*Cladonia impexa* and *C. arbuscula*, Fig. 18), and in higher latitudes is abundant enough to form an important source of winter fodder. A major division within the genus is the colour of the fruits which may be red or brown. Some with red fruits are extremely attractive and take the form of trumpets one inch (25 millimetres) high with 'red beads' round the edge, e.g., *C. coccifera*. Others are branched like candlesticks with large red spherical fruits terminating the branches, e.g., *C. floerkiana* and *C. macilenta* (Fig. 18).

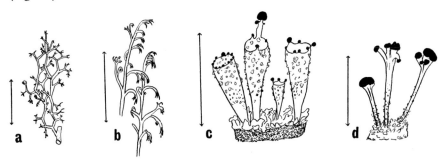

Fig. 18 Some *Cladonia* species common in moorland habitats (a) *C. impexa* (b) *C. arbuscula* (c) *C. coccifera* (d) *C. floerkiana* (Each scale represents ½ inch)

Woodlands

Trees in the Lake District carry a very rich lichen flora, in contrast to trees over most of England which have had their epiphyte flora greatly impoverished by air pollution, sulphur dioxide seeming to be the most toxic fraction. Trees vary considerably in the texture, pH and water-holding capacity of their bark, and this influences the lichen cover. Ash, sycamore and elm have a 'rich bark' and carry a very different assemblage of lichens from the 'poor bark' of birch and most conifers.

One of the most conspicuous tree lichens is *Parmelia caperata*, which forms yellow-green patches up to dinner-plate size on favourable trunks. They form a good display on roadside trees between Eskdale and Wasdale. Another prominent lichen, Old Man's Beard (*Usnea* spp.), has a grey-green intricately branched filamentous thallus and is an excellent indicator of pure air. Its luxuriant growth may be pendulous up to six inches (15 centimetres) or more. *Alectoria* spp. have a similar structure but form tangled masses of brownish-black hair-like strands on poor bark.

The smooth bark of hazel, rowan and beech frequently yields one or two writing lichens (*Graphis, Opegrapha*). Their thin, pale thalli are covered

with black, elongated and branched fruiting bodies which look like hiero-
glyphics. In the Lake District, as elsewhere, native woodland has a far
superior epiphyte flora compared with even the oldest plantations.

Limestone

Weathered limestone is completely covered with a small-scale mosaic of
crustose microlichens, which gives it a most pleasing appearance when
examined closely. Six square inches (40 square centimetres) of rock often
produce ten lichens of various colours: yellow (*Caloplaca*), black (*Verrucaria,
Placynthium*) and white (*Lecanora*). These microlichens are frequently
difficult to name and the beginner is advised to start with the largest lichens
he can find.

FUNGI

by Juliet C. Frankland and T. F. Hering

Fungi are very wide-ranging, so we must not expect to find species unique to Lakeland. The area is, however, rich in natural habitats favourable to the growth and fruiting of a wide variety of these plants without chlorophyll, which depend on dead or living organic material. Under the mild wet climate, soil moisture is permanently fairly high, with accumulation of plant and animal litter under both trees and grass, where many toadstools can flourish. Beatrix Potter has captured the beautiful form and colour of several common species in her paintings of Lakeland specimens, some of which illustrate W. P. K. Findlay's *Wayside and Woodland Fungi*. Identification keys and references to further mycological literature can also be found in this book.

Wild land and rough grazing, which make up most of Lakeland, support far more fungi than arable country. A survey carried out at Merlewood Research Station, Grange-over-Sands, in 1962–64 showed that a woodland plot of 100 square metres can produce over fifty kinds of fruit body each autumn—more than the number of flowering plant species in the plot. The same survey showed that the weight of toadstools found in Lakeland forests is usually smaller than in warmer parts of Europe, but the amateur collector should find plenty of specimens to fill his plastic bags or basket.

The 'damp' oakwoods on soils overlying acid rocks (Plate 13) contain greater quantities of mycorrhizal toadstools than the drier woodlands on Carboniferous limestone. Among these mycorrhizal fungi, closely associated with living tree roots, two genera, *Lactarius* (Milk Caps) and *Russula*, are prominent. Both genera possess distinctive 'cheesy' flesh, and several species are brightly coloured. There are also many toadstools in the genus *Cortinarius* with a 'cobweb' veil protecting the young gills. Several new species have been described from Scottish forests and may well occur in Lakeland also. Unfortunately the identification of many *Cortinarius* species is very difficult. Conifer forests usually have their own distinctive mycorrhizal species. *Lactarius camphoratus*, a reddish-brown species smelling of curry powder as it dries, and *Russula emetica* with a scarlet cap, although associated with conifers over most of Europe, grow abundantly in pure oak stands in Lakeland.

In woodlands on limestone fewer large mycorrhizal species can be found, but the deadly poisonous Death Cap (*Amanita phalloides*) occurs in quantity, although it is generally rare elsewhere in the north of England. The cap is variable in colour, but usually has a pale yellowish hue tinged with green; at the base of the stalk is a cup-like volva, the remains of a sheath which encloses the young fruit body, These woodlands also contain a perplexing variety of small decomposer toadstools, including some brilliant blue species of *Leptonia*. Some of these decomposers may be particularly characteristic of forests with a Lakeland climate, but many more observations are required before we have a good account of them. Since the fruit body is usually the only portion of the fungus organism recorded and may not be produced every year, it will be a long time before a species list approaching completeness can be compiled.

As might be expected, exposed and isolated patches of woodland have fewer decomposer toadstools, but most mycorrhizal species are still present. In Keskadale Oaks, the highest virtually natural woodland in Britain, over thirty species of larger fungi have been recorded and the list is far from complete. Thin acid soils often contain large quantities of the subterranean and more or less globose fungus, *Elaphomyces muricatus*, with its fungus parasite, *Cordyceps ophioglossoides*, which produces little black stalks above the soil and thus reveals the presence of its host.

When the fleshy toadstools have been killed by frost, many woody fungi with pores instead of gills can still be found on trees and rotting wood. The white or brown hoof-shaped brackets of the Razor-strop fungus (*Piptoporus betulinus*), restricted to birch, are particularly common. The corky tissue was used for making strops until the beginning of the last century. Another polypore, *Polyporus brumalis*, is frequent on stumps and branches of various broadleaved trees. In general shape its leathery fruit body, with a cap and stalk, resembles the gilled toadstools.

Fungus-collectors spend much of their time in woodlands, but open habitats, where the characteristic fungi often have a longer fruiting season than woodland species, should not be neglected. On mountainsides, the larger fungi can be found more frequently amongst heather and grass than under bracken. Several species grow on the dung of grazing animals, but there are also a number of brightly coloured toadstools with 'waxy' gills belonging to the genus *Hygrophorus*, which arise from soils and decaying grass roots. Boggy mountainsides have a characteristic fungus flora associated with *Sphagnum* moss and peat. It includes a number of small bright brown toadstools in the genus *Galerina* and a yellow unbranched club fungus up to two inches (50 millimetres) high, *Clavaria argillacea*, found only on moorland peat.

Waterside habitats are often too waterlogged for the continuous growth of many terrestrial fungi. Very common in spring, however, is the bright orange Brook Beacon (*Mitrula paludosa*) on rotting leaves lying in shallow pools. In autumn around roots of Alder small brown toadstools, *Naucoria escharoides*, are likely to be found.

Apart from wild mushrooms, several other wild fungi are good to eat. At least three edible toadstools are occasionally abundant in Lakeland: Blewits (*Lepista saeva*), the yellow Chanterelle (*Cantharellus cibarius*) and Shaggy Parasol (*Lepiota rhacodes*). Even the young egg-like fruit bodies of the Stinkhorn (*Phallus impudicus*), allied to the puff-balls, are edible. This fungus, common in woodlands with plenty of rotting vegetation, usually occurs on the ground but is sometimes found perched in an old coppice stool of Hazel where organic matter has collected. The mature Stinkhorn can be tracked down from a distance of several yards by the foetid smell from its slimy conical cap. A word of warning—fungi must be carefully identified before eating them—there are no useful 'rules of thumb' for distinguishing the poisonous from the edible fungus.

SECTION THREE

LIFE IN THE WATER

LIFE IN THE WATER

by T. T. Macan

The waters of the Lake District fall roughly into three categories: lakes, tarns and streams. Like so many classifications of natural phenomena, this scheme is a useful generalisation that leads to endless and profitless argument when attempts are made to fix exact limits. In general lakes are large and lie in the main valleys, and the most frequent emergent plant is the Common Reed (*Phragmites communis*). Tarns are smaller, lie in side valleys, and are characterised by the Beaked Sedge (*Carex rostrata*). The distinction on vegetation breaks down in those lakes and tarns where there is no emergent vegetation. Nearly all the streams and rivers in the Lake District flow rapidly, with the result that their beds are stony or rocky (Plate 12). The slow stream with a sandy or muddy bottom and a growth of rooted vegetation, familiar to naturalists from flatter parts of the country, is uncommon. The streams running down the fellsides join in the valley to form a river, which is almost always rapid with a stony bottom too.

A stream of the type described is almost invariably well oxygenated. The temperature is variable. It may be low and constant through the year at the spring, if the water comes from deep in the rock or from a thick deposit of peat. It heats up rapidly in the sun, particularly in a sluggish stretch, but may cool down rapidly in a wood or in a deep gorge that the sun does not penetrate. A stream originating in a marsh or a shallow pond may be warm. The litter contributed by both plants and animals (the word was applied to dead leaves long before the advent of the toffee-paper and the cigarette carton) provides food for many aquatic organisms, and any that can establish itself in running water has a steady supply of food constantly carried past it. It must, however, avoid being carried away by means of some modification either of form or of behaviour. There are many tarns high up in the mountains and nearly all these lie in the corrie basins formed during the Ice Age (Plates 3 and 8). The bottom in shallow water is generally stony and superficial observations suggest that living organisms are few, but no proper survey of one of these tarns has been carried out.

Lower down artificial tarns are numerous. Most date from the Edwardian era, when landowners were creating them by damming valleys for various purposes. Open bodies of water thus created were found to produce good sport if stocked with trout, and many were built for this purpose only. Gradually a tarn fills up. At a certain depth floating-leaved and emergent vegetation spoil the fishing and then the tarn is neglected. The dam starts to disintegrate and before long there is no standing water left. This may well be why artificial tarns more than sixty to seventy years old are rare.

The lower tarns are much more productive than the higher ones. There is more soil and more vegetation. Stoneworts (*Chara* spp.), or Milfoil (*Myriophyllum* spp.), may cover the bottom in deep water, and the Canadian Pondweed (*Elodea canadensis*) is another that may be found here. Shore-weed (*Littorella uniflora*) (Fig. 17), and a submerged rush often form extensive swards in shallow water. As vegetation develops, it generally passes through three stages, first submerged plants, then species with floating leaves, and finally emergents. The second and third of these stages in a tarn are almost invariably the same, the plants being Broad-leaved Pondweed (*Potamogeton natans*) and one or more of the larger sedges (*Carex* spp.).

The lakes are of particular interest to the biologist because, although all of the same type, they vary in productiveness. Over forty years ago the late Professor W. H. Pearsall, F.R.S., arranged them in a series according to their productivity. Ennerdale, Wastwater (Plate 2) and Buttermere (Plate 1) are unproductive lakes, which means that the total amount of living matter produced in them during the course of a year is small. This is a matter of regret to fishermen, but of delight to any waterworks engineer who can lay his hands on one, as Manchester Corporation did on Thirlmere towards the end of the last century. The fewer the organisms in the water, the easier it is to filter, and the lower the running costs at the waterworks. Esthwaite (Plate 16) is a much more productive lake and Windermere (Plate 2) comes next to it in the series. The rest can be arranged in order between these extremes.

Map 2 (between pages 44 and 45) helps to explain this difference. The unproductive lakes lie right in among the mountains. Windermere, in contrast, lies away from the high mountains. The rocks around it are softer and have weathered more. The amount of living matter produced in a lake depends ultimately on the amount washed in of nutrient matter which plants can utilise. Obviously rain seeping through the soil around

Windermere will bring to the lake more in solution than rain running over the bare rock and scree which lines so much of the drainage basin of Wastwater. There is a secondary difference that is more important. The flat land round Windermere is suitable for cultivation and settlement, and the fertiliser that the farmer puts on his land and the sewage that human colonies produce greatly increase the production in the lakes.

Most of the lake floor in shallow water is stony, because wave action when the wind is blowing hard carries away finer particles. In sheltered bays reed-beds develop, and the whole of that side of Esthwaite which is sheltered from the prevailing wind is fringed with reeds (Plate 13). Beyond the stones is a quieter zone where finer particles settle and provide a substratum for rooted vegetation, but the great forest of pondweeds that grows on it is narrow because the lake floor soon shelves to a depth where there is not enough light for plant growth. Beyond is a uniform substratum of mud stretching to the greatest depths, where light does not penetrate, the temperature varies but a degree or two in the course of a year, and only the slowest currents keep matter in circulation. This lower cold layer is isolated from the upper warm layer throughout the summer and, in a productive lake that is small, decomposition may use all the oxygen in it. The inhabitants of the mud, the open water and the weeds can be caught only by the possessor of a boat and special apparatus. They are, therefore, not discussed in this book. Groups whose members are so small that a microscope must be used for their examination are also ignored. For the rest it is convenient to take the groups one by one, starting with the simplest and proceeding to the vertebrates, the most complex.

Flatworms

There are ten species of freshwater flatworm (planarians) in Britain and all may be found in the Lake District except one. The largest is about an inch (25 millimetres) long, but most are nearer half that size. They are flat unsegmented worms, brown, black or white in colour, and a characteristic feature is their smooth glide over the substratum, generally stony. They feed on small animals and occasionally on large ones, to overpower which they combine in packs. One of their most notable features is their ability to decrease in size if they do not get enough to eat, a process that can go on till they are one-twentieth of their original length. If the food supply is plentiful, they grow, and at a certain size, produce eggs which, when laid, are protected by a large tough cylindrical cocoon. Sooner or later reproduction leads to a shortage of food, and when this comes about, the production of eggs stops and any developing are resorbed. When that process is complete the animal lives on its own tissues and starts to grow smaller. The result is that the total amount of living flatworm material increases or decreases as the resources of the environment increase or decrease. Most animals, with the noteworthy exception of man, appear to exert some kind of control to prevent their numbers reaching a point where there is no food left, but none achieves this quite so neatly as the flatworm.

The naturalist who turns over stones in the shallow water of Esthwaite will find some of them thickly covered with blackish rather shapeless dots which, when the disturbance stimulates them to start moving, are seen to be flatworms. There is a large white one with two black eyes, *Dendrocoelum lacteum*, and a large black one with light-coloured eyes, *Dugesia lugubris*. The most numerous is likely to be one of two species whose size is a little smaller and whose eyes are a series of black specks round the end of the front half of the body, *Polycelis* (Plate 14). Anyone hunting systematically for these creatures soon notes that both individuals and species are fewer in less productive lakes, and, in places such as Ennerdale, a search for several hours may not reveal any. It is reasonable to suppose that numbers become fewer as the food supply diminishes, but the explanation of the disappearance of species is less evident. However, Dr T. B. Reynoldson and his colleagues at the University of Bangor have demonstrated that, although different species of flatworm normally have distinct food preferences, these distinctions disappear when food is scarce. The different species then come into direct competition and the less successful ones die out.

The flatworms in running water are no less celebrated and one of them, *Planaria* or *Crenobia alpina*, may well be the most intensively studied of any freshwater animal. It is whitish in colour, over half an inch (12 millimetres) long and rather narrow. It can thrive only at low temperatures, and will not breed above a temperature of about 12°C (54°F). The presumption is that it occurred in every stream or river during the Ice Age and that, as the ice retreated and the temperature rose, it retreated upstream until eventually, in a temperate country such as England, the only places it could inhabit were at the tips of the system where the water emerged cold from the ground. As might be expected the consequent isolation has led to genetic differentiation, and different populations vary in temperature tolerance and in the conditions under which they reproduce sexually or asexually.

A *Crenobia* that has found plenty to eat grows and eventually starts to produce eggs, and, when in this condition, it tends to move upstream against the current. Sometimes it reaches the spring and lays the cocoon in which the eggs lie protected, but sometimes the food supply in the upper parts of the stream proves insufficient. Should this happen the flat-worm starts to resorb its eggs and in this condition its reaction is to move with the current and travel downstream. This may lead it to richer feeding grounds, and the process starts again.

Downstream migration may be halted by a good supply of food, by an intolerably high temperature, or by competition with the other common stream-dwelling flatworm, *Polycelis felina*. This is black, shorter than *Crenobia* when full grown, and differs further in possessing numerous small eyes around the rim of the body instead of the dorsal ones. The front end of both species is drawn out into triangular projections and these, with the rounded front end of the body, cause one to recall a cat's head seen in silhouette. *Polycelis* can tolerate warmer water than *Crenobia* but does not extend to the warmest parts of rivers nor succeed in colonising perm-anently the shores of any of the lakes.

Flatworms can lay threads of sticky mucus over the stones on which they crawl and in this way entrap such animals as the Freshwater Shrimp and insect larvae, which may be much bigger than they are. They over-come prey caught in this way by attacking it together in large numbers. However, the main food is undoubtedly something smaller, and evidently something whose numbers are greatly increased by enrichment with sewage. In a stream that was kept under careful observation over a number of years, fewer than five specimens were found in twenty-five minutes' collecting during the course of a regular survey. There was at that time a septic tank to receive the sewage from four houses in a small village beside the stream, and earth closets served the remaining twelve. When mains water came to the village baths and indoor sanitation were installed in all the houses, but all the waste went to the same septic tank. As in Winder-mere the effect was not great enough to be called pollution, but there was undoubtedly enrichment and, as in Windermere, this favoured the flatworms. Their numbers rose from five to round about one thousand caught in twenty-five minutes.

Molluscs

The number of species of mollusc within the Lake District defined in a strict sense, that is the area of the Ordovician and Silurian rocks, is low, and generally specimens are not numerous either, which is to be expected in the soft waters of this area.

The Great Ramshorn (*Planorbis corneus*), and both species in the genus *Bithynia* are absent and the Great Pond Snail (*Lymnaea stagnalis*) has been found only in a few places to the east of Windermere, in an area which is not far from the limestone and in which concentrations of calcium in some tarns is inexplicably high. Other species with a similar distribution are the Nautilus Ramshorn (*Planorbis crista* and the Flat Ramshorn (*Planorbis complanatus*).

Two species might attract naturalists to the district: the Glutinous Snail (*Myxas glutinosa*) which, generally regarded as rare and local, has been found in weed-beds in Windermere, and the Mud Snail (*Lymnaea glabra*) which has been recorded in pools in the Lake District.

Two species which are common elsewhere are noteworthy on account of their distribution in the Lake District. Lister's River Snail (*Viviparus fasciatus*) inhabits slow rivers and canals in calcareous regions, and is therefore not to be expected in the Lake District at all. In fact it is known in one tarn, into which it was probably introduced unintentionally in 1939 when the tarn was stocked with what had been sold as *Lymnaea peregra* to provide food for fish. There were probably a few *Viviparus* among the *Lymnaea*. It has persisted ever since, even surviving the emptying of the tarn in 1948, but it never spread to any adjoining water, Jenkins' Spire Shell (*Potamopyrgus jenkinsi*) was first noticed in Windermere in 1936 and a survey revealed a characteristically dense population on large pondweeds in a trench created by a sand-dredger. On the lakewort in shallow water around the trench numbers diminished rapidly with increasing distance from the trench, until thirty yards (27 metres) away no specimens were found. In 1948 large numbers of this species were found in a stream in which none had been taken during the preceding year, and it was probably emigrants from this colony that established themselves on a fresh stretch of lake shore. Neither colony in the lake has expanded. Within the last few years *Potamopyrgus jenkinsi* has been found in Derwentwater. This snail is spreading extremely slowly, if indeed it is spreading at all, and the infrequency of the dense populations that are often found elsewhere suggests that conditions are not favourable for it. It will be interesting to see whether the progressive enrichment of the lakes makes them more favourable.

Another species that is unexpected because it is very rarely found in water with less than twenty parts per million of calcium is the Keeled Ramshorn (*Planorbis carinatus*) which is widespread in Windermere. The late Professor A. E. Boycott, a great authority on snail ecology, mentions one or two examples where the large size of a water body seems to compensate, as far as snails are concerned, for a low concentration of calcium. This species was first recorded in Windermere by Professor H. P. Moon in 1934 and was probably a fairly recent invader, for it is not in the lists of the earlier naturalists. There is, however, nothing more difficult to establish with certainty than the absence of species. Others in Windermere are the Wandering Snail and the Marsh Snail (*Lymnaea peregra* and *L. palustris*), the White and the Twisted Ramshorn (*Planorbis albus* and *P. contortus*), the Valve Snail (*Valvata piscinalis*) and the Bladder Snail (*Physa fontinalis*), together with the two limpets, *Ancylus fluviatilis*, which lives on stones, and *Ancylus lacustris*, which lives on reed-stems. All these species occur also in the less productive lakes and it is not until the least productive are reached that the list begins to shorten. In Ennerdale only *Lymnaea peregra* and *Ancylus fluviatilis*, both notably tolerant species, have been recorded.

Ancylus fluviatilis is very widespread but is confined to places where there is a stony or rocky substratum. It occurs in most fast streams and has been found in quarry pools and even in a horse trough into which somebody had thrown stones. It is absent from most tarns because there is no hard substratum. In many there are no snails, so tarns also can be arranged in a series. The least favourable, those in which there are no snails, generally have a low concentration of calcium. Increase in the concentration of this substance, increase in size, and submerged rather than floating-leaved or emergent vegetation are factors that appear to make a tarn favourable for snails.

Workers on other groups of entirely aquatic animals also have learnt to recognise certain pieces of water as suitable places for certain species, and they generally find what they expect to find. The conclusion is that these animals have no difficulty in traversing land barriers between isolated pieces of water. Indeed Professor Boycott studied a large number of ponds for many years and found that new arrivals were frequent. How these animals effect these overland journeys is one of the main unanswered questions in the study of fresh water. No doubt some are transferred by naturalists who do not wash their nets properly, others by fishermen who like to introduce new plants or animals that they believe will serve as food for fish, but human agency cannot account for all the transfers. The feet of aquatic birds are the traditional vehicles, but no systematic study of the subject has been made.

Leeches

Of the thirteen species of leech found in Britain ten occur in the Lake District, among them the now rare Medicinal Leech (*Hirudo medicinalis*). Some forty years ago a small tarn was constructed to the east of Windermere, in the region already mentioned on account of its unusually rich snail fauna. The Medicinal Leech, which had been recorded in a nearby pool, appears to have been one of the early colonisers and the owner of the property reported after the war that he and his family never bathed in the tarn because of its attacks. Fortunately it is the only leech that attacks man, and it is not known except in these two places. Another bloodsucker, which feeds only on fish, is *Piscicola geometra*, immediately recognised by its thin form, green colour and exceptionally large suckers, one at each end. A third is the large soft greenish leech, *Theromyzon tessulatum*, which attaches itself inside the throats of ducks. This habit probably accounts for its wide but sporadic distribution. Most leeches do not suck blood but swallow small animals whole; snails and midge larvae are eaten extensively. The Horse Leech (*Haemopis sanguisuga*) (Plate 18) is one of these—and it is misnamed both in English and in Latin. It is common but generally to be found just above the water's edge, resting under stones. Other species attach themselves to stones or to plants in the water, and cling so tightly that a pond net frequently fails to dislodge them. The student of this group must remove and examine the substratum in order to obtain specimens.

The longest list of species is to be found in the productive lakes, and the less productive a lake the fewer the species that occur.

Crustacea

Crustacea abound in the lakes and enormous numbers of small ones, water-fleas and copepods, inhabit the open water, making up part of what is known as the plankton. However, this account is confined to the five large genera in the group. There are four species in the genus *Gammarus*, but only one, *Gammarus pulex* (Plate 14), occurs in the Lake District. It is commonly known as the Freshwater Shrimp, but this is not a good name, for it is not like the shrimps that are caught and eaten at the seaside.

Gammarus pulex is frequently to be seen in pairs, a large male carrying a smaller female. He is not always as gallant as might appear, for sometimes he eats her. The Crustacea, and all the arthropods, the group which includes insects, mites and spiders as well, have their skeletons on the outside. This means that they can grow only by shedding the hard external cuticle and then increasing rapidly in size before the new one underneath has hardened. Only during this soft stage can the female pass her eggs through the oviduct. A male seizes a female who is nearing a moult, and carries her round until this event takes place. She then passes her eggs into a brood pouch between her legs and the male fertilises them. The female, now on her own, carries the eggs for some six weeks at winter temperatures and for about half that length of time in summer. The young remain in the brood pouch for a day or two and then disperse. They grow quickly and, if from an early brood, may be parents themselves before the season is over. The breeding season starts at the beginning of the year and continues until October, when a three-month resting period starts. It is an unusual season. Most freshwater animals breed during the warm part of the year; a few, such as *Planaria alpina* (page 84), and the trout, breed in winter. Such breeding seasons as have been investigated are generally found to be related either to temperature or to changing length of day. The reproduction of *Gammarus*, which starts when the water is at its coldest and the days are just, but only just, beginning to lengthen, and continues throughout the period of highest temperature and longest days, poses interesting physiological problems which have not been investigated.

Gammarus is not found in all Lake District streams. As it can be recognised by those with little knowledge of natural history, considerable aid in mapping its distribution has been received from youth groups of various kinds who wanted to explore the Lake District with a purpose. There is some evidence that the streams where it does not occur are those with the lowest calcium concentration but it is not known whether there is a direct connection or whether some essential food is lacking in the softest waters.

Asellus (Plate 14), the water hog-louse or water slater, is also abundant but less widespread than *Gammarus*. It is often taken as an indicator of pollution, but actually abounds in any water where there is a good supply of organic matter. A weedy pond whose water is rich in those materials which promote decomposition of dead vegetation will be thickly populated with it, although far from any source of pollution.

It is a flat animal whose only method of locomotion is a slow walk. Like *Gammarus* it carries its eggs until they hatch.

A careful record of the distribution of *Asellus* in the Lake District and changes in it in the coming years should yield results of interest and importance for two reasons. In the first place there are two species, *Asellus aquaticus* and *A. meridianus*, and some evidence that the former is replacing the latter. To explain why this is happening involves a good deal of speculation, much of which can probably never be tested. During the last Ice Age England was covered with ice down to the Thames, and it is unlikely that many species inhabiting the island today could have survived those conditions. Some 20,000 years ago the ice had largely disappeared and many species were advancing northwards to recolonise country from which the ice had driven them. The rate of advance would obviously vary greatly according to the requirements of each species. Colonisation of England presented no problem because it was attached to the Continent and the Thames was a tributary of the Rhine. However, not all species had reached Britain when, some 8000 years ago, the sea broke through to form the Straits of Dover. Thereafter invasion was less easy. This is a plausible explanation of the fact that the British fauna today lacks certain species found on the Continent. Some species have certainly crossed the Channel since its formation. It is possible that *Asellus meridianus* gained Britain before *Asellus aquaticus*, possibly before the Channel was cut. It spread into all suitable places. *Asellus aquaticus* appears to be a more successful species, though why is not known, and it may be a comparatively recent arrival. As it has spread, it has replaced *Asellus meridianus*.

If proper records are kept today some future naturalist will be able to discuss the relations between these two species in terms of incontrovertible fact and there will be no need to construct a story consisting largely of hypothesis. It may be that the replacement of one species by the other turns out to be partial and that under certain circumstances *Asellus meridianus* can hold its own. H. P. Moon's observations suggest that *Asellus aquaticus* is replacing *Asellus meridianus* in the shallowest parts of Windermere but not in deeper water.

The second reason why records of *Asellus* should be of interest is because they indicate the enrichment of the lakes. The productive ones are becoming more productive and the process is a rapid one in terms of lake history. It is partly due to increased amounts of fertiliser spread on the land, but mainly due to increased amounts of sewage. The permanent human population of the district will probably not grow fast as there are restrictions on the building of new houses. On the other hand, since the war many houses that were served by earth closets have been connected to a sewage disposal plant. There has also been an enormous increase in the number of camp sites equipped with running water sanitation.

It is not known when *Asellus* first entered Windermere; it was certainly present when H. P. Moon started work on the lake in 1932. A detailed picture of its distribution was not obtained for another thirty years. It was then found to be relatively numerous in shallow water at the north end of the lake together with flatworms. In the middle of the north basin this assemblage was much less prominent and the most abundant creatures were mayflies and stoneflies. Further south this community gave place to the first one, which occurred everywhere in the south basin of the lake. Nearly all the members of it are particularly abundant in the immediate vicinity of the outfall of the Bowness-Windermere sewage works, which discharges into the middle of the south basin. The only other major sewage works, that of Ambleside, discharges into the north end of the lake. The *Asellus*-flatworm community occurs in those regions enriched by sewage and a connection between the two is highly probable though its nature is unknown. Both sewage works mentioned are efficient: the organic matter they receive is broken down into simple constituents before discharge. It is, however, these simple constituents which are utilised by minute floating plants in the water and converted back into organic matter.

It is surprising to discover that *Asellus* was established in Windermere long before it reached Esthwaite, although Esthwaite is the more productive of the two. It was first found during the last war by the annual class of university students who come to the Freshwater Biological Association for a fortnight. Some classes in subsequent years found it and some did not, which probably indicates that a small population was maintaining itself but no more. In 1957 there was evidence that an advance had started, and subsequent events were carefully recorded. The advance was rapid and in 1962 the hog-lice were abundant everywhere. This appears to be the usual sequence: first an establishment which is obviously never recorded unless it is an intentional introduction, then a period when the foothold is maintained precariously, next a period when numbers increase and finally a rapid advance.

Asellus aquaticus also occurs near the inflow of Ullswater (Plate 3). *Asellus meridianus* is widespread in Bassenthwaite and in 1957 *Asellus aquaticus* was found near the inflow.

The next two crustaceans form an interesting contrast of ancient and modern, the first being a newcomer, the second one of the oldest inhabitants of Lake District waters. *Crangonyx pseudogracilis* is a shrimp which resembles closely a small *Gammarus*. With a little practice the naturalist quickly learns to separate the two at a glance, for *Crangonyx* frequently walks right way up whereas *Gammarus* always moves along on its side. A slightly greenish tinge also characterises *Crangonyx*.

It is an American species first recorded in England in 1931 when a specimen emerged from a domestic tap in Hackney. It was submitted to an expert but he was so baffled by the occurrence of a transatlantic species in a London tap that he said nothing about it. Six years later a colony was found in a water purification plant of the Metropolitan Water Board. The invader spread rapidly through the canal system that criss-crosses eastern and central England with outlying branches to Kendal, Llangollen and Bristol. It is more tolerant of oxygen deficiency than *Gammarus*, which is not found in at least the more polluted canals. *Crangonyx* quickly extended its range beyond the canal system and in 1960 it was taken in Windermere. A survey in 1961 showed that it was common in most of the south basin of that lake but absent from the north basin except in the extreme south. A few years later it had colonised the whole lake and also reached Ullswater, Bassenthwaite and Derwentwater.

Our fauna contains several species that have arrived within the last century from other regions of the world. A likely surmise is that freshwater animals such as *Crangonyx* have arrived in consignments of weeds to aquarists, for there are several plants, particularly American ones, which are sold to decorate aquaria. Only a few achieve the spectacular success of this crustacean, probably because they cannot compete successfully with the native species. As far as can be made out *Crangonyx* is not ousting the native *Gammarus* and is, therefore, presumably exploiting the resources of the environment in a way that no indigenous species does. This is a matter of extreme importance to fishermen and others interested in increasing the production of a piece of water. Deliberate introductions of species believed to have this property are frequent but they are generally made without a thorough investigation and usually fail. Occasionally the result is disastrous.

The next crustacean to be mentioned bears the name of *Mysis relicta*, which should appropriately be known as the freshwater shrimp because it is similar to, though smaller than, the familiar marine shrimp. In fact, being confined to a few lakes where it feeds in the open water by night and retires to the bottom in deep water by day, it is an unfamiliar animal that has received no English name. As far as is known it occurs in no English lake except Ennerdale. It occurs in Lough Neagh and Lough Derg in Ireland and in Scotland, and is in fact circumpolar in distribution. Nowhere does it occur south of the most southerly line reached by the ice sheets during the Ice Age, from which it may be deduced that it has poor powers of dispersal and lacks the mysterious ability of most other freshwater animals to cross land barriers.

It is believed to be derived from a marine or brackish water animal that was pushed inland during the Ice Age and isolated in various basins when the ice retreated. The water in these basins gradually became fresh once connection with the sea was severed, and *Mysis* was among the few animals that adapted themselves to this change.

Ingenious theories have been propounded to explain the occurrence of this animal and another, much smaller one which also has marine affinities, in Ennerdale and no other Lake District lake, but they involve a great deal of speculation. *Mysis* was first recorded in 1941 by Dr Winifred Pennington.

Mysis has disappeared within the present century from some Baltic lakes, apparently as a result of their enrichment by sewage and by the fertilisers spread on agricultural land. Warm water is lighter than cold. The sun's rays are quickly absorbed by water and consequently warm the surface layers only. There comes a time in early summer when the difference in density between the two layers is such that wind no longer mixes them, and the lower cold layers are then isolated until the autumn when the upper layer cools. Animals and plants that die in the upper layers sink to the lower ones and decompose, a process which uses oxygen. If production in the upper layers is high, and if the volume of the lower layers is small, this process may use up all the oxygen and the lower layers are uninhabitable by all except a few animals that have adapted themselves to survive a period of oxygen deficiency. *Mysis* is not among these and must therefore remain in the upper layers throughout the warmest part of the year. It has been asserted that it dies out under these conditions because it cannot tolerate the high temperature, but another explanation is that it normally retires to the depths by day to avoid the fish that prey on it and that, when it can no longer do this, predation annihilates it.

The largest of all the British freshwater crustaceans is the Crayfish *Astacus pallipes* (Plate 20), but this is rare in the Lake District, probably because the concentration of calcium is too low, and is known only from a few streams and tarns near the edge of the district.

Most of the animals mentioned have always been aquatic. Their ancestors lived in the sea and adapted to decreased salinity in places like the Baltic which today at the tip of the two main bays has a salinity only one-twentieth that of the sea. The insects and some of the snails, however, are derived from terrestrial animals and the former group particularly have been outstandingly successful in adapting themselves.

Insects

Seven groups, or orders to use the technical term, have sufficient representatives to warrant mention here. The order Plecoptera, or stoneflies, may delight the naturalist whose collecting has been confined to east and south England because he will encounter in abundance a group which previously he has met but rarely, possibly not at all. Twenty-seven of the thirty-four British species are known in the Lake District. One is found in weeds in tarns and in reed beds in lakes, and the rest are confined to running water or to the stony beds of lakes. The eggs are laid somewhat haphazardly on the surface of the water, whence they fall to the bottom to land where chance directs. The group is a primitive one and anybody who has studied insect anatomy will, on seeing a nymph, be reminded of pictures of the archetypical insect. There is a large broad head with typical biting mouth-parts and long tapering antennae, a thorax of three distinct segments each bearing a pair of short legs, and a long clearly segmented abdomen armed at the tip with tapering cerci (Plate 14). The adults are similar to the nymphs except, in most, for the two pairs of wings.

The aquatic stage lasts a year, sometimes more, and there is often a resting stage, either the egg or the very small nymph, which may live deep in the gravel where ordinary collecting methods will not secure it. The resting period is generally the summer, growth takes place throughout the winter and the adults emerge in spring or early summer, but a few species grow during the warm months of the year. The adults are often numerous beneath stones at the water's edge, and are not often seen upon the wing. The sexes call each other by drumming on the ground. The duration of the call and the spacing of the beats appear to be different in each species.

The naturalist who turns over stones in the shallow water of Ennerdale in March or April will be astonished at the number of nymphs of *Diura bicaudata*, a species about an inch (25 millimetres) long, for it is carnivorous, as are the other three common large species, and it is not clear how so unproductive a lake supports so many large carnivores. Under stones above the water may be found nymphs about to become adults, and it is not immediately obvious which is which, for the females have very short wings. This species occurs also, though in smaller numbers, in that part of the north basin of Windermere where *Asellus* and flatworms are scarce, but has not been taken in Esthwaite. Four other species, all smaller and herbivorous, are characteristic of stony lakes, and with them are often found many of the species most abundant in streams. Here stoneflies reach their greatest abundance, both of species and of individuals, particularly in the topmost reaches of streams that rise high in the mountains.

The order Ephemeroptera, or mayflies, illustrates the inexactitude of English names as applied to aquatic insects. For example, according to J. R. Harris in his *An Angler's Entomology* (page 137), the Mayfly includes all three species in the genus *Ephemera*. In addition to bearing this name, *Ephemera danica* is known as a Greendrake when in the subimago or dun stage, and as a Black Drake or Grey Drake in the imago or spinner stage, the former being male, the latter female (pages 135, 136). A spinner that falls on to the water and drowns becomes a Spent Gnat (page 138). The naturalist requires that a name shall refer to one species only and to all stages of it.

It is widely believed that the span of a mayfly's life is but one day. In fact they have a long aquatic life and an adult one which is bound to be short because the mouth-parts are atrophied and feeding is impossible. Those that enter adult life on a fine sunny day are probably dead by evening, the males having exhausted the store of energy laid down in the nymph in dancing, the female in shedding her heavy burden of eggs. If the day is windy and overcast they can survive a few days, lying quiet in the vegetation until conditions are suitable for dancing, mating and egg-laying.

The nymph casts its skin many times during the process of growth. Finally it comes to the surface and splits down the back to permit the emergence of a winged form. This is unique in that it is not fully adult and must moult again before this stage is attained. But it is not true, as is stated in many books, that the cast skin resembles the perfect insect; in fact the wings of the subimaginal skin shrivel.

The eggs are laid haphazardly as are those of stoneflies. Often a mass of eggs is extruded from the oviducts and glued in a mass to the female's abdomen. She flies over the water, drops to the surface, and dips the tip of her abdomen. The egg mass is washed off and the eggs fly apart before falling to the bottom. Subsequent events are diverse and much remains to be found out about them. There are winter growers whose eggs, laid early in the summer, lie dormant throughout the period of high temperature and hatch in the autumn. The nymphs grow throughout the winter. An unusual phenomenon observed in some species is that, although the eggs are laid within a short period, hatching takes place over a much longer one. This has been observed in, for example, *Rhithrogena semicolorata*, a species whose flat nymphs are confined to running water. Nymphs from eggs that hatch early may attain full size by Christmas, and then they wait until May or early June when, together with those from late-hatching eggs which have grown rapidly and continuously, they emerge. Nothing is known about the factors which delay the hatching of some eggs or which trigger off emergence. Other species have a life-history which is similar except that the eggs hatch at once and give rise to nymphs from which adults emerge later in the summer; in other words there is a slow-growing winter and a quick-growing summer generation. Other species appear to have several generations during the summer, the number depending on the temperature. Another variation is seen in species that grow during the summer and over-winter in the egg stage. *Ephemera*, the Mayfly of the angler, is believed to take more than one year to complete development, but there is good evidence that it sometimes does it in one. This is a field in which there is scope for a great deal of further work. Life-histories are different in different parts of the country, and careful observations both of the life-history and of the local conditions may throw light on the factors responsible.

The nymphs of the mayflies are not unlike those of the stoneflies but may be distinguished at once by three appendages at the tip of the abdomen where stoneflies have but two. Moreover, whereas the abdominal segments of the stoneflies are simple rings with a hard curved piece over the top and a similar one beneath sometimes fused with it, those of mayflies bear movable processes at the sides. They often have the form of thin plates and are generally called gills, but such investigations as have been made have shown that they are not the place where oxygen is taken in, as are the gills of fishes. They do, however, play a part in respiration, for they beat rhythmically to keep a current of water flowing over the body of the nymph and the body absorbs oxygen from the water.

All the stonefly nymphs have the same general form. Many mayfly nymphs, in contrast, are modified structurally for existence in particular environments. A sample dredged from Windermere anywhere where the bottom is sandy is likely to contain nymphs of *Ephemera*. The full-grown nymph is large, an inch (25 millimetres) or more long. Its legs are broad and short and strong, an adaptation for burrowing seen also in the mole. The gills are feathery and curved over the back to form an archway that holds up the soil above a tunnel through which their beating keeps water flowing. A few adults may be seen flying over the lake in early June, but there are never the vast swarms familiar to those who live beside some of the south-country chalk streams.

The observer who lifts a stone from the bottom of Windermere near the edge may see a nymph scuttling over the surface with great agility. Its head is large and oval and flat, and the first segment of the legs is also flat and the whole body is well adapted to cling tightly to a flat surface and move rapidly over it. A specimen from the lake will belong either to the genus *Ecdyonurus* (Plate 14) or the genus *Heptagenia*. Both of these may be found also in stony streams together with another, *Rhithrogena*, which is often one of the most abundant animals. It is one of the few creatures that can inhabit a bottom of round stones which roll at every flood. Its nimbleness enables it to avoid being crushed and it has a further device for clinging to a smooth surface, its gills being modified to form a sucker, This means that they cannot beat, as can those of the other two genera, which is probably why it is not found in still water.

Other genera have shorter 'tails' which, fringed with hairs, serve as paddles with which the animal can swim rapidly. One genus is *Cloeon* (Plate 18), the only mayfly to be found in rich ponds. Two species occur in the Lake District: *Cloeon simile* in weeds in deep water, often in the lakes, *Cloeon dipterum* in weeds in shallow water in some of the tarns. The abundant mayfly of the tarns is *Leptophlebia*, a nymph with long 'tails' and gills that taper to a point. It swims by undulating the body and the 'tails', and its progress is much slower than that of *Cloeon*. It occurs also in lakes and may be abundant in reed-beds, and one may speculate why a creature so numerous in the conditions of the Lake District is absent from so many lowland waters. It is one of the species that grow throughout the winter, and the eggs lie unhatched on the bottom for two or three months in the summer. Perhaps they die of lack of oxygen in rich ponds. Perhaps too, *Cloeon* flourishes in these conditions because its eggs hatch so soon after they are laid and the nymph can avoid the unfavourable conditions near the bottom. This, however, is a theory that remains to be proved.

Another quick swimmer is the genus *Baetis* (Plate 15). The eight British species are all confined to running water. They have gills, but they cannot move them, so probably they, like *Rhithrogena*, must rely on current to supply them with enough oxygen.

The order Odonata, or dragonflies, is well known because the adults, unlike those of the two preceding orders, are large and spectacular. They live for several weeks and feed on small insects which they catch on the wing.

There are two divisions: the large 'horse-stingers' or 'devil's darning-needles', two names which indicate the popular misconception that they can sting; and the small delicate 'demoiselles' that are generally bright blue or bright red. Both groups have in common in the nymph a peculiar modification of the mouth-parts, found in no other group. The lowest part is a hinged structure which can be shot forward in front of the head to seize prey by means of two teeth at the tip. All species are carnivores, which lie in wait for their prey and do not pursue it. They therefore inhabit weedy places and are common in tarns and pools but rare in lakes. They do not occur in the weeds in deep water probably because the ovipositing female cannot reach them, but some are found in reed-beds. The small ones terminate behind in three lamellae which are called gills though there is no evidence that they have a respiratory function; nymphs which have lost them do not appear to be inconvenienced. The large ones have a respiratory apparatus inside the end of the abdomen and water is taken in and out. Sudden contraction of this chamber can drive the nymph forward rapidly, but this method of jet propulsion seems to be used for escape rather than for hunting.

The White-faced Dragonfly (*Leucorrhinia dubia*) is the only rarity in the Lake District. All the other twelve species are common and widely distributed in the British Isles. No less than seven of them inhabit a small tarn that has been studied thoroughly. Four of these belong to the large group, and one, the Common Aeshna (*Aeshna juncea*) (Plates 18 and 20), has a long slender abdomen. Of the six British species in this genus, the only other one found in the Lake District is the Southern Aeshna (*Aeshna cyanea*). The other large long-bodied dragonfly is the Golden-ringed Dragonfly (*Cordulegaster annulatus*), recognisable on account of its black and gold abdomen. Its nymph is found in slow streams. The adult may occasionally be seen hawking over the tarn. Somewhat smaller and with an abdomen that is relatively shorter and broader is the beautiful metallic green Downy Emerald (*Cordulia aenea*). The other two species in the tarn are the Four-spotted Libellula (*Libellula quadrimaculata*), and the Black Sympetrum (*Sympetrum scoticum*). The adults hawk over the tarn on sunny days, *Cordulia* in May, and *Libellula* in mid May, *Aeshna* and *Sympetrum* in late July and August. *Sympetrum* is one of the latest species and may be on the wing as late as October.

The three species of demoiselle are among the commonest of the larger animals in the tarn. They are the Large Red Damsel-fly (*Pyrrhosoma nymphula*), the Common Blue Damsel-fly (*Enallagma cyathigerum*), and the Green Lestes (*Lestes sponsa*). The first two have a similar way of life, with an exception to be mentioned later. The eggs are laid in early or mid-summer, but do not hatch until August or September. Generally the nymphs stop growing at a length of two or three millimetres and pass the winter at this size. During the following summer they reach full size, and pass another winter in the water before emerging in the following summer. In years when numbers are large, a considerable proportion may take two summers instead of one to complete development; it may be postulated that shortage of food delays growth. A few nymphs that hatch early may grow sufficiently fast in the summer in which they appear, to emerge the following year. Whether time of emergence is related to length of day, as in some species, or to temperature, is not known. The nymphs do not move far from the place where the eggs were laid.

The life-history of *Lestes* is different. The eggs are laid in late summer, and undergo what scientists call an obligatory diapause. This means that development of the embryo stops at a certain point and does not proceed unless it is subjected to low temperature. In other words there is a mechanism that ensures that the winter is passed in the egg stage. Development starts again in the spring, as the temperature rises, and tiny nymphs appear in April. They grow with great rapidity, compared with the other two, and the adults emerge in July and August, and may still be coming out in September in a cold summer. Another contrast is that the nymphs, which are better swimmers than those of *Enallagma* and *Pyrrhosoma*, quickly spread all over the tarn.

The difference between *Enallagma* and *Pyrrhosoma* is that the former occurs all over the tarn, though in small numbers in beds of sedge, whereas *Pyrrhosoma* is confined to shallow water. This distribution is brought about by the oviposition habits of the adults and the relative immobility of the nymphs. On a still sunny day pairs of the blue *Enallagma* may be seen flying close to the surface of the water and they appear to avoid zones of emergent vegetation, through which they probably find difficulty in flying. In the middle of the tarn a pair may be seen to alight on an inflorescence of Milfoil, which projects a millimetre or two above the surface. The female immediately starts to walk down into the water, a process which dismays the male, to judge from his violent fluttering. Sometimes he drags the female out of the water, but more often he lets go before his wings get wet and flies away alone. The female walks down the stem, now and then inserting an egg into the plant with her sharp ovipositor. After half an hour or so she may be six feet (1.8 metres) below the surface and then she lets go and is brought rapidly to the surface by the bubble of air between her wings. She struggles to the nearest stem, crawls up it and soon flies away.

A pair of *Pyrrhosoma* remains attached during the egg-laying, and there-

PLATE 17

(above right) Common
Wintergreen (*Pyrola
minor*)
(centre right) Yellow
Mountain Saxifrage
(*Saxifraga aizoides*)

above) Bog Asphodel
Narthecium ossifragum)
nd Cross-leaved
Heath (*Erica tetralix*)

ight) Moonwort
Botrychium lunaria)

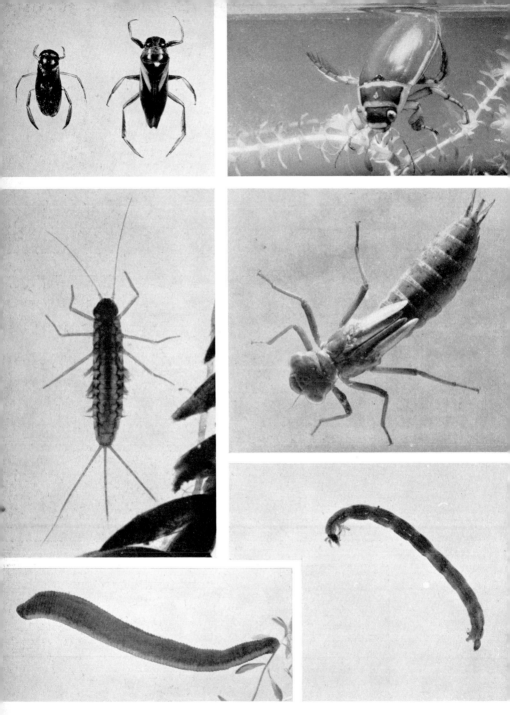

PLATE 18 Some typical animals from a tarn
1 Water bugs, *Corixa* and *Notonecta*
3 Mayfly nymph, *Cloeon*
5 Horse Leech (*Haemopsis sanguisuga*)
2 Swimming beetle, *Dytiscus*
4 Dragonfly nymph, *Aeshna*
6 Midge larva, *Chironomus*

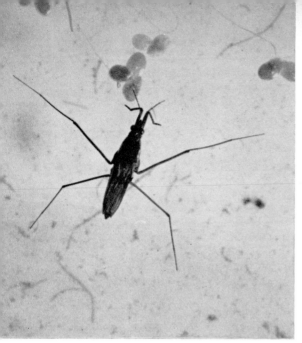

PLATE 19 Animals that dwell on the surface of the water
1 Water strider, *Gerris*
3 Water Measurer (*Hydrometra stagnorum*)
2 Whirligig beetle, *Gyrinus*
4 Water cricket, *Velia*

PLATE 20   1 Freshwater Crayfish (*Astacus pallipes*)
2 Hawker dragonfly (*Aeshna juncea*)   3 Natterjack Toad (*Bufo calamita*)
4 Windermere Char (*Salvelinus alpinus willughbii*)

fore requires a larger perch, the leaf of a sedge projecting above the water, or a leaf of the Floating Pondweed. The female immerses her abdomen but avoids wetting her wings, feels with the tip of her abdomen and inserts her eggs into the leaf or stem.

Mating *Lestes* also remain together but both go into the water, generally down some emergent plant. They walk down into the water and then walk up again into the air.

The emergence of a dragonfly has been described many times. The nymph crawls out of the water by climbing up some suitable support. The back splits and the front end of the perfect insect emerges and hangs helplessly downwards. Then it circles upwards, grips the nymphal skin with the legs, and pulls out the rest of the abdomen. It hangs on, soft and helpless, while the wings expand, which they do at a speed visible to the human eye. Then it must wait until the whole cuticle hardens and it can fly away to safety. Dr P. S. Corbet, studying one of the larger species, observed that many were eaten by birds while in this soft helpless stage. Chaffinches may be seen searching the edge of the tarn mentioned during the time when dragonflies are emerging, and it seems likely that that is what they are looking for, though actual capture has not been witnessed.

The other three species recorded from the Lake District are the Common Ischnura (*Ischnura elegans*), the Common Coenagrion (*Coenagrion puella*), and the Demoiselle Agrion (*Agrion virgo*). The first two inhabit reed-beds in lakes and have also been found in a few tarns. *Agrion*, the beautiful blue dragonfly with coloured wings, occurs in slowly flowing water and may be found in the few places in the Lake District where those conditions obtain.

The bugs, order Hemiptera, may be divided into those that live on the water surface and those that live in the water. Of the first there are ten British species in the genus *Gerris* (Plate 19), sometimes called water boatmen, though a more appropriate English name is water strider. Three are larger than the rest, and of these only one, *G. najas*, is known from the Lake District. It occurs on Windermere in boathouses, and Dr R. Brinkhurst has shown that it is confined to those boathouses with dry stone walls. It is absent from those made of concrete or where stones are cemented, apparently because they do not provide the crannies in which it hibernates. Dr Brinkhurst has also suggested tentatively that it is dying out because so much detergent is tipped into the water from the ever-increasing number of boats on which people live. The detergent lowers the surface tension and the bugs can no longer support themselves on the surface film. *G. najas* is one of the species in which wings are rarely developed.

All seven smaller species are recorded from the Lake District, each having its peculiar habitat, on tarns, lake reed-beds or peat pools.

As far as is known all species of *Gerris* subsist largely on creatures which inadvertently fall into the water and are trapped in the surface film.

The Water Measurer (*Hydrometra stagnorum*) (Plate 19) may be found in emergent vegetation at the margins of lakes and slow rivers. The water cricket, *Velia caprai* (Plate 19), is common on pools in streams, and *V. saulii* occurs at the edges of lakes, generally under stones just above the water.

Of the bugs which live in the water, most swim by means of long hind legs beset with hairs, but two, both known as water scorpions, have unmodified legs and can only walk. They lurk in shallow water among dead leaves or in thick vegetation, and seize anything that comes within reach of their front legs, the fore part of which fits into a groove in the basal part like the blade of a pocket-knife. The long tubular *Ranatra* has not been recorded in the Lake District but the flat *Nepa cinerea*, which resembles a fragment of dead leaf, may be found in suitable places at the edges of lakes and a few tarns. Its breathing tubes open at the end of two long filaments and it can lie concealed with the tip of these just breaking the surface. *Notonecta* (Plate 18) is the true water boatman and is known also as the backswimmer, which is what its scientific name also means. Both names are appropriate, for it swims back downwards and is shaped like a boat. It normally hangs from the surface, the tip of the abdomen and of the first two pairs of legs just breaking through. It waits until some terrestrial animal falls into the water and then, holding it securely with the first two pairs of legs, it sucks it dry through its pointed beak. This mode of life makes it vulnerable to fish, and it is confined to pools where there are no fish or to the thickly vegetated parts of tarns and lakes where it is safe from predation. The species found in pools and tarns is almost invariably *Notonecta obliqua*, and the species in lake reed-beds *N. glauca*. No explanation of this distribution has been put forward.

There are thirty-three species in the family Corixidae, which are sometimes known as lesser water boatmen. They are flat, as are most bugs, and swim rapidly by means of their oar-like hind legs. The characteristic feature of the order is a beak armed with piercing and sucking mouth-parts, but the head of a corixid terminates in a relatively blunt point and their powers of piercing are feeble (Plate 18). They certainly cannot wound the human hand that catches them as *Notonecta* can—an observation which is often among the earliest and most painful that a young pond-hunter makes. They feed by sucking fine particles from the bottom, though a Dutch worker found that he could not rear specimens unless the diet contained a certain amount of the body fluid of other animals. How far in nature they can puncture prey and how far they rely on wounds inflicted by other predators is unknown.

Each species is found within a restricted range of environmental conditions. For example on a sandy substratum in a productive lake *Sigara dorsalis* is often the only species. Within a reed-bed where the increased shelter allows vegetable remains to accumulate and consequently there is more organic matter in the sediment, *S. distincta* and *S. fossarum* are often found as well. If a stream flows into the reed-bed the silt causes the vegetable debris to decay into a black mud on which *Hesperocorixa linnei* occurs. As such a reed-bed fills up with each year's accumulation of dead leaves and stems, it becomes fen, and fen pools are occupied by *H. sahlbergi*. If a reed-bed is situated in a bay into which there is no or little flow and consequently no silt, there is less decay and the bottom becomes unsuitable for reeds, which are replaced by sedge. Under these conditions *Sigara scotti* abounds. This is a very common species on the peaty soils of tarns; the most heavily vegetated regions, where sedge and bogmoss foreshadow the formation of bog, are inhabited by *Hesperocorixa castanea*. These two species occur also in ponds, but above 1500 feet they are replaced by *Callicorixa wollastoni* and *Sigara nigrolineata*. Why each species is confined in this way remains to be discovered.

Corixids and *Notonecta* have on the under surface of the abdomen hairs in which a bubble of air is trapped. It is renewed at the surface periodically and serves as a store of oxygen. It also serves as a kind of gill. As oxygen is used by the body, more diffuses in from the water. Because the bubble is under pressure nitrogen diffuses out, but more slowly than oxygen diffuses in and the bubble, therefore, provides more oxygen than it contained originally. But in time the bubble disappears. If it could be enclosed in something which resisted pressure but permitted diffusion, it would serve as a permanent gill in well-oxygenated water. This problem has been solved by *Aphelocheirus montandoni*, a wingless species somewhat reminiscent of a bed bug, which is generally found in the deeper parts of rivers but which has been recorded in Bassenthwaite. On the underside of its abdomen there is a covering of short fine hairs having water-repellent properties, so that the pressure needed to force water between the hairs is greater than any that the insect is likely to encounter. Gas is secreted into the space between these hairs at the beginning of life, and thereafter all the oxygen necessary is obtained by diffusion and visits to the surface are not necessary. This coating of hairs is known as a plastron.

Members of the orders just considered start active life as nymphs which have the same general form as the adults; the transition from one stage to the other is direct. The rest start life as larvae—caterpillars if they are butterflies—and this stage is so unlike the adult that a resting stage, the pupa (chrysalis in the butterflies) is necessary while the tissues are reorganised.

The order Trichoptera, or caddisflies, is well known on account of the case of vegetable fragments or stones which the larva glues together with a secretion from silk glands. There are about 200 British species. The adults have a general resemblance to moths, but close examination reveals that they are covered with hairs, not scales. Many adults are crepuscular or nocturnal, but some, known to anglers as silverhorns, may be seen in swarms over water during the day. The larva starts to make a case as soon as it is active (Plate 15). Sometimes the form of the case changes as the larva grows bigger, sometimes it varies with the season, and always it must depend on the materials available. It is not, therefore, a good guide to the identity of the inhabitant, though some species make cases that are distinctive at all times.

The larva of *Rhyacophila* (Plate 15), in which genus there are four species, is green. It has a long narrow head and tufted gills at the side of the abdominal segments. This larva never makes a case at all and crawls on the surface of stones in streams. Also common in streams are the larvae of several families that make no case but spin a net to catch food. This way of life is particularly suited to running water where there is a current to fill the net with food, but one or two species that follow it live in ponds.

The scientific naming of animals and plants was started by Linnaeus some 200 years ago. The ideas of Darwin gave fresh impetus to this work and most groups had been studied by the beginning of the present century. Generally, however, the work had not extended to the immature stages, which was a severe handicap to those interested in fresh water because it is the immature stages that they encounter. The nymphs of all the British species of stoneflies and mayflies have been described within the last few decades, but the larvae of many species of caddis are still undescribed and this remains an important gap in knowledge and a barrier to further discoveries.

Several families of the order Coleoptera, beetles, have taken to life in the water and generally both adults and larvae inhabit that medium. The best known are the Dytiscidae, in which *Dytiscus* (Plate 18) is one of our largest species. Most are a great deal smaller. The adults come to the surface to take a bubble of air in between the wings and abdomen. Occasionally they crawl out and take wing. They are carnivores that pursue their prey. The larvae are spindle-shaped creatures that use all their legs for swimming, and seize their prey with two sickle-shaped jaws through which they suck the body fluids. The breathing tubes open at the tip of the abdomen. Most hunt in open water and therefore fall an easy prey to fish, which is probably why most species are confined to small ponds and places with much vegetation. *Dytiscus marginalis* and *D. semisulcatus* may be found in the Lake District. Both are widely distributed, as are most of the species recorded, and the chief interest for the collector lies in such northern species as *Agabus arcticus*, *A. congener* and *Hydroporus morio*, which may be taken in the peat pools high on the fells.

There are ten species in the family Helmidae (Plate 15). All are small but several are numerous. They have evolved a plastron which enables them to live permanently on the bottom where they walk about slowly. As noted, this method of respiration depends on a concentration of oxygen that is always high and it is no surprise, therefore, to find these beetles in streams and on stony lake shores but not in tarns. *Stenelmis canaliculatus* is the largest, and in Britain it is known only in Windermere, where it was discovered a few years ago by a class of students literally within a stone's throw of the laboratory of the Freshwater Biological Association (Plate 2).

There are fifteen British species in the genus *Donacia*. The cuticles of the adults are heavily wrinkled and sculptured, and shot with metallic sheens. They may be found on the stems of reeds and sedges well above the water. If one of the plants is pulled up and the roots are washed, fat white inert grubs may be found attached to them. Close examination shows that they are attached by two black hooks. Actually the breathing tubes run into these hooks, which pierce the roots until they reach one of the air channels. These grubs are the larvae of *Donacia*.

One of the best-known of the water-beetle families is the Gyrinidae or whirligigs (Plate 19). They are small oval steely-black beetles that gyrate rapidly on the surface, propelled by very short and broad legs. When alarmed they disappear beneath the surface. They too live on animals that come to grief on the water surface.

Many families of Diptera spend the larval period of their life in water. One, surprisingly, for its large, fat, round, grublike body is not adapted to the life, is widespread though not numerous beneath stones or in gravel in rapid streams. It is known as *Pedicia rivosa* and a characteristic feature is its ability to inflate the penultimate abdominal segment.

The Culicidae, mosquitoes, are, happily, a family whose members are not numerous in the Lake District, and it is indeed surprising to the naturalist who has been vigorously attacked by species of the genus *Aedes* on damp southern heaths to find none in the apparently similar pools in the Lake District. *Aedes punctor* is occasionally troublesome in the neighbourhood of woodland pools and *A. cinereus* in the infrequent areas of fenland. A rare northern species, *Theobaldia alaskaensis*, has been recorded in the Lake District. Also belonging to this family is the non-biting fly, *Chaoborus*, whose larva is the unique Phantom Larva, an inhabitant of the open water in lakes and tarns. The body is transparent except for air-sacs fore and aft, by expanding or contracting which the larva can maintain itself at any desired depth. It seizes prey with its antennae and digests it outside the body.

The larvae of the Simuliidae, black flies or buffalo gnats (Plate 15), are more adapted to life in a current than any other organism. They are dumb-bell-shaped creatures with a pad of hooks at the end of the body and another on a projection just below the head. They can cover the surface of a stone with a web of silken threads and move across it like a looper caterpillar, gripping alternately with the fore and hind pad of hooks. Firmly attached to a specially secreted pad of silk, the larva hangs in swift parts of a stream, straining the water with rakelike mouth-parts. This highly modified creature is found only in running water, though not in the great abundance typical of richer south-country rivers. Fortunately none of the British species bites man.

There are some 400 species in the family Chironomidae, mostly small

non-biting midges. Needless to say this is a specialist's group. The larvae
(Plate 18) are elongate and cylindrical and may be found almost anywhere
in fresh water. Some of them are bright red owing to the possession of
haemoglobin, and are popularly called 'bloodworms'. Most naturalists
will have seen these in domestic water butts. They occur also in the mud at
the bottom of lakes, including those whose lower layers are depleted of
oxygen during the summer.

Some of the clegs, hover flies and muscids also have aquatic larvae but
little is known about most of them.

Fish

A list of the fish of Windermere, classified in an unscientific but convenient
way, is a good starting point for an account of the fish of the Lake District.

Game Fish	Common Coarse Fish	Small Fish	Rare Coarse Fish
Salmon *Salmo salar*	Pike *Esox lucius*	Minnow *Phoxinus phoxinus*	Roach *Rutilus rutilus*
Trout *Salmo trutta*	Perch *Perca fluviatilis*	Three-spined stickleback *Gasterosteus aculeatus*	Rudd *Scardinius erythrophthalmus*
Char *Salvelinus alpinus willughbii*	Eel *Anguilla anguilla*	Miller's Thumb *Cottus gobio*	Tench *Tinca tinca*

The Salmon is a rare migrant through Windermere, and will not be
mentioned further. As far as is known, and it is necessary to be guarded in
statements about fish that have not been systematically studied, the rare
coarse fish in Windermere are not becoming any more abundant. They
may possibly have been introduced comparatively recently from the bait-
cans of anglers. Not much is known about the small fish in the other lakes
because fishermen ignore them and naturalists have so far done the same.
It is known that sticklebacks occur in Ennerdale, because Mr G. J. Thomp-
son caught them in surprisingly deep water in traps which he had set for

Mysis. They had probably entered the traps in pursuit of *Mysis*, because the crustacean was generally absent when fish were present. The Stone-loach occurs in some lakes.

The remaining species may be discussed first in terms of their occurrence in the various lakes. Esthwaite, it will be remembered, is a small shallow lake which is more productive than any other and which has no oxygen in its lower layers in summer. The Char is absent. Trout, Pike, Perch and Eels are numerous, and Roach and Rudd appear to be more abundant than in Windermere. This is in keeping with what is known about them for they are fish of productive waters.

Passing along the series from productive to unproductive lakes, one finds a diminution in the number of Perch and Pike relative to the number of Trout and Char. The two coarse fish are scarce in Ennerdale and Wastwater, and possibly absent from the latter, but nothing is more difficult to establish than a negative of this kind. There are few suitable spawning places for them in these lakes, but their scarcity may also be related to the poor food supply. Eels are ubiquitous; they occur, for example, in Hodson's Tarn, though to get there they would have had to pass through Windermere, Esthwaite, and Wray Mires Tarn.

The fish fit less well into the lake series than most groups, and there are anomalies in the middle. For example the Pike appears to be absent from Ullswater. So is the Char, though it was certainly there at the beginning of the last century. It is also unknown in Derwentwater and Bassenthwaite. In these three lakes occurs a fish known as *Coregonus*. We shall return to its name. Its fragmented distribution over the north part of the northern hemisphere suggests that, like the Char, it is a fish with poor powers of extending its range, having reached the places where it occurs today during the Ice Age. Both fish occur in Sweden and workers there have observed that the introduction of one into a lake may lead to the disappearance of the other. On the other hand, in Haweswater both occur together in large numbers. Dispute about why these two are distributed as they are is therefore likely to continue indefinitely, unchecked by any incontrovertible scientific evidence. Clearly the two can inhabit the same lake. *Coregonus* inhabits the four lakes that lie in the north-east quadrant of the Lake District; they could be described as two pairs, for Derwentwater flows into Bassenthwaite, and Ullswater and Haweswater discharge into the River Eden. The first two are relatively broad and shallow, which could be why the Char is not found in them. Its occurrence in Ullswater until recently is an established fact. Its extinction has been attributed to pollution of the stream in which it bred, by lead-mining, which could well have happened though it may be wondered why it bred in one stream only. There are, therefore, grounds for supposing that competition between the two has not played a part, and that *Coregonus* reached the Lake District from the north-east at a time when there was no access to lakes whose outflows ran from between the north-west to the south. Any such explanation, however, rests on the assumption that there has been no change during the 20,000 years or so since the ice retreated. Those who find this assumption difficult to accept point out, among other things, that fishermen have a weakness for transporting fish from one place to another, and that this process has been going on for some eight centuries, since the monks were given extensive areas of the Lake District.

Knowledge about the individual species has been largely gained in Windermere, and the following account refers mainly to that lake. It is, therefore, convenient to start with *Coregonus* which does not occur there. Of the rest of its scientific name no more need be said except that experts disagree, and the names change every time a new study is made. The English names are more constant but they too are diverse. The fish from Derwentwater and Bassenthwaite are known as Vendace, those from Ullswater and Haweswater as Schelly or Skelly. In Wales, where *Coregonus* occurs in a few lakes, it is the Gwyniad, in Loch Lomond the Powan, and in Lough Neagh the Pollan. Whether all these names really indicate species distinct in the scientific sense is still *sub judice*.

The one statement about *Coregonus* that can be made without fear of contradiction is that it hardly ever takes anything the angler offers. Until recently records from Derwentwater and Bassenthwaite were based on occasional specimens washed up dead. Then Dr P. S. Maitland brought to the Lake District experience of catching these fish in Loch Lomond and some of the other Scottish lakes in which it occurs. He found large populations in both lakes. *Coregonus* probably feeds on small crustaceans, possibly those which it finds among weeds rather than in the open water. It sheds its eggs rather haphazardly in winter in shallow water.

The Trout of Windermere run up rivers and becks to spawn and the small ones return after one to three years. Some Trout apparently never leave the becks and these always remain small. In the lake there is plenty of food and Trout grow well. The fly fisherman in luck may catch one weighing three pounds (1360 grams), but at about that size they are beginning to ignore small animals and to feed exclusively on fish. The angler who uses a spinner may catch one up to five or six pounds (about 2700 grams), and fish twice that size have been caught in pike nets. Feeding at the surface appears to be infrequent after midsummer.

Specimens of Char from different lakes are not identical, which has led to some controversy over the correct name, but there seems to be reasonably good agreement now that all British Char belong to the species *Salvelinus alpinus*, and that the variation warrants the recognition of no more than subspecies in the various lakes. Char inhabit deep water and feed mainly on the small crustaceans that swim in the open water. Trout occupy the shallow water and feed on the animals of the bottom there. This relationship is found also in many Swedish lakes, but there are a few in which there are no Trout. In these lakes Char inhabit both deep and shallow water, and those in the shallow water feed on the bottom fauna and grow larger than those of the deep water.

Fishermen catch Char on a spinner which is much bigger than anything the Char normally finds to eat. There are usually several on one line, each at a different depth, and the line is attached to a simple rod with a bell which rings when the fish is hooked. The depth at which the fish are varies according to conditions and it may range from near the surface to below 100 feet (30 metres).

Dr W. E. Frost has studied the Char of Windermere (Plate 20) extensively and has shown that there are two races, one of which spawns in shallow water in the autumn either on the lake shore or in rivers not far from the lake, the other in deep water in early spring. The latter also seek gravel that, at the depth at which they spawn, 50–100 feet (15–30 metres), is found only off deltas which are still growing. There is a period of several weeks centred on the winter solstice when the last autumn spawner has spawned and the first spring spawner has not started. Moreover extensive marking indicates that fish return to the place where they themselves first saw the light of day to spawn. There are evidently two distinct races and Dr Frost has found some small structural differences between them.

The Perch spends the winter in deep water and starts to move into shallow water in April. Spawning starts at this time and the eggs are laid on weeds and other objects on the lake floor. In order to reduce the numbers in a lake in Sweden, workers placed brushwood in the lake and took it out when it was festooned with spawn. The Perch is a carnivore and takes larger food as its own size increases, eventually subsisting extensively on smaller fish.

The Pike spawns in reed-beds. Its diet changes in the same way as that of the Perch but it becomes entirely piscivorous much earlier in life. It preys extensively on Perch in summer when that fish is in the shallow parts of the lake, and turns more to Trout and Char in the winter. On this diet it may attain a weight of thirty-five pounds (16 kilograms).

The female Eel spends nine to nineteen, the male seven to twelve years, in Windermere, feeding on the invertebrate animals as do the very small Pike and the medium-sized Trout and Perch. More snails, however, are found inside it than in the other fish, which probably reflects its ability to glide in and out of weed-beds too thick for the species that can only swim to penetrate. At the end of its freshwater life certain changes take place, and then on some dark wet night it enters the swollen outflow of the lake and sets out on its remarkable journey to its spawning grounds on the other side of the Atlantic.

INVERTEBRATES

MOLLUSCS

by Nora F. McMillan

The Lake District is a mountainous area with rocks poor in lime, and therefore a large molluscan fauna is not to be expected. Small limestone areas such as Whitbarrow Scar (Plate 16), which is just within the boundary of the Lake District as defined for the purposes of this book, have a much richer fauna in variety of species and number of specimens.

The history of conchology in the Lakes dates back to at least the early part of the last century, when J. Bulwer found the rare and local freshwater snail *Myxas glutinosa* in a 'pond near Windermere', as chronicled by J. G. Jeffreys in *British Conchology*: the snail still lives in Windermere. Later, Captain Farrer, who lived at Bassenthwaite in the 1890s, published a good list of Mollusca from the Lake District, and of course the presence of the Freshwater Biological Association's headquarters in the district has ensured a good coverage of the freshwater species (page 86).

The numerous lakes, tarns and pools, representing many kinds of habitat from the primitive austerity of Ennerdale to the rich variety of Esthwaite, have about thirty-two species of Mollusca. The Pearl Mussel (*Margaritifera margaritifera*) lives in some of the rivers and becks and sometimes yields small pearls. The River Irt in Cumberland is celebrated for pearl fishing and in the sixteenth century the famous circumnavigator Sir John Hawkins had a patent for fishing that river.

The land Mollusca are fairly well represented in the Lake District, about sixty-five species occurring in the two counties of Westmorland and Cumberland, mostly in the sheltered valleys and wooded gills. Indeed, on the open fells there are no snails and only one or two species of slug.

Among the terrestrial species one of the most interesting is the tiny snail *Vertigo alpestris* (Fig. 19) which has its British headquarters in north-west England. In Britain it lives on old walls, limestone or slate indifferently, and apparently nowhere else, although on the Continent it is not confined to walls. However the Lakeland valleys were not cleared and divided until relatively late (sixteenth, seventeenth or even eighteenth century), so the question arises: where did *V. alpestris* live before the walls were built? The answer probably is that the species did occur in the area in the pre-enclosure days but was very rare. Human influence has furnished a habitat which is particularly suitable for the snail and it has increased in number accordingly. The present range of *V. alpestris* in Britain, therefore, probably includes rare natural habitats and 'secondary' ones such as Lakeland walls, to which it has spread during the last 200–300 years.

 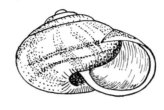 

Fig. 19 (left) *Vertigo alpestris* (centre) *Monacha cantiana* (x 2) (right) *Helicella itala* (x 2)

Several species of land-snails were introduced about Bassenthwaite by Captain Farrer in 1895. He remarks that a year or two later two of the species, *Monacha cantiana* and *Helicella itala* (Fig. 19), were well established and increasing, but that *Marpessa laminata* and *Helicella virgata* had apparently failed. It would be interesting to know if these introductions still survive.

PLATE 21 (*reading from the top, left to right*)

PLATE 22

Wheatear, male

Buzzard

PLATE 23   Curlew
Ring Ouzel, male

PLATE 24 MOTHS AND BUTTERFLIES (*reading from the top, left to right*: 1 Red Carpet (*Xanthorrhoe munitata*) 2 *Crambus margaritellus* 3 *Crambus furcatellus* 4 Netted Carpet (*Eustroma reticulata*) 5 Antler Moth (*Cerapteryx graminis*) 6 Brown Argus (*Aricia agestis*) 7 Haworth's Minor (*Celaena haworthii*) 8 Yellow-horned moth (*Achlya flavicornis*) 9 Brown Argus, underside 10 Northern Dart (*Amathes alpicola*) 11 Wood Tiger (*Parasemia plantaginis*) 12 Silver-studded Blue (*Plebejus argus*) 13 The Saxon (*Hyppa rectilinea*) 14 Wood Tiger (var. *hospita*) 15 Silver-studded Blue, female 16 Scarce Prominent (*Odontosia carmelita*) 17 Large Heath (*Coenonympha tullia*) 18 Large Heath, moorland form 19 Small Mountain Ringlet, male (*Erebia epiphron*) 20 Large Heath, underside 21 Large Heath, moorland form, underside 22 Small Mountain Ringlet, female

INSECTS

by N. L. Birkett

There are probably about 10,000 different species of insects living within the confines of the Lake District National Park. It is obviously impossible to deal with all these within the confines of a short chapter, indeed it would require more than the whole book for an adequate discussion of the species. This subsection, then, must be highly selective and attention will be focused on those species which the ordinary walker will be likely to meet in his rambles. The butterflies and moths will be considered in most detail, but some attention will be directed to the more obvious members of the other orders of insects such as the beetles and flies. Though relatively small in area the Park contains many varied habitats supporting considerable and often specialised insect populations. Many orders of the class Insecta have been scarcely investigated so that even a simple statement of the numbers of species occurring cannot, in the present state of knowledge, be given. Some orders, such as the butterflies and moths (Lepidoptera), beetles (Coleoptera), and true flies (Diptera) have been relatively well worked, especially in restricted localities, perhaps known to harbour interesting species, while other areas, possibly of equal or greater significance, have scarcely been studied at all.

Very little field or experimental work has been done on the ecology of terrestrial insects in the area, and there is great scope here for both professional and amateur students. It can safely be said that in the present state of knowledge an ecologically coherent account of the insect fauna cannot be given. There are one or two exceptions to this generalisation which will be noted in due context later. Much more ecological work has been carried out on aquatic insects (see Section III, pages 94–107).

It might be useful at this point to give a census of the numbers of insects of the different orders occurring in the Lake District. The following table gives some indication of these where known, either with reasonable accuracy or by a process of reasoned guess-work in the case of orders rather neglected in our area. In the 'Check List of British Insects' (Kloet and Hincks, 1945) are listed something over 20,000 species occurring in the

British Isles. Since that list was published more species have been discovered and others continue to be discovered each year.

Table of Insects

Order	British★	Lake District	%
Orthoptera	38	c. 10	24
Dermaptera	9	1	11
Plecoptera	32	25	78
Ephemeroptera	46	25	54
Odonata	42	c. 20	48
Megaloptera	6	4	66
Neuroptera	64	c. 38	60
Mecoptera	4	4	100
Trichoptera	188	106	56
Lepidoptera	2187	1382	65
Coleoptera	3690 (now over 4000)	c. 1800	50
Diptera	5199	Not known	
Hymenoptera	6191	Not known	

★Figures from Kloet and Hincks, 1945

The numbers of British species of Diptera (true flies) and Hymenoptera (bees, wasps and ants) are indicated, but the numbers occurring in our district are not known even approximately. Various families of these orders have been worked, more or less intensively, but no over-all totals are available. For example, of the well-known hover flies (Syrphidae) nearly 70% of the British total of about 240 species have been recorded. The non-biting midges (Chironomidae) are represented by well over half of the British total of about 400 species. Intensive collecting of a group by a specialist invariably reveals numerous species unsuspected in the area. One can thus estimate that at least half the total British species occur in our district.

It may be advisable here to point out that many species of insects have no vernacular names and that scientific names must at times be used. It is hoped that the necessity of using these will not detract from the interest of the general reader to whom this book is addressed.

Insects of the Mountains

Much of the Lake District lies above an altitude of 2000 feet (600 metres). The flora and fauna of these regions often exhibit affinities with those occurring at lower levels at higher latitudes and for this reason the term arctic-alpine is commonly employed in their general characterisation. Climatic factors are probably dominant in explaining this affinity but little work seems to have been done on the specific aspects involved.

In any specialised region ecological factors of various kinds must be considered—factors such as soil type, vegetational cover, physical characteristics of temperature, humidity, cloud, precipitation and sunshine are all relevant. These factors may be interrelated and all have some bearing on the fauna and flora present.

Our mountains have a decidedly acid soil and the principal cover is provided by such grasses as *Nardus* and *Molinia*. Earthworms are virtually absent, their place and function being filled by larvae of insects (particularly the dipterous families Tipulidae and Chironomidae), there are few or no ants and general grazing is carried out by sheep. The absence of lime prevents the occurrence of snails but black slugs (*Arion* spp.) are common.

There occur a number of Lepidoptera typically of montane habitat and rarely, in these latitudes, found other than at high level. The Small Mountain Ringlet butterfly (*Erebia epiphron*) (Plate 24) is of widespread occurrence and tends, like many of its congeners, to form local colonies. The genus *Erebia* consists of essentially arctic-alpine insects most numerous in the Alps, but with representatives at higher latitudes in Europe, Asia and America. In Britain we have only two species of the genus, the second being the Scotch Argus (*Erebia aethiops*) which does not occur within the boundaries of the Park but has two flourishing colonies just outside. The Small Mountain Ringlet occurs usually above 1800 feet (550 metres) and is quite abundant in some of its colonies, as on Langdale Pikes, Red Screes and in the Honister Pass area. An exception to the altitude rule is a colony occurring in Cumberland on a hill of about 700 feet (213 metres). All adult members of this genus require sunshine for activity and even a thin cloud cover will stop all flight. The species is on the wing in late June and early July and with its gentle flight among the grasses and flowers of the mountain meadows it makes an attractive sight, but this same gentle flight makes it also an object of easy prey for the collector. While at present it seems to be sufficiently widespread and common where it occurs not to be in immediate danger of extinction by over-collecting, it should nevertheless be afforded protection for the benefit of future visitors. Perhaps the greatest danger to the species is the increased grazing by sheep. On the Continent this species is widespread in mountainous regions, including the Pyrenees, but in Britain it only occurs in the Lake District, Highlands of Scotland and very locally and rarely in Ireland. There appears to be no record of its occurrence in Wales, where apparently suitable mountain habitats are found. The females lay their eggs, usually singly, on Matgrass (*Nardus stricta*), the food upon which the young larvae feed. After a short period of feeding in the autumn the little caterpillars go into hibernation and spend the winter quiescent, deep in the tangled vegetation below their food plant. Increasing warmth in the spring rouses the larvae, which then feed rapidly and, on reaching full growth, pupate deep down in the grass inside a frail silk cocoon. After about three weeks the adult insect emerges. There is some evidence that sometimes the larvae hibernate for two winters before attaining full growth. Probably the length of the larval stage is climatically determined.

A number of moths of montane affinities are worthy of note, especially as they may be observed at the same time and in the same places as the Small Mountain Ringlet. The Red Carpet (*Xanthorrhoe munitata*) (Plate 24) may be disturbed from low vegetation or rocks where it rests during the day-time. In England this is a northern species but it is widespread throughout Scotland. The larvae feed on various low plants, but species of lady's mantle (*Alchemilla* spp.) seem to be the preferred food plant.

Various grass moths of the genus *Crambus* occur on the mountains. While many of these are of almost universal occurrence on grassland there is one essentially mountain species, *Crambus furcatellus* (Plate 24). This moth occurs in North Wales and Scotland as well as the Lake District. In this country the food plant of the larvae is not known with certainty but on the Continent it has been recorded on Sheep's Fescue (*Festuca ovina*), a grass of alkaline habitat, however.

Perhaps one of the most interesting species of moth on the mountains was discovered on the slopes of Skiddaw as recently as 1958 when a visiting coleopterist, Mr F. T. Vallins, found a specimen of the Northern Dart (*Amathes hyperborea*, according to Kloet and Hincks but now known by the trivial name of *alpicola*) (Plate 24). Mr Vallins was searching under stones for beetles when, to his great surprise, he found a fine specimen of this moth. Further intensive search did not reveal any more specimens. This species has long been known to live at high levels in the Scottish mountains and is an object of quest by collectors. The larvae of the Northern Dart feed on various mountain plants such as Crowberry, Bilberry and Bearberry. It is a species which takes two years to develop from egg to adult and is reputed to occur only in alternate years in its Scottish haunts. Since its discovery on Skiddaw much search has gone on, especially in the original locality, but no further specimens have been found. However, another specimen has been taken recently in a moth trap high on the Pennines just outside our area. With insects of powerful flight, such as this is, it is natural to wonder if the occurrence of occasional specimens, far from their known breeding haunts, may be stray or migrant specimens rather than locally bred. No firm answer can as yet be given, and only if the larvae or pupae are found on our mountains can we unhesitatingly claim the species as native. On the whole it seems quite likely that we have a small breeding population which has been overlooked, due to the secretive habits of the larvae, the nocturnal flight of the adults and their occurrence at high altitudes where night collecting is not easily prosecuted. Abroad the species is a northern one extending, in Scandinavia, well north of the Arctic Circle.

Numerous species of beetles, the order best known after the Lepidoptera, are to be found on the mountains. Perhaps most characteristic and most often observed will be members of the family Carabidae or ground beetles. The beetles of this family (Plate 21) will often be noticed by fell walkers as they are quite large and will be seen running about in the open on the mountain tracks and sheep walks. It should be emphasised at once that many species are small and secretive and will be found only by careful search by the specialist in the subject. The three most likely species to be seen are *Carabus nemoralis*, *C. catenulatus* and *C. consitus* (Plate 21). These are large, black or bronzy in colour and run about actively in the sunshine. They are all carnivorous and will often be found with black slugs as prey. The very elegant *Carabus nitens* has been recorded from one locality only. This species has the thorax and head a coppery-red colour while the elytra or wing-cases are shining metallic green becoming coppery towards the sides. It is of very local occurrence in marshy places in Great Britain and it is in such a habitat that it is found in the Lake District.

Various species of dung-feeding beetle are common on the mountains, their frequency no doubt correlated with the abundance of sheep droppings. The large and ponderous dor beetles of the genus *Geotrupes* are often observed moving in slow ungainly fashion. *Geotrupes stercorarius* (Plate 21) is probably the most common of the genus while *G. vernalis* is also frequent, particularly on the northern fells of the Skiddaw-Saddleback group. These species form a considerable item in the diet of foxes.

Where the bracken is common on the mountains will be found the handsome click-beetle, *Corymbites cupreus* (Plate 21), and the Garden Chafer (*Phyllopertha horticola*) (Plate 21). Click-beetles are so-called from their habit of leaping with a clicking noise when handled.

True flies, Diptera, especially of the sub-order Nematocera (thread-horns), are plentiful in both numbers and species. Various species of crane-fly (daddy-long-legs) are fairly characteristic. Some are quite large, such as the species which come to a lighted room in summer, others are small and one species is almost wingless, *Molophilus ater*. This latter may be caught in numbers by sweeping a net through the low herbage on the higher mountain regions. Midges of the families Chironomidae (non-biting) and Ceratopogonidae are abundant. The latter family includes species of the genus *Culicoides*, the females of which are well known for their biting propensities, especially on warm humid days. It is these midges which make the Highlands of Scotland almost uninhabitable at times, but it should be added that they are nothing like such a nuisance in the Lake District! In still conditions large swarms of these midges may be observed. The swarms generally consist of males awaiting a female to fly into their midst for the purpose of pairing. Often swarms may be seen at the highest point of a mountain, even over the summit cairn. On a really calm day these swarms are quite audible and their hum has more than once been mistaken for the sound of a passing aeroplane. Winter gnats of the family Trichoceridae occur at all times of the year. These resemble small daddy-long-legs in appearance and are, indeed, quite closely related to them. At lower altitudes they are mainly winter insects but the higher one goes the later in the year they seem to occur, so that many of them are seen in the summer at the tops of the mountains. Their curious up and down dancing flight is characteristic and makes them recognisable. The dung of sheep and other animals provides food for the larvae of the Common Yellow Dung fly (*Scatophaga stercorarium*). This is the familiar yellow fly which swarms up from dung at one's approach. One or two species of the family Empididae (another family of predatory flies) are known to occur only on mountains. *Anachrostichus verralli* and *A. lucidus* both occur in our area. These two species are also found in North Wales and the Scottish Highlands.

Among the less well-known orders of insects numerous species occur on the mountains and some are even restricted to such a habitat. They are not likely to be observed by the ordinary visitor to the fells.

Moorlands

The habitat area dealt with in this section consists of upland from about 750 feet to 2000 feet (230 to 600 metres). Much of the Lake District Park comes within these limits. Among the insects there is much overlap with other habitats: upwards into the true montane region and downwards, especially where heather is still plentiful, there is close faunal affinity with the low-lying mosslands bordering Morecambe Bay. Heather moor is a fast disappearing habitat in the face of excessive grazing by sheep.

The numerous species of Lepidoptera occurring on the moorlands are quite well known and documented. The Emperor moth (*Saturnia pavonia*) is frequently seen in the spring when the males fly at great pace during daylight, seeking the lethargic female, whose flight period is at night. Rather later in the year, the Northern Eggar (*Lasiocampa quercus*, ssp. *callunae*), exhibiting similar habits, is common where heather is plentiful. Both these species exhibit marked sexual differences particularly of wing pattern and antennal structure. When the females emerge from the pupae they sit about on the heather and other low vegetation and by means of special scent glands emit an odour which attracts the males from a considerable distance. The males detect this scent by means of the much-branched and highly sensitive antennae. The female Emperor lays her eggs round a stem of heather in a neatly arranged mass. The female Northern Eggar flies over the area dropping her eggs haphazardly. The caterpillars of these species are often noticed. When full grown the Emperor larva is handsome, being bright green with black markings; there are numerous warty outgrowths from which blackish bristles arise. It feeds from June to August on various low plants but heather appears to be its favourite food. When full grown the caterpillar spins a flask-shaped cocoon with a trap-door arrangement at one end permitting emergence of the adult insect but preventing ingress of marauders. The larva of the Northern Eggar is clothed with brownish fur, beneath which the dark brown colouring of the skin may be seen. Between the segmental rings the colouring is velvety black. In the Lake District this caterpillar takes nearly two years to become full grown, when it spins an egg-shaped cocoon of silk in which pupation occurs. Heather again is a favourite food-plant though it will feed on various plants and in captivity is quite content with ivy. Other species of frequent occurrence on heather moors are the Heath Rustic (*Amathes agathina*), Grey Rustic (*Amathes castanea*), Scarce Silver-Y (*Plusia interrogationis*), Beautiful Yellow Underwing (*Anarta myrtilli*) and True Lover's Knot (*Lycophotia varia*). Numerous small moths will be seen but their identification is not simple for the non-specialist.

The Wood Tiger moth (*Parasemia plantaginis*) is an elegant moth of the moorlands and occurs also on some of the limestone hills of southern Lakeland. Two distinct forms of the male occur (Plate 24), the typical form and the form *hospita* in which the usual yellow markings are replaced by white. This white form is perhaps at the southern limit of its range in the Lake District and the further north one goes, both in this country and the European mainland, the greater proportion of the population is of the white form. North of the Arctic Circle the white form is the only one occurring. This variation is connected with the sex of the insect and only occurs in males. What factors are responsible for this, whether climatic or otherwise, are not known.

On heather moor the beetle most likely to be found is the Heather Beetle (*Lochmaea suturalis*). As a larva this species can do much damage to the heather cultivated on grouse moors. Some measure of control of its population is effected by the ladybird, *Coccinella hieroglyphica*, which is a predator of the larvae of the beetle. No doubt also birds, spiders and various Diptera take their toll and so help to keep the beetle population within reasonable proportions. The presence of the Heather Beetle also gives some indication of the climate because the adequate hatching of the eggs requires a damp climate with an average relative humidity of about 70%.

When the heather is in flower it provides a great attraction for many insects, particularly bees and flies. It is still the habit of local beekeepers to place their hives on the edge of a heather moor to obtain heather honey, a reputed delicacy. As well as hive bees many species of bumble-bees accompanied by the bee-like hover flies (Syrphidae) feed avidly on the flowers. In the extensive areas where heather no longer occurs a smaller fauna is found, but one which is fairly characteristic and not without interest. A spectacular feature of some of these upland areas is the cotton-grasses (*Eriophorum* spp.). This plant may be present over considerable areas and provides a fine sight when in fruit. Two moths (not one only, as recorded by Pearsall, 1950) are dependent on this plant. Haworth's Minor (*Celaena haworthii*) (Plate 24) is common in August and may be found flying at dusk or just after. It will come to a bright light and is also attracted by that mixture of beer and treacle which entomologists employ when 'sugaring'. The larvae tunnel inside the stems of the cotton-grass, feeding on the pith and so damaging a plant that it may readily be recognised by its wilting appearance. The other moth is the elegant, though tiny, *Glyphip-teryx haworthana*. This moth is not often seen in the wild but may be bred simply by collecting a bag full of cotton-grass heads in the spring and awaiting the emergence of the moths during the summer. The larvae feed, and also pupate, in the downy heads of this sedge.

Plateaumaris discolor (Plate 21) is an interesting beetle attached to the *Eriophorum*. These plants live in ground usually waterlogged and deficient in oxygen. The beetle larvae live in the wet mud at the base of the plants and have developed a special breathing tube which is inserted into the roots of the plant where there are large air spaces. In this way they are able to live in an otherwise uninhabitable environment.

Another interesting and common moth of the grasslands is the Antler (*Cerapteryx graminis*) (Plate 24). The larvae of this moth feed on various grasses and at times occur in immense numbers. The great Swedish naturalist Linnaeus knew this species as a pest of grassland and Newman (1869: 293) gives the following translation of Linnaeus' description: 'This is the most destructive of our Swedish caterpillars, laying waste our meadows and annihilating the crops of hay.' In Sweden the ravages were so great in 1741 and 1781 as to be termed national calamities. Newman also quotes a description of a plague of these caterpillars in the Keswick area (l.c. 293). He describes how a large area on the side of Skiddaw was seen to have a discoloured, parched appearance, visible even from Keswick itself. So marked was this line of demarcation that its progress could be watched as the caterpillars ate their way down the mountainside. Large flocks of rooks were also observed visiting this area of abundant food. Similar population explosions of this species have been recorded in the district in 1917 and 1937. A close study of the former outbreak was made by the late Frank Littlewood of Kendal who suggested that little real damage was done and that in spite of lurid press reports the plague was not financially disastrous to the hill farmers.

There are few species of butterfly on the moorlands. The almost ubiquitous Small Heath (*Coenonympha pamphilus*) is the most common. Double-brooded at lower levels it seems to be single-brooded on the higher ground. The Green Hairstreak (*Thecla rubi*) is common about all moors in May and is also to be seen on the low-lying mosses. The Large Heath (*Coenonympha tullia*) (Plate 24) deserves special mention in the present context. There is, so far is as known at present, only one small colony occurring at about 1000 feet (300 metres), on moorland within the Park area. The species also occurs, quite commonly, on the mosses to be dealt with later. The specimens in this moorland colony resemble those occurring in lowland Scotland and the Borders. They are quite different from the mossland form, showing reduction of the underside spotting and a generally lighter ground colour of the upper side. This high-level race flies about a fortnight later than the mossland form. In view of the interest of this colony and its limited extent, its whereabouts is a secret.

Various characteristics are evident in insects living at high level. They are often of dark and sombre hue, which may be related to the restricted sunlight in a region of much cloud. It will also be recalled that a dark body absorbs more radiant heat from the sun than a light-coloured one. Also the background tone of peat and rocks is dark so that better camouflage is achieved. Mountain insects are often small. This may be due to a short growing season or reduced feeding opportunity consequent on adverse climatic factors. Small size also aids concealment from predators. Reduced flight activity also seems to be a feature and this factor may well aid survival in reducing the chances of being blown away.

Woodlands

The extensive deciduous woodlands occupying many of the valleys of the Lake District support a rich and varied insect fauna. The most studied woodlands, especially as regards the higher insects, are those extending southwards and westwards from Windermere. Earlier in the century considerable entomological exploration was carried out in the rather similar woods between Keswick and Borrowdale. As usual the Lepidoptera are the best-known order of insects and the number of species is considerable. In spring the Orange-tip butterfly (*Anthocaris cardamines*) is common on the margins or in the clearings. In due season various fritillaries are to be seen—the Pearl-bordered (*Argynnis euphrosyne*), Small Pearl-bordered (*A. selene*), High Brown (*A. cydippe*) and Dark Green (*A. aglaia*) occur in these woodlands though some are not confined to such habitats. It is difficult to give any real indication of the richness of the moth fauna. The Great Prominent (*Notodonta trepida*) has been found in recent years to be common, and it is of interest also that the melanic form *fusca*, first described by the late Dr Cockayne from a specimen taken by the late Dr Lowther at Newby Bridge, represents about 10% of the population. The Satin Lutestring (*Tethea fluctuosa*), the Square Spot (*Ectropis consonaria*) and the Saxon (*Hyppa rectilinea*) (Plate 24) are other uncommon species of these woodlands recently found to be well established. The first two have a southern distribution in England and the fact that they are reasonably common in our district has become apparent mainly through the use of mercury vapour light for attracting moths. The Saxon is more widespread and common in Scotland than in our area.

The presence of Yellow Balsam (*Impatiens noli-tangere*) in certain woods bordering Lakes Windermere, Coniston and Derwentwater is responsible for the occurrence of two unusual moths in our area. The Netted Carpet (*Eustroma reticulata*) (Plate 24) is restricted in Britain to the Lake District. (There are old records of its occurrence in North Wales but apparently no recent ones.) The Netted Carpet was first discovered in this district by T. H. Allis in 1856 and was then taken regularly for some fifty years by all who sought it. Early this century it was reputed extinct, and perhaps because of this generally held opinion no one bothered to go and look for it. This myth, as it proved, may well have helped to preserve the species from true extinction. In 1945 it was rediscovered, and in strength, so that it is now known to be common so long as certain specialised conditions are satisfied. J. Heath (1959) has done considerable work on the ecological requirements of the species and in his interesting paper shows that not only must the foodplant be present but the habitat should have a mean annual rainfall of at least sixty inches (150 centimetres) for the species to thrive. Experiments indicated that in drier conditions pupal emergence was prevented or the pupae died before emergence was attempted.

The small tortricid moth, *Argyroploce penthinana*, also used to be taken freely by breeding from stems of *Impatiens* collected during the winter months. The dirty white larvae of *penthinana* fed and pupated within the stems of the plant. In spite of persistent search during the last decade no further specimens of this species, which was apparently common in the nineteenth century, have been found. Absence of evidence is not evidence of absence, so perhaps, as in the case of the Netted Carpet, the species may still be present though overlooked.

Many species of Diptera and Coleoptera occur in the woodlands. Representatives of these orders fill various ecological niches—leaf feeders, bark feeders, timber feeders, predators, leaf-mould feeders and dung feeders are all represented. The recent discovery of the dung beetle *Aphodius nemoralis* in the Finsthwaite Woods is of considerable interest as previously it was known only from the north of Scotland. The longicorn, *Rhagium inquisitor*, is an interesting member of its family, recorded from Finsthwaite, Tilberthwaite (near Coniston) and Glencoyne Woods. It would appear to be a species widespread judging from these records, but it is seldom observed. The cardinal-red beetle, *Pyrochroa coccinea* (Plate 21) has in recent years been found in some of the southern woods of the district.

Numerous other species of longicorn beetle occur in the district and their larvae are concerned in certain stages of the break-down of dead or diseased timber. The larvae live on the cellulose of the wood, a substance not normally digestible. However they are provided with a special digestive ferment (or enzyme) called cellulase which is able to effect the breakdown of the cellulose to soluble sugars which are readily absorbed and utilised by the larvae. The larvae of some other wood-feeding species possess a pouch in the gut in which live certain bacteria which are able to effect the breakdown of the cellulose and release soluble substances which the host larvae can use as food. Longicorns are also noteworthy for the fact that the larvae may live for many years before changing into the adult insect. Two or three years is quite usual and some species are recorded as living from five to twenty years. The ground beetle, *Pterostichus niger* (Plate 21), is also frequently found in rotting wood.

In various parts of the Lake District the mounds made by wood ants are frequently noticed. In the southern part of the district, and now occurring almost exclusively on Carboniferous limestone formation, the species will be *Formica rufa*. Formerly it occurred in a number of woods away from the limestone but these colonies have died out in the last forty years, possibly due to changing methods of management of the woods. *Formica rufa* is a common species in southern Britain, but here it is at the northern limit of its range. In the northern half of the area mounds made by *Formica lugubris* may be found, especially in woods of the Keswick area. This is a northern species widespread in Scotland and also occurring east of the Pennines, in North Wales and in Ireland. Interesting details of the distribution and history of these species are given by Satchell and Collingwood (1955).

A walk through any wood in summer shows at once that the fly population is very great. Many species are observed and it is a sobering thought to remember that the life histories of the majority are still unknown. Some of the more attractive flies, such as the hover flies, Syrphidae, may be seen resting on or flying about the flowers of umbelliferous plants in sunny clearings. Other flies congregate on tree trunks—especially towards evening when they sit basking in the rays of the setting sun. Characteristic of these is *Mesembrina meridiana* (Plate 21). Under the trees, often in the shade of branches, many species are seen flying. Some of these will be bent on mating while others will be predators catching prey while in flight. Many of the latter will be found to be members of the Empididae.

Some interesting work has been carried out in the Roudsea Wood Nature Reserve which lies in the southern part of the Park area. Dr J. E. Satchell (1952) investigated the depredations of oak trees caused by the larvae of the common Green Tortrix moth (*Tortrix viridana*). At times larvae of this moth occur in great profusion, completely stripping the leaves from the oak trees. Dr Satchell's work confirmed results of earlier continental research, that there is close correlation between the time of bursting into leaf of the trees and the presence or absence of an infestation by the caterpillars. Trees leafing early in the year were highly susceptible to attack and showed severe damage. Later leafing resulted in less damage, presumably because the larvae hatched from the eggs before the food supply was available for the young larvae. There was some evidence of differential resistance of trees depending on whether they were in a pure stand or a mixed wood. At Roudsea the pure stand occurred on acid soil and the mixed on alkaline. The former appeared more susceptible than the latter.

The essential plant features of woodland and open scar on the Carboniferous limestone formations have been noted (Section II, page 58) and these features are reflected in the insect fauna. The presence of Common Rock-rose (*Helianthemum chamaecistus*) provides food for the larvae of the Brown Argus butterfly (*Aricia agestis*) (Plate 24) as well as for those of a number of interesting small moths. The Brown Argus is of considerable zoo-geographical interest. In the north of England and in Scotland it is single-brooded, whereas further south in England and on the Continent it is double-brooded. The Scottish form is further differentiated by being of highly distinctive appearance. Recent work indicates that the southern English form is a different species from that of the north. Much theorising concerning the invasion of this country by this species in relation to various phases of glaciation has been published on evidence which, to the writer at least, seems slender in the extreme. The presence of Cowslip (*Primula veris*) on the limestone provides food for the elegant little Duke of Burgundy Fritillary (*Hamearis lucina*). This butterfly is commonly seen in late May and early June throughout the southern limestone areas. A little moth of these areas is the Least Minor (*Phothedes captiuncula*). It is seen flying in numbers in the sunshine especially in the late afternoon. Its larvae feed on the Glaucous Sedge (*Carex flacca*) which is a common plant of this habitat.

Two species of hover fly are worthy of mention on the limestone hills. *Microdon mutabilis* (Plate 21) is a peculiar bee-like fly whose behaviour mimics small bumble-bees. The larva is a scavenger in ants' nests where the strange mollusc-like creature feeds on pellets ejected from the mouths of the ants. The other hover fly, *Doros conopseus*, is a great rarity; as an adult it probably mimics some species of parasitic wasp. Though little definite information is known of its habits and life-history, it has been suggested that this species is also associated with ants. Two or three speci-mens only have been taken in southern Lakeland and its recorded English distribution indicates it to be rare everywhere.

Larch is of frequent occurrence on the limestone and supports a numer-ous and characteristic fauna. In recent years the longicorn beetle, *Tetropium gabrielli*, appears to have established itself in the district. It may have been introduced with imported timber. A specimen taken at Grange-over-Sands in 1947 constituted the most northerly record but since then the species has extended its range into southern Scotland.

The Raised Bogs or Mosses

The areas of peat bog, known generally in this district as 'mosses', bordering Morecambe Bay have long been famous among entomologists as the habitat of a large number of insects of considerable interest. The entomological exploration of these areas commenced early in the nineteenth century and it is safe to say that there is still much of interest to be discovered on them.

The mosses are both raised and valleys bog of peat which overlie silt, as described in Section I, page 32. This peat layer varies in thickness but in places must be about thirty feet (9 metres). Growing on the peat are numerous plants which provide the basis of the insect food-chains (Section II, page 51).

Nowadays, with some considerable fall in the water table, occasioned chiefly by extensive agricultural drainage of the surrounding land, drier conditions are occurring and with them much growth of birch and pine, the latter appearing to be the natural vegetational climax. Many of the original mosses have disappeared to become first-class agricultural land, but some still remain and efforts are being made by the Lake District Naturalists' Trust and the Nature Conservancy to preserve these for the benefit of future generations of naturalists.

From early spring until autumn a succession of interesting insects occurs, many of which are peculiar to the habitat. Some of these are the object of quest by students and collectors from other parts of the country.

In early spring the Orange Underwing moth (*Brephos parthenias*) flies actively and erratically about the birch trees. It is often seen but not so often caught owing to its wild, high flight. At the same time every step in the vegetation will disturb examples of the predatory empid fly, *Platyptera borealis* (Plate 21). Females of this species have the habit of swarming, especially in the late afternoon sun, and these swarms are a conspicuous sight. Empids are all predatory flies and their courting behaviour is curious and interesting. The male will capture a small fly, usually of another species (but occasionally of its own), and present this gift to the female. While the female is actively engaged in sucking the juices of this gift, mating takes place. This kind of behaviour is common in many species of the family Empididae and various elaborate modifications of this courting behaviour occur. Apart from the empids there are usually numerous other species of Diptera on the wing in early spring; many of these will be hibernated insects.

The Yellow-horned moth (*Achyla flavicornis*) (Plate 24) is also common and may be found newly emerged resting on twigs and small branches of birch trees on the first few really warm days of spring.

During April the numerous sallows (*Salix* spp.) bordering the mosses are in full bloom and their catkins provide a great attraction to many insects—flies, bees and beetles by day, moths by night. Female bumble-bees, hover flies (particularly of the genus *Eristalis*) and other flies are commonly encountered. The moths at sallow are principally the quakers of the genus *Orthosia*, which occur sometimes in large numbers. Some of the species of the genus are exceedingly variable.

By early May the Green Hairstreak butterfly (*Thecla rubi*) and the Emperor moth (*Saturnia pavonia*) are common, flying in the sunshine. These two species have already been noted as occurring on moorland where heather is common and are representatives of that considerable number of insects common to both habitats. At night the Scarce Prominent moth (*Odontosia carmelita*) (Plate 24) is a frequent visitor to light.

By midsummer the mosses are alive with insects of many orders. Apart from Diptera, to be dealt with later, the Lepidoptera are most in evidence. The Common Heath (*Ematurga atomaria*), the Grass Wave (*Perconia strigillaria*), the Clouded Buff (*Diacrisia sannio*), the Purple-bordered Gold (*Sterrha muricata*), the Manchester Treble-bar (*Carsia sororiata*) and various species of the grass-moth genus *Crambus* will be observed. In the last-named genus *Crambus margaritellus* (Plate 24) is a typical moss-land in-habitant.

Perhaps the mosses are most famous entomologically for the occurrence of two butterflies, one of which may, however, now be extinct. It was on the mosses bordering Morecambe Bay that a fine race of the Silver-studded Blue butterfly (*Plebejus argus*) occurred. This race, named *masseyi*, was characterised by its small size, coupled with a beautiful blue suffusion of the wings of the females (Plate 24). The race is very similar in appearance to that occurring in Corsica. The Silver-studded Blue is given to the formation of local races and the even smaller race *caernensis* is well known from limestone regions in North Wales. The food-plant of this butterfly in our area was never discovered despite careful search by the collectors of the day. The last of the race seems to have been noted about 1940, after which it disappeared more or less simultaneously from all its known locali-ties. The reason for its demise is uncertain. Over-collecting was at one time suggested, but the fact of its disappearance from all localities, some of which were not generally known, and certainly not heavily collected, militates against this view. The larvae hibernate and complete their growth in May and early June. Sometimes quite severe frosts occur at this time of year, especially on low-lying areas, and it has been suggested that such a late frost occurring at the critical time of pupation may have been responsible for the widespread destruction of the species. Complete extermination of a population is not necessary to precipitate its final decline. If a population falls below a certain critical level insufficient individuals are left to carry on the race, which then dies out.

The other butterfly for which the mosses are famous is the Large Heath (*Coenonympha tullia*), one form of which has already been noted on a restricted area of moorland. The form occurring on the mosses, known as *philoxenus*, is characterised by the large size of the spots on the underside (Plate 24). On the mosses the species is common and the larvae feed on the White Beaked Sedge (*Rhyncospora alba*).

The Marsh Oblique-barred moth (*Thalomiges turfosalis*) is a small moth which occurs in abundance on the mosses. Although it is so common nothing is known about its early stages and food plant. It is not easy to observe when and where the females, being small and crepuscular, lay their eggs among the rank vegetation among which they fly.

One cannot omit from this account a consideration of the numerous blood-sucking flies which are so prominent a feature on the mosses. During the summer months a visit to the mosses can be quite an ordeal due to the attentions of these creatures. The most common is the cleg, *Haematopota pluvialis*, the females of which bite viciously and can do so through a considerable thickness of clothing. Its congener, *H. crassicornis*, is slightly less common. The closely related and elegant tabanid, *Chrysops caecutiens* (Plate 21), is also a bloodthirsty nuisance at times. The larger tabanids, or horse flies, *Tabanus sudeticus* (Plate 21) and *T. bisignatus* are both common and at times attack man. Though not a biter, the muscid fly, *Hydrotaea irritans*, lives up to its trivial name. Vast numbers settle on exposed parts of the body for the purpose of imbibing sweat. The constant irritation of these flies can be well-nigh intolerable at times.

At dusk another cohort of blood seekers takes over. Species of the tiny flies of the genus *Culicoides* are common and vicious. Standing water provides breeding grounds for various species of the true mosquito, the females of which are eager for a meal of blood.

Hover flies (Syrphidae) are numerous on the mosses. *Volucella pellucens* and *V. bombylans* (Plate 21) are two striking species often seen visiting flowers in the sunshine.

Very many beetles occur on the mosses. The birches are regularly attacked, sometimes to the point of defoliation, by the Birch Weevil (*Luperus longicornis*). The heather, here as on the moorland, is similarly attacked by *Lochmaea suturalis*. Pine and birch stumps will be found to harbour larvae and adults of the longicorn beetles *Rhagium mordax* and *R. bifasciatum* (Plate 21). Various species of bark beetles of the family Scolytidae are found under bark or flying in the sunshine. The characteristic galleries made by their larvae are often seen if a piece of bark is examined on its underside.

The Salt-marshes

The insect fauna of these areas is not numerous as regards species though some of the insects occur in considerable numbers. The habitat is highly specialised and many of the species have to be able to withstand occasional immersion by high tides. The Sea Aster (*Aster tripolium*) is a common plant and supports a number of insect species. The moths *Phalonia affinitana*, *Coleophora tripoliella* and *Bucculatrix maritima* are common and may be bred by those who know how to find the larvae. Any butterflies seen are usually strays from various habitats adjoining. None appears to breed on the salt-marshes themselves.

A numerous and rather specialised dipterous fauna occurs on the salt-marshes. Species adapted to breed in brackish water find conditions suitable. The soldier flies (Stratiomyidae) are represented by a number of species, most common being *Chloromyia formosa* (Plate 21).

The Sand-hills

The areas of sand-hills occurring in or adjacent to the Lake District National Park have already been indicated. The Lepidoptera are the best known of the insects though the beetles and flies have not been entirely neglected and are represented by interesting species. Our sand-hills differ little from those of other parts of the country, but entomologically they are of interest as being areas of either extreme northern or southern distribution of some species. The Common Blue butterfly (*Polyommatus icarus*) is abundant in two broods. The sand-hill specimens perhaps represent the finest forms of the species occurring in the district, especially the females. The Grayling butterfly (*Eumenis semele*) is common and perhaps brighter, especially on the underside, than those occurring elsewhere in the district on darker backgrounds. The Gatekeeper (*Maniola tithonus*), once widespread in the district, now seems to be restricted to the lanes bordering the dunes and to the dunes themselves. The following moths are all more or less common and are all characteristically sand-hill species: Portland moth (*Actebia praecox*), Satin moth (*Leucoma salicis*), Dark Tussock (*Dasychira fascelina*), which seems to be a species of sand-hills in England but of heather moor in Scotland, Coast Dart (*Euxoa cursoria*), White-line Dart (*Euxoa tritici*), Archer's Dart (*Agrotis vestigialis*), Sand Dart (*Agrotis ripae*) and Shore Wainscot (*Leucania litoralis*). Two recent discoveries are perhaps of greater entomological interest. The White Colon (*Heliophobus albicolon*) and the Oblique-striped (*Mesotype virgata*) are both frequent on our sand-hills. The latter is probably at the extreme northern limit of its range in Great Britain. Numerous species of so-called microlepidoptera occur but they are of interest to the specialist only.

Many of the usual dune beetles occur. At Drigg the tiger beetle, *Cicindella hybrida*, occurs and is one of the less common species of the genus. Species of the genus *Aphodius* are associated with rabbit dung, which is plentiful. *A. borealis* and *A. ictericus* are examples. The latter is of southern distribution in the British Isles; it has recently been suggested (Angus, 1964) that its northern limit is determined by a minimum summer temperature requirement, but it can withstand cold winters. The sand-hills presumably provide a hotter summer microclimate than other ground in the north, hence this species can maintain itself at a higher latitude than would otherwise be the case. *Philan gibbus* (Plate 21) is another dune species.

Many kinds of flies occur on the sand-hills. One of the most obvious species on a summer day is the large robber fly, *Philonicus albiceps* (Plate 21). This is a large predatory fly which sits about on the hot sand indulging in frequent short flights either when disturbed or when darting after prey, which consists of other insects. The family Therevidae is fairly well represented on the dunes with *Thereva annulata* and *T. nobilitata* (Plate 21) being most often observed. The latter species also occurs in woodlands. These flies are also believed to be predatory and to feed on other smaller flies, but the evidence to date is not conclusive and there is scope for observational work in solving this problem. The larvae of this family are partial to damp situations and on the dunes they presumably live in the damp, marshy slacks.

Various Hymenoptera, especially wasps, find conditions on the sand-hills ideal. Many species of solitary bees and wasps occur and the holes made by them in the sand, in which they install a paralysed caterpillar as food for their own larvae, are often seen. Larvae of Lepidoptera are the most commonly selected food. *Chlytochrysus planifrons* (Plate 21) is an example of a solitary wasp of the sand-hills.

Migratory Species

Some mention of migratory Lepidoptera which are noted from time to time in the Lake District may not be out of place. The problem of migration, whether in insects, birds, fishes or other groups of animals, is a fascinating one. For fuller details of insect migration the reader is referred to Dr C. B. Williams' excellent book (1958).

Regular visitors Usually seen every year, sometimes in great abundance.
Red Admiral (*Vanessa atalanta*)
Painted Lady (*Vanessa cardui*)
Large White (*Pieris brassicae*)
Small White (*Pieris rapae*)
Death's-head Hawk-moth (*Acherontia atropos*)
Humming-bird Hawk-moth (*Macroglossum stellatarum*)
Dark Sword-grass (*Agrotis ipsilon*)
Pearly Underwing (*Peridroma porphyrea*)
Angleshades (*Phlogophora meticulosa*)
Silver Y (*Plusia gamma*)
Gem moth (*Nycterosia obstipata*)
Diamond-back moth (*Plutella maculipennis*)

Occasional visitors These include well-known migrants which do not regularly reach this northern area.
Camberwell Beauty (*Nymphalis antiopa*)
Clouded Yellow (*Colias croceus*)
Convolvulus Hawk-moth (*Herse convolvuli*)
Bedstraw Hawk-moth (*Celerio galii*)
Striped Hawk-moth (*Celerio livornica*)

Silver-striped Hawk-moth (*Hippotion celerio*)
Dark Bordered Straw (*Heliothis peltigera*)
Scarce Bordered Straw (*Heliothis armigera*)
Vestal (*Rhodometra sacraria*)

In general members of this second group are extremely rare in our district, some of them indeed having been recorded only once or twice.

No useful information is available on migratory species of other insect orders. Many of these are known to migrate and it is reasonably certain that records for these will eventually be forthcoming for the Lake District.

Conclusion

In this sub-section only the merest outline of some of the more interesting and obvious species of insects has been possible. Some orders of insects have not been mentioned at all and it has not been possible to deal with any in great detail. It is hoped that some indication has been given of the many fields of study still open to entomologists before it can be considered that an adequate knowledge of the class Insecta has been obtained. Even the mere collecting of insects (and identifying them correctly) can add to the knowledge of distribution and the whole field of ecology is practically untouched. It is large enough to provide many years of interesting work for many people.

Insects serve many functions in the community of plants and animals. Such functions as fertilisation of flowers, and consequent formation of fruit, scavenging of all kinds of organic matter both vegetable and animal, and providing honey all come to mind. In agriculture and gardening there are many pests which upset man's efforts to grow food and timber. Insects can transmit various diseases both of plants and animals. It is the writer's earnest hope that perhaps his contribution to this book may encourage other collectors and students to study the insects of the Lake District and so build up on the foundations already laid by workers in the last hundred years.

SPIDERS AND ALLIED FORMS

by J. R. Parker

Unlike the Lepidoptera, the Arachnida have never earned the popularity which provides English names for species. Any English names in use refer to families such as wolf spiders, crab spiders, jumping spiders and so on. Of the 300 or so spiders recorded for the Lake District (out of a total of over 600 British species) at least half are of the great family Linyphiidae which is the dominant family in the temperate climatic regions of the Northern hemisphere. In general, representatives of other families become inversely evident in proportion with an increase in latitude towards the Arctic Circle.

In addition to Araneae (spiders), the class Arachnida also includes the orders Opilionidae (harvestmen), Pseudoscorpionidae (chelifers) and Acari (mites), the latter being too complicated a study and too minute in size to be considered here, but all occur in the Lake District area and harvestmen and chelifers will be referred to later.

All spiders and most other arachnids are predators and their distribution is directly relative to the population density of those other invertebrates which form their food. In the preceding sections it has been shown that the distribution of plants is dependent on drift geology, the composition of the top soil and climatic conditions. The distribution of insects, to a lesser or greater degree according to species, is in general dependent on plants in all states of growth or decay and the spiders are almost entirely dependent on the insects. Therefore areas rich in plant and insect life will be often rich in Arachnida.

Because both spiders and harvestmen are very indiscriminate in their selection of invertebrate prey, it is simply the manageable size and quantity of the latter which are the fundamental factors for the food supply and this is one of the reasons for the very wide distribution of many of the common or more competitively successful spider species. The restricting factors, apart from the limitation of food, are the availability of certain types of habitat which specialising species have evolved to require, the presence or absence of humidity, salinity, temperature and light being contributory.

Spiders are found almost everywhere in the Lake District: many on trees, bushes and woody plants; in woodland leaf litter and lichens; under stones on shingle beds; on exposed stony mountain wastes and crags; in the debris of tidal drift lines on the shores of the sea and lakes; at the bottom of herbage on peat mosses, fens, sand dunes, salt marshes and reed-beds; in houses, gardens, cellars, sewers and caves; in sphagnum moss and

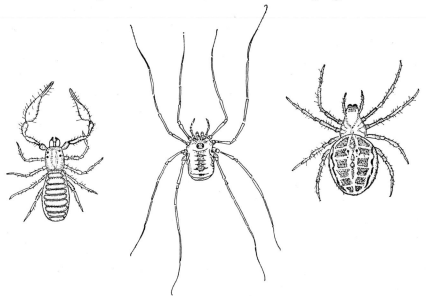

Fig. 20 (left) Pseudoscorpion (body length 3 mm approx.) (centre) Harvestman ♀ (body length 5 mm approx.) (right) Wheel web spider ♀ (body length 8 mm approx.)

heather on moorlands; and spiders occur in myriads in the microclimates provided by the close herbage on heaths and grasslands. Those species occurring under the stones of eroded river beds are frequently submerged for periods during the winter when torrents of meltwater from the snow-covered fells fill the rivers; and others on the estuarine salt-marshes are likewise submerged at the time of High Water Spring tides.

The invertebrate food supply is hunted in the day-time by species which have developed a keen eyesight and speed of movement, or at night by species which wander in the darkness or wait to make contact with their prey, having developed a delicate sense of touch, or at all times by species using web snares. One or other of these methods is peculiar to each family. The hunters are lithe and lean, the jumpers are short limbed and squat, while the trappers are relatively slow, heavy and soft bodied.

The Argiopidae (Fig. 20) spin wheel webs in open situations exposed to the sweep of the wind, and their vertical snares are both open in structure and somewhat elastic in texture offering little wind resistance. The Linyphiidae on the other hand wait on the underside of their horizontal sheet webs which are of relatively close texture built within the shelter of woody shrubs, in low herbage, across depressions in the ground and in crevices below stones and in mosses. The Dictynidae spread matted lace webs on the faces of old walls and tree trunks. The Theridiidae build open scaffold webs in semi-sheltered situations in prickly shrubs, below overhanging heather and in nooks and crannies of rocks, walls and stone heaps.

In discussing briefly the distribution and ecology of spiders in the Lake District it is necessary to make some remarks on the separation of species in three dimensional space and in both diurnal and seasonal time. Consider a very small area of a typical Lakeland habitat such as a few square yards of deciduous woodland below a weathered crag face. The ground cover will consist of mossy tussocks, grasses and herbs growing round fallen pieces of slate or other rock talus with an understorey of woody plants among which the tree trunks stand, providing a leaf canopy overhead. A large number of spider species will be found in this habitat at almost any time of the year, the smaller species being most abundant in the moss, grass bottoms and below stones, while the large species, with some exceptions, will be commoner in their webs spun on the woody plants, on the tree trunks and upwards into the leaf canopy. The bark crevices and the lichens of the tree trunks will, however, provide a sub-habitat for small species. Some of these spiders will be active in the hours of daylight while others restrict their hunting activities to night-time in the same habitat niche. Not only is there both spatial and diurnal separation of species active in the same habitats, but there is also some seasonal separation relative to the peak period of sexual activity.

From the time of emergence from the eggs, young spiders grow as they feed and this growth is accommodated by ecdysis, the casting off or moulting of the exoskeleton. Between infancy and maturity a spider passes through five or six or more of these instars. The complete sexual organs do not appear externally until after the final moult when activity in the quest for food becomes secondary to the active search for females by the male sex. Fertilised gravid females become rather less active in web spinning or hunting at the time of using silk for egg cocoons.

This peak period of sexual activity occurs at different times of the year for different species, and although there is overlapping and coincidence to a very considerable extent there is nevertheless a succession of peak periods of sexual activity throughout the seasons, even in this single type of woodland habitat under consideration. At any time of the year at least some species will be adults, but when sample-collecting is made from a given habitat more than half the catch will consist of immature specimens and to a very considerable degree these small immatures are themselves a secondary source of food for the larger species. In general, however, there are two seasonal peaks in June and late September when many spider species become mature annually, just as there are peak periods at such times for the seasonal blossoming of flowering plants.

The build-up of a spider population (immatures and adults) for any habitat increases proportionately with the seasonal build-up of insect prey. This is most evident in the vegetation strata above the herb layer, but at ground level below the leaf litter and under accumulations of loose stones there is less exposure to wind and less variation in temperature and all invertebrate populations tend to be more static. Here the food supply for spiders is maintained. Here the immature of the surface-running spiders such as the Lycosidae (wolf spiders) over-winter, while many of the very small linyphiids and litter species are reaching maturity all the year round.

In all the topographical areas referred to in this and in the previous chapters there are some species which are rare and others, 'the successful species', which are abundant. It is a remarkable fact that there is quite often in the same spider genus one rare species which is very closely related to another species which is ubiquitously common. The common species and the rarity are not always limited to the same type of habitat; one may be montane and the other maritime; associated with man, or with trees; and each may also be isolated from the other by seasonal separation.

Some of the rarer species are no doubt on the verge of extinction, having reached those limits of evolution which no longer enable them to compete with other 'successful species' in the same habitat. Other rare species are no doubt relict in isolated 'pockets' which have been less affected, following a general change of either climate or local conditions. One cannot overlook the agency of man's interference during the past 1500 years—a view which is supported by the fact that many of our spider rarities are found in areas which have never been suitable for land utilisation, such as the raised bog mosses and the high moorlands or those places left undisturbed since Neolithic times. Pre-historic sites do often shelter uncommon spiders.

On the other hand, many of the small linyphiids as well as some species of other families are capable of extending their range by aerial dispersal. This usually takes place when bright morning sunshine follows a still cold night without frost. The sharp rise in temperature seems to stir the little spiders into great activity and they climb from ground level habitats up the plant stems, from the extremities of which they project a stream of silk into the convecting air currents. As soon as the silk becomes long enough to provide sufficient 'lift', the little creatures sail away, borne upwards by the air currents, often to heights of hundreds or even thousands of feet and horizontally to great distances. Contrary to popular opinion it is usually the adults of the tiny spider species which disperse in this way, and dispersal can take place at almost any time of the year for those species which have no fixed period of maturity; but the procedure is most evident for many autumn-maturing linyphiids when the right conditions prevail during the first two weeks of October, and the bushes, grasses and fences of the Lake District are seen to be smothered in the silky strands shimmering in the autumn sunshine.

It is not possible in the limited space available to give either a full list of the spider species to be found in the Lake District area or to provide a guide to identification, for which recourse must be made to the bibliography provided on page 207, the authoritative work covering identification and distribution of British Spiders being the two volumes by Locket and Millidge. A third volume, which will include distribution maps, is in the course of preparation.

Both rare and common species are not infrequently being newly recorded for the Lakeland area and these include *Atypus affinis* from limestone outcrops at Silverdale, *Lepthyphantes pinicola* and *Theridion bellicosum* from the shattered rock slabs on the summit of Helm Crag at Grasmere. In Grasmere village *Pholcus phalangioides* occurs in outbuildings at the northern limit of its range of distribution; *Lepthyphantes expunctus* is uncommonly found on the juniper trees above Easedale Tarn. Recently newly identified for Britain are *Cornicularia clavicornis* from the heights of

Helvellyn and the Pennine Hills (a species with a range of distribution beyond Lat. 80°N. inside the Polar circle), and the minute *Maro lepidus* from a sphagnum habitat on the National Nature Reserve at Rusland Moss.

At the beginning of this section reference was made to two other orders of the class Arachnida, the Opilionidae or harvestmen and the Pseudoscorpionidae or chelifers. Harvestmen are easily distinguished from spiders because the head and abdomen are in one compact unit in the former, whereas spiders have these parts of the body separated by a narrow waist or pedicle. Harvestmen also possess those remarkably long spindly legs which can so easily become detached in an emergency, and the loss of one or two of the eight seems to cause little inconvenience (Fig. 20). In general harvestmen are usually nocturnally active and, like the true spiders, prey on small invertebrates including insect larvae, worms and small molluscs. They are also scavengers, feeding on dead invertebrate and vegetable material, as well as on bird droppings, seeds and fungi. So far sixteen of the twenty-one British species have been recorded for the Lake counties and all these have a very wide distribution in fields, woods, marshes, bracken, heather, gardens, sand dunes and moorland right to the mountain tops, without any marked habitat preference other than humidity, which is essential for their survival.

Chelifers or pseudoscorpions (Fig. 20) are very small animals quite distinctly different from the other Arachnida referred to, and bear a superficial resemblance to tropical scorpions, having pincer claws but lacking the stinging tail. Most of them are less than 3 millimetres long and occur in decaying vegetable debris, at grassroots, under tree bark, in rock crevices and sand hills, where these little predators feed on minute invertebrates such as psocids, Collembola and Acari which share their habitats. Eleven of the twenty-five British species are recorded from within or just outside the Lake National Park area, but the order has been so little worked in our region that no doubt others will be discovered by systematic collecting.

VERTEBRATES

AMPHIBIANS AND REPTILES

by T. T. Macan

The Common Frog (*Rana temporaria*) occurs throughout the district, extending nearly to the top of the mountains. Spawn has been recorded in January, but is not laid until March in cold winters, when the waters are icebound till then. It is laid in shallow water in tarns and in smaller places, even cart-ruts. The latter dry up and, in the former, most of the tadpoles are eaten by fish as soon as they start to move about. A small number which remain in the shallow water among thick vegetation survive.

The Common Toad (*Bufo bufo*) is also abundant though it is not found as high as the frog. It breeds in the same sort of places but in deeper water and later. Fair numbers enter parts of Windermere to spawn, and may be found in water twenty feet (6 metres) deep, though spawning does not often take place in depths below ten feet (3 metres) (Frazer 1954).

The Natterjack Toad (*Bufo calamita*) (Plate 20) occurs on either side of the Solway and along the Cumberland coast to the south. According to Smith's map (1951, Fig. 42, page 118) it does not occur again until the coast of Lancashire south of Morecambe Bay is reached. However, it is now known that it is abundant on the Cumberland sand dunes between Drigg and Eskmeals, which are within the National Park.

All three newts, the Smooth, Palmate and Great Crested (*Triturus vulgaris*, *helveticus* and *cristatus*) are known in the Lake District, and they used to occur together in a pond near Wray Castle. As its level has since been reduced, this may no longer be true. The Palmate Newt is the commonest. Adults enter tarns to breed during the summer. Most come in April but breeding appears to extend over a long period. The first larvae to appear are probably ready to leave the water in August, but many have not reached full size before winter and they remain in the larval state until the following year. Trout apparently eat few larvae, probably because they are too well concealed in the vegetation, but they take a comparatively heavy toll of the adults.

Not enough is known about them to justify a separate chapter on the reptiles. Zoologically they come between the amphibians and the birds, and as they are cold-blooded it seems more logical to include them with the former.

The Adder or Viper (*Vipera berus*), the Grass Snake (*Natrix natrix*), the Slow Worm (*Anguis fragilis*) and the Viviparous Lizard (*Lacerta vivipara*) all occur in the Lake District (Taylor, 1948), though none has been the object of particular study there. The Sand Lizard (*Lacerta agilis*) is still to be found on the coasts of Lancashire, but there are no reliable records north of Morecambe Bay (Smith, 1951, Fig. 62, page 192). However, much of that part of the Cumberland coast which falls within the National Park is inaccessible, notably the area to the south of Ravenglass where naval guns are tested, and, as there are extensive dunes in this region, the possibility that the Sand Lizard does occur cannot be ruled out.

Redstart, male

PLATE 25

Grey Wagtail, female

PLATE 26   Pied Flycatcher, male

Dipper

PLATE 27

Common
Sandpiper

Short-tailed Vole

PLATE 28

Badger

BIRDS

by J. A. G. Barnes

Birds are the most mobile of vertebrate creatures, and one of the attractions of bird-watching as a hobby is the chance of finding interesting species in unexpected places. Although a few species fit into a narrow ecological niche, for example the Bearded Tit, which is practically restricted to large reed-beds, most birds are much more adaptable in their requirements. The Wren, for instance, flourishes in a high mountain gully, a wood, a farm-yard, a town garden or on the edge of a salt-marsh. But even if the local distribution of birds is less predictable than that of plants and insects it is still true that certain species are especially associated with particular kinds of habitat, and it is the aim of this sub-section to give a brief account of the most characteristic birds of the main types of environment represented in the Lake District National Park.

The Fells and Moorlands

The Lake District can claim no breeding species confined, like the Ptarmigan in Scotland, to the summit plateaux of the mountains. It is doubtful if the Dotterel has ever been a regular breeding bird in the Lake District mountains in historical times (Macpherson, 1892): now it should probably be regarded only as an occasional passage migrant.

Thirty years ago the three characteristic 'big birds' of the open fells were the Peregrine, the Buzzard and the Raven. These three species were all, in a sense, refugees from human persecution. In medieval times the Raven was a familiar tree-nesting bird in the lowlands, and the Buzzard (Plate 22) was common all over Britain 150 years ago. With the development of game preservation and improved firearms in the nineteenth century both Raven and Buzzard were practically exterminated in England as tree-nesting species, and, like the Peregrine, which has been under pressure from falconers over a much longer period, they only survived where they could nest on cliffs difficult of access for humans. In England the only considerable inland refuge was provided by the Cumbrian

Mountains. The rugged crags of this highly glaciated region afforded suitable nest sites for all three species, and the sparse human population and limited game preservation were further advantages. An additional attraction for the Raven was the extensive sheep-grazing: both observation and the analysis of pellets show that the staple diet of the Lake District Ravens is sheep carrion, and its abundance is probably the reason for the Raven population being denser here than in the Scottish Highlands. Fell-breeding Buzzards also eat carrion; and sheep contribute indirectly to a secondary food supply for both species—the dor beetle (*Geotrupes* spp.), which lays its eggs in sheep droppings.

Wordsworth (1835) tells of rewards offered for dead Ravens in his schooldays at Hawkshead, but the tolerant attitude of local farmers towards these big birds in more recent times has helped their survival. The Raven's intentions towards new-born lambs may be no more charitable than the eye-pecking Carrion Crow's, but its reluctance to come down to the lambing fields near the farms makes it comparatively harmless in practice.

All three species have been constantly persecuted by egg-collectors, but in spite of this the Buzzard has greatly increased its numbers and expanded its range over the past fifty years, both in Britain as a whole and the Lake District in particular. The increase may have begun here with reduced interference during the war of 1914–18, and it was probably helped by a similar respite in 1939–45, but the expansion continued during peace-time. It was in the 1930s that the Buzzard returned to breed in the Winster and Crosthwaite districts of south Westmorland, almost exactly a hundred years after its extermination there by game-preserves (Pearson, 1863), and by 1945 woodlands all round the Lake District had been recolonised. The virtual disappearance of the rabbit, the supposed main item in the Buzzard's diet, with the myxomatosis epidemic of 1954–56 caused only a temporary check. There is no doubt that the Buzzard is now a characteristic bird of the woodlands rather than the fells of the Lake District, and there is some evidence that the crag-nesting population has recently declined as the tree-nesters have increased.

Ravens have at least held their own in the last fifty years. In addition to the breeding population, which has been estimated at about sixty pairs (Blezard, 1954), flocks of non-breeding birds appear on the fell-tops, especially in spring and autumn. Occasional nests in trees have been found in recent years, but Lake District Ravens have not become woodland birds like Buzzards, although from the past history of the species there is no apparent reason why they should not do so.

The Peregrine population seems to have remained remarkably constant for the first fifty years of this century, with the same crag ledges in regular, if not continuous, use decade after decade. The territorial requirements of of these falcons seem to inhibit any considerable increase in their numbers in this restricted area.

In spite of the desertion of some nest sites because of increasing disturbance by rock-climbers, the outlook for these three species in the 1950s was quite favourable. And at that time a new and intriguing possibility arose—the return of the Golden Eagle to the Lake District as a breeding species. After appearing only as rare vagrants for 150 years eagles were seen each year from 1957, when an empty nest was found on a Lakeland crag. Many of the sightings were over the lower hills and moorlands of the south, where food is probably more abundant than in the typical eagle country of the central fells. At last, in 1969, two eggs were laid, the first recorded in England since the eighteenth century. Most unfortunately they were deserted, and it is abundantly clear that if there is to be successful breeding in future there will have to be a well-organised plan to give the eagles the seclusion and freedom from disturbance that they require. It is to be hoped that responsible efforts to achieve this will have the widest possible support.

In 1961–62 a national enquiry on the Peregrine (Ratcliffe, 1963) showed almost complete breeding failure and a drastic reduction of numbers in the south of England and similar conditions spreading to Wales and northern England. Since then the decline of the Peregrine in the Lake District has been catastrophic. In 1963 and 1964 only a negligible remnant of the former population succeeded in bringing off young. Analysis of eggs and bodies of birds has proved the cause of this change beyond all reasonable doubt: a build-up of persistent toxic chemicals causing abnormal breeding behaviour, infertility and eventually death. The cumulative effect of these organo-chlorine compounds is most severe in birds at the end of the food chain, for example falcons, which eat numbers of other birds that may be individually only moderately contaminated by poisoned seeds or insects. More recently it has been shown that many different species, including the Golden Eagle, are being affected in varying degrees, and in particular eggs of Lake District Ravens and Buzzards have been found to be seriously contaminated by chemicals used in sheep-dip (Ratcliffe, 1965). In 1963 there seemed to be a very real danger that these fine birds, which must have added to many a tourist's delight in the Lakeland scene by their mastery of the art of flight, having survived centuries of conscious human persecution, might be exterminated unintentionally by an indiscriminate use of chemicals in agriculture. Fortunately there has been a recent improvement in the situation, following restrictions on the use of certain pesticides, but continued vigilance will still be necessary.

The commonest breeding bird of the fellsides is the Meadow Pipit. It is found on any open ground with rough grass, heather or bracken, from the valley floor to all but the highest mountain tops. But it is only a summer visitor, arriving among the fells in March and April, when flocks may be seen moving slowly up the valleys or along the hillsides by a sort of leap-frog progress, some birds settling briefly to feed while others fly over them. Emigration has already begun in August, and by the end of September few are left on the fells. Some Meadow Pipits winter on lowland fields or by the sea, but the great majority of our native birds leave the district entirely.

The only other abundant breeding bird of the bare mountainsides is the handsome and conspicuous Wheatear (Plate 22). It also ranges from the valley bottoms to nearly 3000 feet (900 metres) above sea-level and may occur anywhere where there are stone walls or boulders to provide perches and nest sites. But it must be admitted that the sheep-walk of the Lake District fells is poor in total bird population as well as in variety of species, and in places even Meadow Pipits and Wheatears are thinly distributed. The featureless fells of West Cumberland are perhaps the nearest thing in England to an ornithological desert.

Ring Ouzels (Plate 23), though less plentiful than on parts of the Pennines, are not uncommon in more broken country, breeding chiefly between 1500 and 2000 feet (450 and 600 metres) up on low crags, in gills or deserted quarries and mines. While nesting they are chiefly insectivorous, in the wide sense in which this word is generally used by ornithologists, but in autumn they range widely in search of berries and may then associate in loose flocks up to sixty strong. Juniper scrub is a favoured habitat at this season.

The Sky Lark is a bird of the grassy tops, but not of the valleys or hillsides. It is claustrophobic by nature and frequents wide open spaces at any height. On a fine summer day Sky Larks may be heard singing all along the summit ridge of the High Street range, at over 2500 feet (760 metres) above sea-level, over lower fell-tops and foothills and, most abundantly of all, over the sand dunes and salt-marshes of the Cumberland coast.

Finally there is an abundant non-breeding summer visitor to the mountain tops that many fell-walkers must have noticed—the Swift. Parties of them suddenly appear over the summits and high slopes in pursuit of flying insects. It seems likely that these parties consist of non-breeding yearlings, although the distances involved would not be a serious obstacle to adults nesting in the Lake District villages. Swallows and House Martins sometimes visit the high tops in the same way.

Such are the typical birds of the central fells in summer. In winter the picture is very different. Except for Ravens and Buzzards, and an occasional Wren foraging in rock clefts or heather clumps, the high slopes are practically deserted. But there is one winter visitor to the mountain-tops, the Snow Bunting. Though never plentiful, small parties appear each winter on the high slopes and summit plateaux, feeding on seeds, especially those of the Heath Rush (*Juncus squarrosus*), which bears its fruits on stiff stalks which project through the snow. Although Snow Buntings are occasionally seen on lower fells at about 1000 feet (300 metres), and not infrequently on the seashore, they avoid valleys even in the severest weather.

Before leaving the open fells one should mention three birds which are not by any means confined to mountains but nevertheless breed on them and frequent at least the lower slopes through the winter. The Carrion Crow nests in crags or isolated hawthorns far up the hillsides and has increased its numbers. The Jackdaw breeds in colonies in crevices in the lower crags, as well as in chimneys in farms and villages, and has also multiplied in recent years. Both these corvids have an extremely varied diet, and the crow in particular shows a wary cunning that has helped it to survive the hostility of gamekeepers and farmers. The third species is the Kestrel, the most adaptable of our raptorial birds. It is common from the coastal flats to the mountain-tops, breeding on crag ledges at least up to 2000 feet (600 metres). Its staple diet in the fells is the Field Vole, so the risk of serious contamination by toxic chemicals is fortunately small.

The hills and moorlands on the lower fringes of the Lake District, between 500 and 1500 feet above sea-level (150 and 450 metres), have a rather different bird population from the central fells, although several species, for example the Meadow Pipit and its frequent parasite, the Cuckoo, are common to both. The most characteristic breeding bird of the foothills and rough pastures is the Curlew (Plate 23). But although they are still plentiful on some moorlands, Curlews now nest regularly in the enclosed fields right down to the valley bottoms. In south Westmorland this change of habitat has been most marked since about 1940. It is difficult to account for. Pressure of increased numbers seems an unlikely cause in view of the abundance of corvids in the breeding areas and the fact that some former moorland haunts are now deserted.

The Golden Plover has always been scarcer in the Lake District than in the Pennines and numbers seem to have declined in recent years, but several pairs still breed on a few of the higher moorlands near the northern and eastern borders of the National Park.

Two closely related passerine species, the Stonechat and the Whinchat, are more typical of the foothills and moorlands than of the central fells. One of the chief strongholds of the Stonechat in north-west England has always been the Cumberland coast, where pairs or individuals are normally to be found throughout the year among scattered gorse bushes. After a succession of mild winters there is a spread inland, and during the 1930s Stonechats were not uncommon on bracken-covered slopes even in the central valleys. But four severe winters in the forties exterminated the inland breeders and greatly reduced the coastal population. By 1962 Stonechats were again beginning to breed inland, but the species was almost wiped out in the Lake District counties by the great frost of 1963. Although the numbers of Stonechats elsewhere in Britain have been reduced by other factors, especially the destruction or disturbance of their heathland habitat, in the Lake District the correlation of numbers and distribution with winter weather seems unmistakable.

Whinchats, which are summer migrants, are reported to have become increasingly scarce recently, but they are still widely distributed on the lower slopes of the fells, especially where there is bracken and gorse, and they are locally abundant on the south-eastern outskirts of the National Park. In 1965 seven pairs could be seen in a half-mile (800 metres) walk on a hillside a few miles north of Kendal.

Two birds are specially associated with heather, but for different reasons. For the Merlin it provides cover for eggs and young, preferably with rocky outcrops nearby for perches and plucking stations. But the Merlin population seems to have been declining steadily for many years, for no obvious reason, and more recently (Ratcliffe, 1965) Merlin eggs from two Lake District nests showed heavy contamination with organo-chlorine residues, presumably picked up by Meadow Pipits and Wheat-ears, the Merlin's commonest prey, on their winter travels. So the outlook for this attractive little falcon is far from promising.

For the Red Grouse, heather provides not only concealment from enemies and protection from the weather but also food. Recent research has shown that the quantity and quality of food available is the controlling factor in grouse population: the effects of disease and predation seem to be negligible. In particular the mortality of chicks has been correlated with the die-back of heather during the previous winter, and the density of grouse population with the content of the soil as well as the apparent quantity of heather. Controlled burning of heather has long been recog-nised as a means of increasing the production of the fresh shoots that are the chief food of the Red Grouse, and the only places in the Lake District where there are any considerable numbers of Red Grouse are those where heather burning is practised, notably a few fells of the Skiddaw group and one or two Westmorland moorlands. The birds are only thinly distributed over the extensive heather slopes of the Skiddaw slate mountains of the north-west.

It will be convenient to mention here the Black Grouse, which is sometimes found on open grassy moors, though it is more typically associated with the woodland fringes: scattered larches on limestone plateaux or birches and rowans on moorland. For the last century the species has been reported on the verge of extinction, and certainly several former haunts have been deserted in the last ten years, but either by fresh introductions or natural recovery small groups still survive in widely scattered areas, mainly on the outskirts of the Lake District.

The Woods

The Black Grouse is only one of a whole range of new species that appear with the first trees on the fellside. Trees are of vital importance to a wide variety of birds. They supply food in the form of buds, fruits and insects in their various stages of development; they provide shelter from the weather and protection from predators on the ground or in the air, nest sites in holes or in the branches, nesting materials, perches—especially for singing males in spring—and roosting places. Even isolated rowans or hawthorns on a bare fellside will often accommodate a pair of Chaffinches. The sessile oakwoods, so familiar a feature of the Lakeland scene from the valley floor to over 1000 feet (300 metres) above sea-level, with their lichen-covered trees and lack of 'shrub layer' (Plate 13), have rather a sparse bird population, but even the stunted Keskadale oaks (see page 47) at about 1300 feet (400 metres) harbour not less than three or four pairs each of Chaffinches, Willow warblers and Blackbirds, and at least one pair of half a dozen other species. Yapp (1962) concluded that the dominant species of this type of woodland in summer are, in order of frequency: Chaffinch, Wood Warbler, Pied Flycatcher, Robin, Coal Tit, Tree Pipit, Willow Warbler, Wren and Redstart; but the bird-watcher should not expect to find these birds plentiful in a pure oakwood on the Lake District fells, especially if the trees are young and sound. Where the oaks are mixed with other trees, such as birch, rowan, hazel and sycamore, the bird population is often denser and more varied.

Four of the summer migrants in this list are typically, though not exclusively, hill-country species. The Wood Warbler provides something of a mystery. Miss M. L. Armitt, writing of the Rydal district between 1897 and 1901, described the Wood Warbler as 'extremely common in favourite spots' and 'thickly dotted over oakwoods of any size'. But this is certainly not true today. The species is only thinly distributed over most of the Lake District, including the Ambleside-Grasmere area, and one can search many apparently suitable oakwoods without finding a single Wood Warbler. Even in the neighbourhood of Ullswater, which seems to be its chief stronghold, it is generally less numerous than the Willow Warbler. One can only conclude that there has been a drastic reduction in the Wood Warbler population during the present century.

The attractive Pied Flycatcher (Plate 26), which has become a kind of ornithological emblem of the Lake District, poses problems too. Campbell (1954) showed that its habitat requirements, including food supply, protective cover, nest sites and suitable perches for song, display and feeding sallies, are most likely to be satisfied in the open deciduous woodlands of the foothills of Highland Britain, with a high rainfall and an average daily maximum temperature in May of not less than 59°F (15°C).

Around Ambleside and Grasmere, and in Patterdale, Borrowdale and some other valleys the Pied Flycatcher seems to find all these amenities supplied by a wide variety of woods and gardens or scattered trees on a fellside. In these central valleys it has become locally abundant, especially where nest-boxes have been put up, but it has remained surprisingly absent from apparently suitable oakwoods to the south and west. However, since 1966 the provision of nest-boxes by the Lake District Naturalists' Trust and the Forestry Commission in open deciduous woods has produced a marked extension of the species' range, and boxes at over 1200 feet (365 metres) above sea-level have been occupied. The fact that over 92% of the L.D.N.T. nest-boxes were promptly occupied by tits or Pied Flycatchers suggests that competition for nest sites may be an important limiting factor on the range and population of the latter species, though it is possible that a strong homing instinct or a conservative attitude to the wider environment of the breeding territory may also tend to restrict expansion.

The Tree Pipit is certainly found in the oakwoods, but it is perhaps more typical of, and is much more conspicuous in, the scattered trees and bushes on a fellside. It is, indeed, as characteristic a bird of the lower slopes and valleys of the Lake District as the Meadow Pipit is of the open fells. Redstarts breed not only in woods, where they compete with tits and Pied Flycatchers for nest-holes in trees, but in open country with scattered large trees. They are common along roadsides and round farms and houses, where they nest in holes in stone walls, including those of buildings. In spite of this association with man they are shy birds and the song is usually delivered from a concealed position in a tall tree, so it not infrequently happens that non-ornithologists who have lived in the Lake District for years are puzzled and astonished by their first close view of the brilliantly coloured cock Redstart (Plate 25).

A different type of high-level habitat for perching birds, with a generally denser population than the oakwoods, is provided by the juniper scrub which is found on several fellsides up to about 1500 feet (450 metres) above sea-level. Personal observations suggest that one of the commonest breeding species is the Dunnock, or Hedge Sparrow, which nests in juniper at least up to 1300 feet (400 metres). This seems a surprising habitat for a bird usually associated with roadside hedges and gardens, but odd pairs are also found at remote farms without hedge or bush cover, and even on treeless crags. Other birds found in juniper at about this height include the

Blackbird, Mistle Thrush, Song Thrush, Robin, Greenfinch, Linnet, Coal Tit and Goldcrest.

The plantations of the Forestry Commission (Plate 11) have had a considerable effect on the bird life of the Lake District. There is no doubt that they generally support both a denser population and a more varied list of species than the sheep-walk they have replaced. The first effect of planting is the exclusion of sheep and consequent growth of heather and long grass, which harbours large numbers of Field Voles, and they in turn attract predators: Kestrels, Buzzards and Short-eared Owls. These owls are otherwise practically restricted, at least in summer, to a few outlying moorlands. The long grass also provides cover for nests, and Meadow Pipits and Sky Larks continue to breed in the plantations until the trees are about four feet (1.2 metres) high, by which time Tree Pipits, Willow Warblers, Redpolls and other species are appearing as breeders. After the trees have been 'brashed', i.e. have had the lower branches cut off close to the trunk, there is a reduction in bird population and the Chaffinch is then the only abundant breeding species. Young healthy conifers naturally provide no holes for nests, but nest-boxes have been put up in some plantations to attract tits and other insectivorous birds.

Artificially planted conifers have also provided occasional nest sites for more unusual species, for example for many Crossbills and probably some Siskins near Coniston in 1957–59, and for a pair of Golden Orioles in the Grizedale Forest in 1958–59, much the most northerly breeding record for the species in Britain.

The bird population of the extensive mixed woodlands of the southern part of the Lake District is generally richer than that of the fellside oak-woods or the conifer plantations. There is much more undergrowth, and this attracts Chiffchaffs, Garden Warblers and Blackcaps. The Yews on the limestone scars are attractive to the Marsh Tit, which is notably abundant in some of these woods. The elusive Hawfinch is by no means rare on the outskirts of the woods. If there has been a heavy damson crop in the Lyth and Crosthwaite districts of south Westmorland flocks of Hawfinches collect in the orchards in winter to split the damson and cherry stones with their powerful beaks and eat the kernels; sixty have been seen in a single flock. The Sparrow Hawk, which has suffered a severe decline in southern and midland counties in recent years, is still not uncommon in the woods of south Lakeland.

Two crepuscular birds deserve mention, the Woodcock and the Nightjar. Woodcock, which were only known as winter visitors a century ago, are now common breeders both in the oakwoods of the central fells and the southern woodlands. Nightjars on the other hand have declined seriously during the last twenty years, for no obvious reason. However several pairs still breed in the bracken and scrub woodland of the limestone and Silurian country.

The three species of woodpecker found in Britain provide examples of changing distribution. At the end of the last century the Great Spotted Woodpecker was known only as a scarce winter visitor (Macpherson, 1892), but by 1943 it was well established as a breeding bird in woods throughout the district. It was about this time that the Green Woodpecker, which feeds more on the ground and prefers more open country, began a spectacular northward advance. It was a very rare bird in the Lake District in Macpherson's time, and still uncommon in 1943, but by the middle 1950s its unmistakable call could be heard in almost every valley, even well up the fellsides where trees are few and small. Green Woodpeckers were badly hit by the severe winter of 1962–63, but they have now almost recovered their former numbers. The Lesser Spotted Woodpecker is still uncommon, but it has been recorded more frequently in recent years. The Lake District is at present on the extreme northern border of its distribution in Britain. The same can be said of the Nuthatch, which is now appearing with some regularity on the southern fringes of the National Park. Summer temperature seems to be a limiting factor on the distribution of both these species.

The Lake District also lies approximately on the northern boundary of the present distribution of the Little Owl. This bird, which was introduced into Britain in the nineteenth century, began to appear quite commonly on the outskirts of the Lake District in the 1950s and showed every sign of becoming a common resident. However, the expected expansion has not taken place, and although Little Owls still breed in some localities, especially in west Cumberland, they have disappeared from several former haunts in south Westmorland. It would appear that this latitude is about the limit of their natural range.

So far we have considered the summer bird population of the woodlands. In winter the warblers, redstarts and flycatchers have of course emigrated, and other birds have changed their habits and their habitats.

The Chaffinch, for instance, is no longer a territorial, insectivorous bird of the woods, but a gregarious, seed-eating bird of the lowland fields and gardens. There must, in fact, be a large-scale emigration of Chaffinches from the Lake District in autumn, for the finch flocks round the farms have been smaller in recent years, and wintering Chaffinches are now found chiefly round houses and popular car parks.

One can walk for some distance through a Lake District wood in winter and find it as desolate as the open fells, but sooner or later in any type of wood at any level one finds a flock of tits, sometimes with all five common species represented, moving through the trees. The Coal Tits, usually the most numerous species, show a brilliance of plumage that one rarely sees in the specimens that feed in village or suburban gardens, and an occasional individual has the yellow tinge of cheeks and nape that characterises the Irish race. Often associated with them are some Goldcrests and one or two Tree Creepers, and it is interesting to watch how this mixed flock keeps its cohesion, with Blue and Long-tailed Tits feeding in the tree tops and outer twigs, Great Tits in the lower branches and on the ground and Tree Creepers on the trunks. Individuals of other apparently incongruous species seem to be attracted by the flock: Bullfinches and even Robins will follow it for a time.

Woods, especially evergreen conifer plantations, also serve as dormitories for birds in winter. Where such plantations are near farm land, such as parts of the Grizedale Forest (Plate 11), a stream of Wood Pigeons, Fieldfares, Redwings and finches can be seen flying in from the fields at dusk to roost in the spruces.

The Farms and Lowlands

There has been a serious decline in the bird population of many parts of rural England owing to post-war agricultural developments. The effect upon birds of prey of the persistent toxic chemicals introduced in the 1950s has already been mentioned, but the loss of breeding habitats for a wide range of species through the destruction of hedgerows and elimination of 'waste land' has also had far-reaching effects. In the Lake District these changes have been much less marked than in eastern and southern England. Arable land within the National Park is practically restricted to an irregular fringe on its outskirts, and even here the fields have not, so far, been enlarged by the removal of hedges.

Nevertheless the reclamation of marginal land during and after the 1939-45 war has affected certain species in limited areas: breeding Snipe and Redshanks have disappeared from former haunts because of the draining of marshy fields, and Whinchats, Linnets and Yellowhammers have lost nest sites where gorse and juniper have been cleared to provide improved grazing. Over a longer period the Corncrake, so familiar with its rasping call in our hayfields fifty years ago, has practically disappeared as a breeding species, though an occasional male can still be heard craking in the spring or early summer. Almost certainly the disappearance has been due here, as elsewhere in Britain, to mechanical hay-cutting and the tendency to cut earlier in the year. Few farmers can be as considerate and fortunate as the south Westmorland man who, some years ago, picked up a Corncrake's nest and eggs intact on the cutting bar of his machine and transferred it successfully to the hedge bottom. The Partridge may well be another victim of changing farming methods. Always scarce among the fells and valleys, the Partridge has recently become noticeably less common even in the agricultural margin of the Lake District, as it has throughout Britain. The occasional small coveys found among the Cumberland sand dunes may have better prospects than the more conventional birds on the farmland.

The Lapwing is a species that is affected by severe winters as well as by drainage of marshy ground and more intensive cultivation. However, the sharp drop in numbers that occurred in the Lake District in or about 1957 is difficult to account for. As a breeding species the Lapwing is now rather thinly distributed in most parts of the National Park, although there are fluctuations from year to year and large flocks may still be seen at migration times, especially on the southern estuaries.

Another drastic decrease, not easily explained, is that of the Barn Owl. A common bird, especially in the southern valleys, thirty years ago, it is now scarce throughout the Lake District and has disappeared from considerable areas where it was formerly abundant, although there is no evidence of human persecution or lack of nest sites in farm buildings. When they were more plentiful many Barn Owls were killed by cars and trains, owing to their habit of taking prey on the open spaces afforded by roads and railway tracks; and toxic chemicals and the severe winters of 1947 and 1963 may have accelerated a slower previous decline. Nevertheless it is strange that the Tawny Owl has survived these hazards and has, if anything, increased in numbers during the same period.

On the sheep farms of the fells there have been few changes that affect bird life. In summer the farm buildings themselves often attract Pied Wagtails, Swallows, and sometimes a colony of House Martins, and the familiar cluster of sycamores round many farmhouses may provide a nest site for a pair of Mistle Thrushes. In winter, when the surrounding fellsides and woodlands are almost deserted, even the remotest farmyard has its little collection of tits, finches and other common birds, drawn by the food that is charitably or unintentionally provided for them. But the large flocks of finches and buntings that used to frequent the lowland stackyards before the time of the combine-harvester are no longer in evidence, although smaller parties are still seen in early spring on fields dressed with farmyard manure.

Gardens, whether in villages or more open countryside, often have a much denser bird population than field, fell or wood. Apart from the widespread inducements of bird-tables and nesting-boxes, the combination of tree and shrub cover, exposed soil and close-cut lawn in a garden makes it a favourable habitat for a wide range of species. For example the Goldfinch, much more numerous since its capture for caging became illegal, the Greenfinch, which has developed an addiction to peanuts, and the Bullfinch, with its well-known taste for the buds of fruit trees and flowering shrubs, are becoming increasingly common as garden birds.

Another attractive feeding habitat, particularly noticeable in a tourist area like the Lake District, is provided by car parks and popular picnic sites. The composition of the population of bird-scavengers varies with the environment, but wherever there are a few trees or bushes at hand Chaffinches will appear. A flock of fifty or more, often accompanied by Yellowhammers, frequents the Tarn Hows car parks, and some individuals will feed confidently from a hand extended from a car window. At White Moss, between Rydal and Grasmere, there are also tits, which perch on car bonnets and wing mirrors, Robins, Dunnocks, Blackbirds and Jackdaws, with Black-headed Gulls and occasional Mute Swans from Rydal Water. Even on the bleak roadside strip opposite the Kirkstone Inn at 1500 feet (450 metres) above sea-level, without a tree or bush in sight, a pair of Pied Wagtails can sometimes be seen pecking about among the parked cars.

Becks, Tarns and Lakes

Water, falling, running or standing, is such an important feature of Lake

District scenery that the birds particularly associated with it deserve special consideration.

The Dipper (Plate 27) is so universally regarded as the typical bird of mountain torrents and waterfalls that it seems almost heretical to suggest that in the central Lake District its favourite habitat is a shallow, tree-lined river in the lower part of a valley, with broken water, moss-covered stones and perhaps rooted water weeds, preferably with rocky outcrops on the banks. In the volcanic rock areas the upper course of a beck is usually bare of vegetation (Plate 12), the bed consisting of smooth rock basins or rounded stones that are swept along by floods—rolling stones that gather no moss—and these stretches of stream are generally poor in animal life, which is the Dipper's food. (Macan and Worthington, 1951, page 153). For example, a search of the Borrowdale streams in April 1965 revealed one pair of Dippers on the Langstrath–Stonethwaite beck near Rosthwaite, and three pairs on the Derwent, all between Longthwaite and Grange, none in the apparently attractive Styhead and Hause Gills or the steep rocky sections of Stonethwaite beck. Dippers do, of course, occur on high level streams, even nesting at over 2000 feet (600 metres), but they frequent the hill-streams more in the softer rock districts, and indeed the population seems to be denser on the outskirts of the Lake District than in the centre. In winter many Dippers keep their summer territories, but others move down in autumn to the shores of lakes.

The Grey Wagtail's habitat preferences are very similar to the Dipper's. It is found by clear, shallow, swift-running streams, but more often by the wider, tree-lined rivers than on the narrow becks. The nest is usually in a rock crevice, occasionally some distance from water (Plate 25). Grey Wagtails seem to have declined in recent years, especially after the severe winter of 1962–63. Most of them leave the Lake District in autumn but a few spend the winter on the lower reaches of the main rivers.

A wagtail seen on the bare stony upper course of a beck is more likely to be a Pied, which is also a very characteristic bird of Lake District road-sides, where the dry stone walls offer abundant nest sites. Most of the Pied Wagtails also leave the district in autumn. Yellow Wagtails are now common summer visitors, especially on low-lying meadows by lakes and rivers. They have noticeably increased in numbers in the last ten years.

The Common Sandpiper (Plate 27) is one of the most characteristic and widespread waterside birds of the Lake District, nesting by the shores of lakes and tarns, rivers and becks, both wooded and open, and even by stony beaches on the estuaries, where small parties collect in early autumn before migration. However, there are signs that the Sandpiper population is being affected by increasing human disturbance.

The Kingfisher, which used to be seen on many of the deeper, slower rivers and lowland dykes as well as by the lakes, has steadily declined in numbers for some years, and since the winter of 1962–63 must be regarded as a very rare bird. Occasional Herons may be seen at any season on lakes, tarns and streams. There is only one regular heronry in the central Lake District, near Derwentwater, but there are three well-established colonies near the southern estuaries, the largest, the historic Dallam heronry near Milnthorpe, being just outside the National Park. The siting of these colonies suggests that tidal waters and lowlands offer the best feeding for Herons. They suffer severely in hard winters and numbers were slow to recover from the drastic reduction in 1963.

Another bird which includes a proportion of fish in its diet, the Great Crested Grebe, has nested regularly on Esthwaite Water (Plate 16) since 1908 and intermittently on Blelham Tarn, but although odd pairs have bred from time to time on other lakes and tarns they have not become established on any of them. A breeding pair seems to require a minimum area of about five acres (2 hectares) of water, mostly under ten feet (3 metres) deep.[1] On some lakes disturbance, especially by holiday-makers in boats, is a major factor in preventing breeding. The Little Grebe, which is satisfied with smaller pools, is very thinly distributed in summer but numbers are found on lakes, especially Windermere, in winter.

Five species of duck now breed in the Lake District. Mallard are common, Teal local, and Tufted Duck scarce, but probably now regular, breeders. The Shelduck, familiar enough on estuaries and muddy shores round Britain, is of special interest in the Lake District because of the development of the habit of inland nesting. Breeding at the south end of Windermere was first recorded in 1918 (Garnett, 1946); now families of young appear each year on Windermere, Coniston Water and some of the southern tarns, and pairs of adults prospect for nesting sites in woods some distance from any water.

The Red-breasted Merganser made its first appearance as a breeding

---

[1] Most of our waters lack adequate nesting cover; some are too small for the grebes' requirements, and others are probably deficient in accessible food.

PLATE 29   Red Squirrel

An exceptional hill stag, photographed in September

Fourteen-pointer Red stag from limestone woodlands, October 1965

PLATE 30

Martindale stag at sunset

d Roe buck in
ch scrub

e family in
dwinter *Buck,*
o has recently
antlers, in
tre, doe on left,
ale fawn of
vious spring on
t

Vixen

bird in the National Park in the early 1950s, when one or more pairs began nesting in the sand dunes near Ravenglass. Since 1960 family parties have been seen regularly on Windermere, and other waters have also been colonised. Several species of duck have extended their breeding range southward in recent years, and it is not unlikely that the Goosander, which is already breeding in north Cumberland, will soon spread into the Lake District.

Both Canada and Grey Lag Geese have been introduced into the district in recent years by the Wildfowlers' Association and now breed in a feral state. An account of the Grey Lag as a winter visitor is given in the section on the estuaries (page 171).

The bird population of the lakes and tarns is greatly increased during the winter months. The most striking and conspicuous of these winter visitors is the Whooper Swan. From mid October to April small parties, often apparently families with both adult and immature birds, may be found on almost any lake or tarn up to 1500 feet (450 metres). Although a party may settle on a suitable water for some weeks, there is usually much movement from one place to another, and Whoopers may be seen on a dozen different waters without spending more than a few days on any of them. Herds of more than twenty appear in some winters, especially when the freezing of the smaller waters drives the birds on to the big lakes. Whoopers have been well known in the Lake District for at least 150 years (Wordsworth, 1835), but they have become much more regular and numerous in the last thirty years.

The smaller Bewick's Swan is only an occasional visitor. The native Mute Swan may be regarded as semi-domesticated in such places as Bowness Bay, but ringing has shown that there is some movement between Windermere and the Lune, and even between the Lune and the Thames.

The only surface-feeding duck that regularly spends the winter on the lakes in any numbers is the Mallard: flocks numbering from a dozen to over a hundred winter on most of the larger lakes, the majority of them resting in mid-lake by day and feeding, often ashore, by night. Wigeon, and, on a much smaller scale, Shoveler, are chiefly passage visitors in spring and autumn, and it is at these seasons that most Teal are seen.

But it is the diving ducks that provide the chief interest on the lakes in winter. Tufted Duck and Goldeneye arrive in about equal numbers in October, Pochard rather later. The Tufted and Pochard may associate in flocks of thirty or forty, the Pochard usually with an excess of drakes; the Tufted feed busily through the day while the Pochard are usually resting over deep water. Night-feeding would presumably be easier for the latter, a chiefly vegetarian species, than for the other two, which have to find a large proportion of animal food.

It must be admitted that the numbers even of these diving ducks are small compared with the population, for example, of a London reservoir; and the limiting factor again seems to be depth of water. The largest numbers are found on the shallowest lakes: Rydal Water, Esthwaite, Bassenthwaite; or the shallow reaches of larger ones, for example within half a mile (800 metres) of Belle Isle on Windermere (Plate 2); or on some of the artificial southern tarns. On the deeper waters a few diving ducks can often be found off the delta area at the head of the lake. Tufted Duck and Goldeneye must take the bulk of their food either from the bottom or from rooted weeds. Goldeneye often dive regularly in areas of water without vegetation and take caddis larvae (Garnett, 1946), while Pochard are restricted by their diet to areas where there is submerged vegetation. Although the maximum diving depth for these ducks is said to be about sixteen feet (5 metres), which is also about the maximum depth for rooted plants in Windermere (Macan and Worthington, *loc. cit.*, page 96), the normal depth of dive is less than eight feet (2.5 metres). Consequently nothing but a narrow fringe round the shores of most lakes and natural tarns can provide food for diving ducks, and even there it may be very scanty.

Much the most numerous bird on the lakes in winter is the Coot, which, as a diving vegetarian, has a distribution similar to that of the ducks. Several pairs breed on many of the quieter waters with suitable cover for nests, but the native population could not account for the numbers seen on the lakes in winter. Well over a thousand sometimes collect in a single flock near the islands in Windermere. These must include immigrants to the district, though there are as yet no ringing recoveries to indicate their origin. It is noteworthy that the autumn influx begins a full month later on Windermere than on smaller waters near the coast.

The only regular fish-eating duck among the winter visitors is the Goosander. These handsome saw-billed ducks arrive late and few are seen before the New Year, but in February and March forty or more may appear on some of the larger lakes, especially Coniston Water, Ullswater and Haweswater. Being shy and cautious, they keep well out from the shore in the day-time.

Cormorants are winter visitors to many lakes and twenty or thirty may sometimes be seen together, although numbers vary from year to year. P. H. T. Hartley found that Cormorants on Windermere fed chiefly on perch, but some char were also taken. On Windermere and Ullswater divers are occasional winter visitors, the Black-throated and Great Northern being the more usual species on Windermere, although the Red-throated is much the commonest on Morecambe Bay. Slavonian and Black-necked Grebes have been recorded several times on these two lakes, more rarely on other waters.

Gull roosts are a conspicuous feature of some lakes in winter. The largest and most impressive is the one on Ullswater, which may extend in a broad line down the middle of the lake for nearly a mile (1600 metres). The majority of the birds here in midwinter are Common Gulls. Towards dusk thousands of them stream in from the eastern foothills and the Eden valley, where they feed particularly on the drier pastures. Black-headed Gulls, the dominant species at the smaller Windermere roost, show a preference for waterlogged fields or for scavenging round towns and villages. In recent years there have also been roosts on Haweswater, Derwentwater and Bassenthwaite. The 'big gulls' are becoming increasingly common at these roosts with the growth of the inland feeding habit. There have recently been over 200 Herring Gulls and twenty Great Black-backed on Windermere, and fifty Lesser Black-backed on Ullswater in January, an example of the increasing tendency of this formerly completely migratory gull, which is a common scavenger on the fells and lakes in spring and summer, to spend the winter in inland localities in England.

The Coast

The Lake District National Park includes about twelve miles (20 kilometres) of sea coast between Drigg and Silecroft. Space does not permit any discussion of the marine species that might be seen from this beach, but with Eiders breeding on Walney Island to the south and Fulmars, Puffins, Black Guillemots and commoner sea-birds on St Bees Head to the north, one can expect a varied tally. The special interest of this stretch of coast lies in the sand dunes across the estuaries of the Rivers Irt and Mite from Ravenglass. They are the site of the largest breeding colony of the Black-headed Gull in the British Isles.

An aerial survey in 1963 showed a total of about 8000 breeding pairs. A few years earlier the population was estimated at about 14,000 pairs, but predation by foxes then took a heavy toll. However, the foxes were eliminated in 1963 and breeding success has since been much higher. Dr N. Tinbergen and his assistants from Oxford, who made detailed studies of bird behaviour in this gullery for several years, found that the fox is the only predator seriously affecting the numbers of gulls. The destruction of eggs and young by the bigger gulls, crows and hedgehogs is comparatively unimportant: the communal attack of the adult Black-headed Gulls upon these predators is very effective.

Various reasons could be suggested for the growth of this huge gullery. Black-headed Gulls normally nest on tussocks of vegetation in lakes or bogs where expansion is limited by the number of available nest sites. There are several small gulleries of this kind in the Lake District, but they frequently move from one tarn to another after a life of only a few years, and the rate of breeding success is low owing to human interference, and probably to predation by birds, which is more effective in a small colony. In the Ravenglass dunes there is room for unlimited expansion, and although there has been extensive egg-collecting at times it has always been controlled to some extent by the difficulty of access by land and by the policy of the landowner. The whole area is now included in a Nature Reserve managed by the Cumberland County Council with assistance from the Nature Conservancy and the Lake District Naturalists' Trust, and the gulls and their eggs are more effectively protected than ever before.

The food requirements of the great number of adults and young are chiefly met by the estuaries and the wide coastal strip of arable land and pasture, but the fells also provide food, sometimes on a generous scale with a plague of Antler Moth larvae. The extraordinary success of gulls in exploiting human activities as a source of food and their consequent low mortality rate through the year must also be an important factor in the increase in numbers during the present century.

Visitors to the Reserve should be particularly careful not to disturb the terns, which may nest in compact colonies or in isolated pairs. They can be watched from Ravenglass village as they fish for sand-eels in the estuary.

Terns are notoriously fickle and erratic in their breeding habits, and the numbers of each species present on Drigg Point vary considerably from year to year, but recently there have been from thirty to fifty pairs of Common Terns and smaller numbers of Arctic and Little Terns. The bigger Sandwich Terns have flourished here for some years, and a recent count showed over 500 pairs. One or two pairs of Roseate Terns have occasionally nested among the other species. It is unfortunately true that it is now impossible for a colony of ground-nesting sea-birds to prosper anywhere on the coast of England without some form of protection, and one must be thankful that arrangements have been made for this at Ravenglass.

Although there are few published records of the passage of migrants along this stretch of coast it seems highly probable, from the results obtained at Grune Point on the Solway and at the recently established bird observatory on Walney Island, that there will be considerable movements of birds through the dunes in spring and autumn. One would expect this from the geographical situation, with the Lake District mountains forming a barrier between the Solway Firth and Morecambe Bay. It might be thought that hills of this height would not be a serious obstacle to migrating birds, but although the actual height of the fells may not present much difficulty, the cloud that so often caps them certainly does. Anyone who has heard the distracted piping of waders when the tide comes in on the estuaries on a foggy night will realise how much birds are affected by loss of visual contact with the ground.

There is undoubtedly some migration through the central Lake District. From a vantage point on Cartmel Fell, north Lancashire, one can follow skeins of Grey Lag Geese as they fly up the Winster valley from the Kent estuary and finally disappear in the north heading for the Dunmail gap, and in spring Lesser Black-backed Gulls can be seen following the same route. The appearance of marine ducks and divers on Windermere, and, more surprisingly, on Ullswater, also indicates overland movements, and the fact that the White Wagtail, the continental race of the Pied Wagtail, occurs in spring in various valleys shows that passerines traverse the Lake District and do not only enter it to breed. But in spite of this evidence of some birds' taking the short cut, the main stream of migrants is more likely to follow the coast route. It would be interesting to have this supposition tested by regular observations at Drigg Point.

The Estuaries

In addition to this stretch of the Cumberland coast the National Park includes the head of the Leven estuary and about five miles (8 kilometres) of the north-west shore of the estuary of the River Kent (Plate 16). The sandy silt of the Morecambe Bay estuaries, so different from the soft ooze of the estuaries of eastern England, dries out quickly in sun or wind, and this affects the distribution of the wading birds that provide the chief interest for bird-watchers at migration seasons. The dry, corn-coloured sand-banks are used only as resting places: feeding is restricted to areas still silvery-grey with moisture.

The first sign of autumn movement is the arrival of Lapwings, Golden Plovers and Curlews from their breeding quarters. The Curlews build up to a total of two thousand or more in July, spending much of the day resting on the sand-banks or salt-marsh at the head of the estuary. They feed mainly in neighbouring fields: the pellets which litter the sand-banks, with occasional crumpled yellow gizzard-linings, are composed of grit, cow-dung and wing-cases of beetles. In autumn mixed flocks of Lapwing and Golden Plover regularly feed on the estuary itself, but in March and April the flocks of Golden Plover, up to a thousand strong and including many of the strongly marked northern race, feed almost exclusively in the fields—an interesting seasonal difference in habits.

The volume and variety of the autumn passage varies from year to year, but usually among the mixed flocks of Dunlin and Ringed Plover on the open sands there are Curlew-Sandpiper and Little Stint, normally in ones and twos but occasionally a party of a dozen or so in late August or early September. Scattered Greenshank feed in shallow water on the estuary or the salt-marsh. Ten, or even twenty, may join in a compact flock in flight but they separate again as they alight. With them one or two Spotted Red-shanks can be found in most autumns, and sometimes a Ruff or a Green Sandpiper. These last six species are much less frequently seen in spring. Whimbrel on the other hand occur almost equally in spring and autumn, and it is only in May and June, if at all, that Sanderling appear on the estuary in any numbers. Rarer visitors have occurred, for instance Avocets and Spoonbills, and no doubt some vagrant wader from America will eventually be recorded on these estuaries.

The turbulent waters by the Kent railway viaduct have a special attraction for some birds: Black Terns are not infrequent there in autumn (they prefer inland waters in spring), and Little Gulls and Long-tailed Ducks are occasional visitors.

There is only a gap of a week or two between the end of the spring passage of waders and the beginning of the autumn one, if they do not actually overlap. During this low water of seasonal movement interest is provided by packs of young Shelduck out on the sands. After their perilous journey down from the woods and hills the ducklings collect into parties, sometimes as many as sixty of mixed ages, in charge of a single adult or a pair, while the rest of the adults migrate to the Heligoland Bight to perform their moult. On fine evenings in July small flocks of adults may be seen flying up the Kent estuary and turning east up the Bela valley towards the North Sea.

In winter, too, ducks and geese are the most noticeable birds on the estuary. Mallard have been present through the summer, and these are joined by other surface-feeding ducks, Teal, Wigeon and Pintail, in August and September. The adult Shelduck begin to reappear in late October.

The history of the wild geese on the Kent estuary is of some interest. Up to 1920 geese of any kind seem to have been scarce in the Morecambe Bay area, the few that were shot being White-fronted, with an occasional Pink-footed or a Bean Goose. But about that date the rapid extension of salt-marsh on the sands on the Lancashire/Westmorland border and the flooding of Leighton Moss near by attracted numbers of Grey Lag Geese, and they have returned each winter since 1922. This is surprising in view of the fact that the predominant grey goose both on the Solway and in south Lancashire is the Pink-footed.

The annual pattern of the movement of the geese changes from time to time, but in recent years it has been approximately as follows. The first geese to appear over the estuary in September are Pink-footed, but they only stop briefly, if at all. The Grey Lags arrive about mid October. There are usually less than a hundred for the first month or so and their movements tend to be erratic. Midwinter overland flights to the Solway are not uncommon. In the New Year they begin to graze regularly in fields near the estuary in the National Park and in the following three months about 250 can often be found there. In a national count of wild geese in March 1965 these were the only Grey Lags reported in England. (The main population is in Scotland). They leave during April, many of them not until the second half of the month. Odd individuals of other species, including Brent and Barnacle, may appear among the Grey Lags at any time, and small gaggles of Pink-footed Geese sometimes stop for a day or two in spring, but there is no sign of their replacing the Grey Lags as the wintering species.

Foulshaw Moss, the raised bog between the Kent estuary and the foot of Whitbarrow Scar, was of some ornithological interest before 1940 as the site of a breeding colony of several hundred pairs of Lesser Black-backed Gulls, a few Herring Gulls and two or three pairs of Great Black-backed Gulls. At that time there were numbers of Red Grouse on the bog, an unusual situation almost at sea-level. But excessive egg-collecting during the war and a series of summer heath fires caused the extinction of the gullery by about 1946, and the grouse seem to have disappeared too, perhaps because the area of open heather and moss has been reduced by the rapid growth of birch scrub. There is little now to reward the bird-watcher for his laborious progress through birch and bog.

Conclusions

A survey in a few pages of the bird life of so diversified an area as that of the Lake District National Park must inevitably be sketchy and selective, but certain conclusions may perhaps be drawn from it. The first is that, although the avifauna of the Lake District is not as rich as that of some parts of southern England, it does include birds of particular interest and beauty that cannot be found in lowland districts. Secondly, the central fells offer the bird-watcher the opportunity of studying familiar birds in an unfamiliar environment, for instance the Chaffinch, Wren and Dunnock as high-level breeding species. Thirdly, it is clear that the bird population of the Lake District is very far from being static; in fact it is probably changing more rapidly now than it ever has in the past. There have been some gains. Woodpeckers, coming from the south, have occupied the whole district, and new species of duck, from the north, are becoming established as breeding birds. The Collared Dove is now breeding on the outskirts of the National Park and is moving up into the central valleys. Meanwhile several other kinds of birds have seriously declined in numbers and some are approaching local extinction. In several cases this decline is clearly due to human influence, either directly upon the bird, as by the use of the chlorinated hydrocarbon pesticides which had such disastrous effects in the decade from 1957, or upon its habitat, for example by the increasing use of beaches, lakes and mountain crags for recreational purposes. In other species the causes of decline are obscure.

In order to understand, and perhaps modify, these changes much more detailed knowledge is required, both of trends in local bird populations and of alterations in the total environment that might account for them. The amateur bird-watcher can help towards this end by taking part in national enquiries organised by the British Trust for Ornithology or the Wildfowl Trust, and also by keeping careful personal records of the numbers of breeding pairs of certain species present each year in a given area. In some circumstances ornithological form-filling may become a rather tedious chore for the less dedicated amateur, but there can surely be few more agreeable ways of acquiring useful information than searching a Lake District valley for Wood Warblers or Grey Wagtails on a fine May morning.

Scientific Names of Birds Mentioned in This Section

Avocet, *Recurvirostra avosetta*
Blackbird, *Turdus merula*
Blackcap, *Sylvia atricapilla*
Bullfinch, *Pyrrhula pyrrhula*
Bunting, Snow, *Plectrophenax nivalis*
Buzzard, *Buteo buteo*
Chaffinch, *Fringilla coelebs*
Chiffchaff, *Phylloscopus collybita*
Coot, *Fulica atra*
Cormorant, *Phalacrocorax carbo*
Corncrake, *Crex crex*
Creeper, Tree, *Certhia familiaris*
Crossbill, *Loxia curvirostra*
Crow, Carrion, *Corvus corone corone*
Cuckoo, *Cuculus canorus*
Curlew, *Numenius arquata*
Dipper, *Cinclus cinclus*
Diver, Black-throated, *Gavia arctica*
—, Great Northern, *Gavia immer*
—, Red-throated, *Gavia stellata*
Dotterel, *Eudromias morinellus*
Dove, Collared, *Streptopelia decaocto*

Duck, Long-tailed, *Clangula hyemalis*
—, Tufted, *Aythya fuligula*
Dunlin, *Calidris alpina*
Dunnock, *Prunella modularis*
Eagle, Golden, *Aquila chrysaetos*
Eider, *Somateria mollissima*
Flycatcher, Pied, *Ficedula hypoleuca*
Fulmar, *Fulmarus glacialis*
Goldcrest, *Regulus regulus*
Goldeneye, *Bucephala clangula*
Goldfinch, *Carduelis carduelis*
Goosander, *Mergus merganser*
Goose, Barnacle, *Branta leucopsis*
—, Bean, *Anser fabalis fabalis*
—, Brent, *Branta bernicla*
—, Canada, *Branta canadensis*
—, Grey Lag, *Anser anser*
—, Pink-footed, *Anser fabalis brachyrhyncus*
—, White-fronted, *Anser albifrons*
Grebe, Black-necked, *Podiceps nigricollis*
—, Great Crested, *Podiceps cristatus*
—, Little, *Podiceps ruficollis*

Grebe, Slavonian, *Podiceps auritus*
Greenfinch, *Carduelis chloris*
Greenshank, *Tringa nebularia*
Grouse, Black, *Lyrurus tetrix*
—, Red, *Lagopus lagopus*
Guillemot, Black, *Cepphus grylle*
Gull, Black-headed, *Larus ridibundus*
—, Common, *Larus canus*
—, Great Black-backed, *Larus marinus*
—, Herring, *Larus argentatus*
—, Lesser Black-backed, *Larus fuscus*
—, Little, *Larus minutus*
Hawfinch, *Coccothraustes coccothraustes*
Hawk, Sparrow, *Accipiter nisus*
Heron, *Ardea cinerea*
Jackdaw, *Corvus monedula*
Kestrel, *Falco tinnunculus*
Kingfisher, *Alcedo atthis*
Lapwing, *Vanellus vanellus*
Lark, Sky, *Alauda arvensis*
Linnet, *Acanthis cannabina*
Mallard, *Anas platyrhyncos*
Martin, House, *Delichon urbica*
Merganser, Red-breasted, *Mergus serrator*
Merlin, *Falco columbarius*
Nightjar, *Caprimulgus europaeus*
Nuthatch, *Sitta europaee*
Oriole, Golden, *Oriolus oriolus*
Ouzel, Ring, *Turdus torquatus*
Owl, Barn, *Tyto alba*
—, Little, *Athene noctua*
—, Short-eared, *Asio flammeus*
—, Tawny, *Strix aluco*
Partridge, *Perdix perdix*
Peregrine, *Falco peregrinus*
Pigeon, Wood, *Columba palumbus*
Pintail, *Anas acuta*
Pipit, Meadow, *Anthus pratensis*
—, Tree, *Anthus trivialis*
Plover, Golden, *Pluvialis apricaria*
—, Ringed, *Charadrius hiaticula*
Pochard, *Aythya ferina*
Ptarmigan, *Lagopus mutus*

Puffin, *Fratercula arctica*
Raven, *Corvus corax*
Redpoll, *Acanthis flammea*
Redshank, *Tringa totanus*
—, Spotted, *Tringa erythropus*
Redstart, *Phoenicurus phoenicurus*
Robin, *Erithacus rubecula*
Ruff, *Philomachus pugnax*
Sanderling, *Calidris alba*
Sandpiper, Common, *Tringa hypoleucos*
—, Curlew, *Calidris ferruginea*
—, Green, *Tringa ochropus*
Shelduck, *Tadorna tadorna*
Shoveler, *Anas clypeata*
Siskin, *Carduelis spinus*
Snipe, *Gallinago gallinago*
Spoonbill, *Platalea leucorodia*
Starling, *Sturnus vulgaris*
Stint, Little, *Calidris minuta*
Stonechat, *Saxicola torquata*
Swallow, *Hirundo rustica*
Swan, Bewick's, *Cygnus bewickii*
—, Mute, *Cygnus olor*
—, Whooper, *Cygnus cygnus*
Swift, *Apus apus*
Teal, *Anas crecca*
Tern, Arctic, *Sterna paradisea*
—, Black, *Chlidonias niger*
—, Common, *Sterna hirundo*
—, Little, *Sterna albifrons*
—, Roseate, *Sterna dougallii*
—, Sandwich, *Sterna sandvicensis*
Thrush, Mistle, *Turdus viscivorus*
—, Song, *Turdus philomelos*
Tit, Bearded, *Panurus biarmicus*
—, Blue, *Parus caeruleus*
—, Coal, *Parus ater*
—, Great, *Parus major*
—, Long-tailed, *Aegithalos caudatus*
—, Marsh, *Parus palustris*
Wagtail, Grey, *Motacilla cinerea*
—, Pied, *Motacilla alba yarrellii*
—, White, *Motacilla alba alba*

Wagtail, Yellow, *Motacilla flava*
Warbler, Garden, *Sylvia borin*
—, Willow, *Phylloscopus trochilus*
—, Wood, *Phylloscopus sibilatrix*
Wheatear, *Oenanthe oenanthe*
Whimbrel, *Numenius phaeopus*
Whinchat, *Saxicola rubetra*
Wigeon, *Anas penelope*

Woodcock, *Scolopax rusticola*
Woodpecker, Great Spotted, *Dendrocopus major*
—, Green, *Picus viridis*
—, Lesser Spotted, *Dendrocopus minor*
Wren, *Troglodytes troglodytes*
Yellowhammer, *Emberiza citrinella*

MAMMALS

by P. Delap

Many of the Lake District mammals, like those of other wild areas of the British Isles, have long been isolated from stocks elsewhere, with man unconsciously exerting intense selective pressure upon these small groups of isolated survivors. Such conditions compel the rapid development of specialised ecotypes—strains adapted to existence in the particular environment; in our area they must combine extreme caution and unobtrusiveness with a tolerance of man's constant proximity. Species unable to meet this challenge have vanished altogether.

Regretfully, little specific information on distribution within the area can be provided. All naturalists have to guard their rarities from the obsessional collector, but the survival of many mammals within their tenuous and ever-altering habitats can be imperilled by even benevolent intrusion.

It is impossible in the available space to provide standard information on the morphology and routine activities of Lakeland mammals; these are easily available elsewhere, and suitable publications are listed in the bibliography at the end of the book. What follows is a brief description of the co-existence of man and ten of his fellow mammals within our area.

The Rabbit

Locally the recent fortunes of this animal have followed the familiar pattern of the country as a whole. Myxomatosis did not become a generalised epidemic here until 1955, but within a couple of years the Rabbit was a rarity. After about five years local resurgences were common, these in turn being checked by progressively less lethal outbreaks of the disease. The Rabbit is now omnipresent once more, but the population remains well below its original level, and although it formerly could be found on dry, sunny fellsides to about 1800 feet (550 metres) above sea-level it has not yet recolonised to this altitude.

There is a strong impression that it is less gregarious than formerly; indeed, since myxomatosis is spread by the rabbit-flea there is an obvious bias in favour of asocial strains. It is possible, however, that we are witnessing a return to an ancient normality, as it is easy to overlook the amount of human manipulation to which the Rabbit has been subjected since its introduction to the British Isles by the Normans. The ownership of a warren was for centuries a rare and prized status symbol to be maintained and guarded by a whole-time warrener of comparable social standing to today's head-keeper. Such men would have deliberately eliminated outliers and bred from the most sociable and disease-resistant strains.

It is our profound good fortune that few in these islands today can envisage our ancestors' lust for protein. Apart from the short period of autumn stock-killing, nearly all our forebears had to survive on a year-long diet of the coarsest and dreariest of carbohydrates, a pattern which had itself been imposed upon us only by the very recent Neolithic revolution. Our physiology remains geared to the age-long hunter's predilection for meat. The deer-park, the warren, the dovecot and the fishpond were not established for sporting, still less for aesthetic reasons. They were savagely treasured protein-banks monopolised by the establishment, and the extra stature and vigour imparted by their constant availability contributed significantly to the maintenance of the *status quo*.

Even today the Rabbit has an invaluable role to play as buffer between the human predator and more vulnerable members of our vertebrate fauna. Although we manage increasingly to sublimate our palaeolithic urges, a substantial minority still demands symbolic hunting outlets: money and talent lavishly applied since the war have perfected techniques for mass-killing of hand-reared pheasants, satiating the affluent on a more than Edwardian scale. For the casual local gunner the Rabbit and the Wood Pigeon must remain the standard targets; but for these resilient creatures the Red and Black Grouse and the Partridge would be vanishing even more rapidly from Lakeland than at present seems the case.

The breeding potential of the Rabbit is proverbial; less well known is the flexibility conferred by the female's ability to resorb a variable number of young from each litter within the uterus. This admirable form of metabolic thrift is shared with the Hare, and the degree of its utilisation presumably corresponds to the current population pressure.

Another remarkable capacity of the lagomorphs (Rabbit and the hares), only officially recognised for twenty years but presumably known to the writer of Leviticus, is refection. This involves the transmission of all food through the gut twice over. After its first passage, soft mucus-covered globules are collected by the owner direct from the anus and reingested: on the second emergence the familiar flattened spheres of hard, coarse vegetable debris are deposited at the rabbit's individual 'latrine', often a stump or similar prominence where considerable accumulations occur. This physiological 'double-take' is as valuable to the Rabbit as rumination to other herbivores, enabling the animal to benefit from both bacterial breakdown and synthesis by other micro-organisms of essential food-elements lacking from the original poor-quality vegetable intake.

Although the Rabbit's most obvious landscape gardening, barked saplings, annihilated crop margins and bare woodland floors, may well distress us, botanists at least appreciate that many plants would be rarer than they are but for its selective grazing and the fresh foothold supplied by the earth spilling from its burrows. At least three direct predators, Fox, Stoat and Buzzard, seem commoner for its resurgence. Perhaps we should, after all, be thankful that the Rabbit still evades our awesome controls.

The Brown Hare

Remembering that this comparatively large mammal spends its entire life above ground, it is humiliating to admit that most estimates of its population remain mere guesses. However, there seems a general consensus that the decline of the Rabbit was followed by an increase in hares; within the Lake District the situation is obscured by the fact that the Brown Hare is largely a woodland dweller. For much of the year our hillsides and pastures are too bare for even the most exiguous 'form'. The Hare, largely a nocturnal feeder, needs a prolonged diurnal rest to complete the complex digestive processes described earlier; in our much disturbed countryside its woodland refuges seem essential.

The casual visitor sometimes asks, 'How can such a creature ever get enough sleep?' In fact potential victims of round-the-clock predation, such as hares and deer, habitually survive with only the most fleeting moments of recurrent somnolence. An analogy with the mammalian heart, active for a lifetime with rest-period measured in microseconds, may be an over-simplification; but it is reasonable to suppose that the very rare but well-authenticated cases of human beings who have lived for years in good health without sleep are demonstrations of an archaic aid to survival once available to the human race also.

Such analogies with human pathology may be risky, but it is tempting to invoke another. The hare is an excellent mammalian example of the prey that escapes detection by total immobility. When capture becomes imminent the victim nearly always displays its magnificent evasive burst of speed, but very rarely all activity remains inhibited and the animal can be picked up, limp and inert. In a few mammals this response is common enough to have reached everyday usage in the phrase 'playing 'possum'. Anecdotes of total motor inhibition induced by sudden frightening stimuli exist for a surprising variety of species and, of course, this represents the standard response to stress of many helpless young. Certain rare and otherwise inexplicable forms of human psychopathology involving temporary insensibility or paralysis may well represent a reactivation of this ancient escape-mechanism.

Sometimes, when threatened by a Stoat, the leveret can exhibit a startling reversal, leaping repeatedly high in the air while squealing shrilly. This may disconcert the predator long enough for the doe to return and drive it off with her formidable hind legs. Even the mother Rabbit will be pugnacious in the same circumstances, instead of submitting to the Stoat with the traditional hypnotic inertia.

As with most species, albino hares are not very uncommon; three at least have occurred in the Lake District during the past ten years. This may account for the recurrent rumours that the Blue or Mountain Hare (*Lepus timidus*) survives in the area. This native of the Highland hilltops was indeed introduced into the Coniston district in 1903 and certainly survived until the First World War. Its subsequent failure is a little surprising, as it would meet no direct competition from the Brown Hare among the higher fells. Perhaps its long exile upon the summits has rendered it overspecialised. It would be interesting to see whether the introduction of its cousin the Irish Hare (*L. timidus hibernicus*) would be more successful. Owing to her early geological separation from the European land-mass, Ireland received only a limited influx of mammals and lacks the Brown Hare; in its absence the Irish Hare flourishes from sea-level to mountain top and might well prove more resilient here than the Blue Hare. In view of some well-known disastrous introductions we are currently scared of alien fauna to the point of total prohibition. As always, the pendulum will eventually reverse its swing. Impoverishment by extermination superimposed on the original misfortune of the premature flooding of the Straits of Dover a mere eight thousand years ago has left us with dreary gaps in our fauna which cannot now be filled without human intervention. Let us hope we shall soon gain the courage and the know-how to refill these blanks in our ecosystems.

Short-tailed or Field Vole

Surprisingly this plump, unobtrusive scuttler in the grass-roots is Britain's most plentiful vertebrate (Plate 28). Man, hardly aware of its existence, has made this so by curtailing the richer habitats needed by its main rivals the Bank Vole and the Long-tailed Field Mouse.

Wherever coarse grass cover exists the Field Vole thrives from tide-mark to mountain top, its runways proliferating between soil and herbage-layer.

It is indeed completely unspecialised except for teeth that grow throughout life to enable its survival on the coarsest grasses. Working for seven years with vole-free plots and control areas, Summerhayes demonstrated that, in the rodents' absence, the commonest grasses became predominant, while their presence actually encouraged a diversification of plant species. But throughout Lakeland the vole's most invaluable role is the conversion of vegetation into handy little concentrations of protein without which our more romantic predators would vanish.

Unlike that newcomer, the Rabbit, the vole does not suffer direct human persecution; indeed man has brought upon himself disastrous vole plague years by eliminating his natural enemies. Swarms of voles have in the past devastated the Cheviot sheep-walks, but in Lakeland the habitats are too diverse and the predators too numerous. Much work has been done on the population dynamics of the vole. Commonly a three-year or four-year oscillation occurs around an optimum level, the density varying from under fifty voles per acre (0.4 hectare) in the trough to over five hundred at the peak.

Foxes, Stoats, Weasels, Buzzards, Kestrels, owls and Adders will all concentrate into vole-infested areas; and the forester is particularly thankful to see this happen in his Rabbit-free enclosures, where an excessive vole build-up may otherwise cause disastrous bark-stripping before the closing canopy of young tree eliminates the grass-cover.

With a breeding-season of at least six months, a gestation-period of only three weeks, and an average litter of five, the vole is so prolific that it is reassuring to learn that a single pair of breeding Weasels could eliminate two thousand of them annually. But let us not forget that this obscure creature saved the ecological pyramid from collapse when myxomatosis eliminated the Rabbit, and that the vole's absence from Ireland may well account for the continuing failure of the Buzzard in that otherwise suitable habitat. The vole remains the infantryman in an endless war—ecologists should erect a memorial to him!

Red Squirrel

With this tantalising creature it is difficult to do more than parochialise Monica Shorten's splendid monograph; nevertheless, as the cult-animal of the Lakelander and on account of its peculiar status, it is doubly impossible to omit him.

At present the Red Squirrel (Plate 29) seems to be reaching one of its peaks of abundance throughout our area and all local naturalists should make what observations they can during what may be its last renaissance. Miss Shorten produces considerable evidence that these peaks are reached at eight-yearly intervals, and before the next one the Grey Squirrel may have established itself here. There are at least six records of this intruder in and around our area over the past ten years, and, although overt hostility seems rare, there is no doubt that the robust foreigner invariably supplants the native one once it has established itself.

Actually the status of the Red Squirrel as a true native is a little uncertain. In Scotland and Ireland destruction of its habitat led to its extermination in the sixteenth century, and no records exist to prove its survival of the equally drastic devastation of our own woods culminating in the iron-smelting period. Certainly widespread reintroductions occurred in the early nineteenth century.

The Red Squirrel is a typical inhabitant of the climax forest, sharing many characteristics with Roe Deer (page 189): for instance a dislike of high winds (less for the discomfort than for the masking of the sounds of approaching danger), and, most notably, an intolerance of over-crowding.

It is almost impossible for us to visualise the lost deciduous forests of Western Europe, and yet these dominated our world until yesterday. In a mere thousand years the wild life of Europe found its habitat reversed from a limitless jungle with scattered human clearings to a desert with shrinking oases, even these heavily infested by man. Obvious enough; but we tend to forget that the climax woods were not a rich mammalian habitat and the inhabitants were correspondingly non-gregarious, with genetic inhibitions against overcrowding and denudation. In this crisis the superior mobility of the birds has proved of supreme advantage.

Hence the irony of the Red Squirrel's fate today. We have almost completely destroyed its natural enemies, the Pine Marten and the Wild Cat; and, apart from a shrinking clique of 'keepers and foresters, human predation has also ended. Yet, even without the Grey Squirrel, disastrous 'crashes' occur regularly. During severe winters successive waves of migrant birds denude the woods on their southward passage (the relative success of Red Squirrels in the big conifer woods of Eastern England may lie in their dependence on pine seed, for which their only avian competitor is the rare Crossbill); but starvation is less lethal than the epidemics of stress diseases induced by overcrowding. Miss Shorten records cataclysmic years (e.g. 1910) when mange or coccidiosis eliminated the squirrels from whole counties.

Elsewhere she records numerous observations of squirrels traversing treeless mountains and swimming far out to sea as if attempting to find the lost forests. She remarks on the persistence of the legend of the squirrel voyaging with its tail for a sail, tracing the story from Topsell (1607) to Beatrix Potter's *Squirrel Nutkin*. This persistence is not surprising, for, at fairy-tale level, this is the universal epic of the turbulent young hero redeeming himself by hazardous journeyings. Miss Potter treats this potent figure with her inimitable astringency and would have been positively caustic to hear of Nutkin as an archetype. Yet so he is—let him stand for all the valiant little Kon-Tikis that perish unsung among our man-made desolations.

The Fox

The Fox (Plate 32) obviously deserves a place in our list as the only predator universally successful although in direct competition with man. Orthodox hunting, carried out on foot in the Lake District, is a picturesque and ineffectual method of control. Behind the scenes no mercy is shown, sheep-farmers until recently using the gin-trap and poison throughout the year. The former is now illegal, but strychnine is still readily procurable 'for poisoning Moles'. Gassing with 'Cymag' (freely available for Rabbit eradication) is another favourite method. Nevertheless the Fox remains omnipresent, man going to great expense and trouble to skim the surplus and keep the survivors fit and cunning.

Survival in hill-country is aided by the presence of 'borrans'—traditional lairs among huge rock-falls, impregnable even to dynamite. Adaptability in feeding is another factor, the Fox being a true omnivore, flourishing on many things from fruit to dustbin scavenging if his invaluable stand-by, the Rabbit, is absent.

In Lakeland his evil reputation depends to some extent upon the coincidence of lambing-time with his growing family needs. Even so, much of the damning rubbish around the earth represents still-born carrion. Ultimately, in sheep-farming areas, the solution might be the release of marked sterilised males, each of which could be expected to pair with a normal vixen and monopolise a large territory for many years, within which no breeding and therefore no increased spring predation would occur.

Today the heavy population of hill sheep provides another, indirect, bonus for the Foxes. During late summer that large, succulent, sluggish beetle *Geotrupes* is plentiful everywhere, flourishing upon the sheep-droppings and providing almost the entire diet of the newly independent young foxes, who otherwise might well starve before attaining full hunting efficiency.

The Badger

The Badger (Plate 28) has had a very chequered history. Nowadays thinly distributed among the higher fells, using the same unassailable 'borrans' as the Fox, it is patchily plentiful in most low-lying areas.

The Badger's survival was certainly aided by the large areas of eroded limestone pavement in our countryside, among whose endless crevices neither trap nor gas can prevail. We cannot be complacent about the splendid recovery of this amiable beast. Many important setts are still regularly attacked, sometimes by old-style digging, but much illegal gassing certainly occurs. The attempt to reoccupy these lethal sites must be a considerable drain on the population; the writer knows of one sett still periodically reopened after nearly a century of ferocious game-preservation in the area.

It is instructive to read Macpherson on the Badger (1892). That invaluable recorder fully believed it had been exterminated in the Lakes by 1850 and attributed a dozen records over the subsequent forty years to 'escapes'. The animal's rare appearances astonished its captors, and it is significant how soon its former well-recognised place in the local fauna was forgotten, which must have favoured the survival of a few outstandingly cunning individuals.

The Otter

This is one of the most difficult of all mammals to study in the wild: the recently published (1969) report of the Mammal Society underlines the dearth of observations at even the most superficial and transient level. This report attempts an assessment of current population trends: surprisingly it suggests that in the north-west, unlike the rest of England, there has been some increase in numbers. Only four reports were available for nearly 1500 square miles (3900 square kilometres). The writer, living for the past twenty-three years on the banks of the River Eden, feels that this estimate may be euphoric as far as this sector is concerned.

The over-all fall in numbers, catastrophic in the south and east, is attributed to many factors: riparian disturbance, pesticide pollution, hard winters and trapping are regarded as more serious (though less controllable) than losses through conventional hunting. Foolhardy as it may be to query even one aspect of such a masterly analysis, the writer cannot but suggest a possibly serious underestimate of human predation outside conventional Otter-hunting circles, on whose evidence so much reliance is unavoidably placed. A country-wide barrier of silence meets all investigators into the fate of otters. Gin-traps are freely and legally available for sale across the Scottish border and are in constant, if discreet, employment south of it. Very recently a local head-keeper was vociferously indignant at his inability to prosecute an underling who, on dismissal, absconded with a dozen of his traps! Even if this revolting instrument is eventually banned in Scotland its elimination will take a generation: a pole-trap of a pattern illegal for forty years was destroyed this year on the estate referred to in the preceding sentence.

In parenthesis, it may be that the lack of tangible evidence for the local survival of the Pine Marten stems from a natural reluctance to display the corpse of a rare mammal bearing the unmistakable stigmata of the gin-trap.

Unfortunately Otters tend to utilise the same holts, landing-places and defaecation-sites for generations: at these points they can easily and unobtrusively be trapped and destroyed by a simple technique known as a 'drowning-set'. Otters have always been tacitly accepted as perquisites of the 'keeper—nowadays a skin may be worth half a week's pay, and live cubs vastly more. Furthermore the huge rents paid for salmon- and trout-fishing by syndicates and clubs makes intervention by their members on the Otter's behalf increasingly unlikely.

Finally it may be suggested that while the Otter stocks of Scotland remain high by recruitment from the relatively invulnerable population of its extensive and unravished coastline, England, already largely deprived of such a reserve, may soon find the species finally eliminated by pollution.

Pine Marten

Our failure to protect this creature (Plate 32) will sadden our grand-children. It was a rarity even in Macpherson's time. 'When foxes is rank, marts is scarce,' said the old fell-farmers. Less concisely we talk of the inability of two species to share the same ecological niche. Foxes are still rank, and the Rabbit-famine will have intensified their urge to 'chop' a Marten caught in the open.

Leckie, working in Ross-shire, found that small rodents formed the bulk of the Martens' diet and over 90% of these were Field Voles; so food supply cannot be a limiting factor.

Lamentably, its reproductive capacity seems geared to a safe, stable environment now forever lost. Martens do not breed until their fourth year and produce only two or three young annually. By contrast the scavenging opportunist Fox mates in the winter following its birth, and a litter of five commonly results.

Authentic sightings in the Lake District confirm its survival but are too few to allow predictions. The only view vouchsafed the writer was in Ross-shire and this individual displayed the suicidal indifference so often observable in the smaller mustelids. In the Stoat and Weasel this boldness should not surprise us; it is the age-long privilege of the predator. Until the advent of universal, cheap firearms and game-preservation these small beasts went unharmed, and a century's persecution has been too short to quench that bold serenity.

We can only pray that the Marten will achieve discretion before extinction.

Red Deer

The Lake District is probably the best area in Britain for the study of our native deer, because of the variety of habitats occupied and because the deer have shown such a heartening capacity to survive in a relatively densely populated area.

Martindale is the only English deer-forest and it has been maintained as such for over three hundred years by the Hasell family. Its stock of Red Deer came originally from Royal forests in the Eden valley which were opened up for agriculture in the Middle Ages, the surviving deer presumably shifting westwards into the higher hills. Nearly 300 deer inhabit an area of some hundred square miles (260 square kilometres) (along with a vastly greater sheep population). To see a mountainside at sunrise bright with a hundred feeding deer has impressed many a Continental and American naturalist, for only in Britain are deer still successfully maintained upon the open hills. The forest is entirely unfenced, but owing to the stabilising influence of the hind-parties the population remains remarkably static in numbers and distribution. There is little contact between these deer and their cousins of the woodlands to the south and west.

Stags (Plate 30) are reluctant to remain in areas well populated by females (except, of course, during the autumn rut), and gravitate to the periphery of such areas; as they become heavier and slower the older stags seek out any available woodland. Thus a successful colony expands behind a screen of pioneering males, many of which can be lost without detriment in a polygamous species. The inward concentration for the autumn rut prevents loss of contact. Unfortunately many of the Martindale stags find their way into areas where no protection is available and poaching has of recent years produced an increasingly serious imbalance of the sexes.

Elsewhere in the Lake District perhaps 150 Red Deer are widely scattered in much smaller groups. The deer society is a matriarchy of interlocking family parties each under its senior hind. No territorial jealousy exists and within groups an order of dominance is quickly established, minimising friction. Also disease-resistant strains have long predominated, permitting high local densities. Should this gregariousness convert forest into savannah and finally open grassland, no harm results; indeed a larger stock can be carried for grassland is the most efficient converter of solar energy into a form suitable for herbivores. When we remember how social ungulates such as the American Bison and African Springbok dominated huge areas of the earth before civilised man eliminated them, we should be cautious before we follow custom and describe the Red Deer as a forest animal.

Even when compelled to frequent woodlands the efficient social network of Red Deer still concentrates them into attractive but perhaps undesirable areas. Many a disgruntled farmer and forester has prefaced the death-sentence with—'I don't mind two or three, but half-a-dozen of the beggars . . .' Consequently our woodland Red Deer seldom survive in more than small parties, and their existence for a long time depended on another old landowning family, the Sandys of Graythwaite Hall, whose efforts are now ably and generously reinforced by the Forestry Commission at Grizedale.

The status of groups surviving around Thirlmere and elsewhere is precarious; indeed the finest deer of the whole countryside, those of the limestone escarpment south-west of Kendal, have recently been almost exterminated. Such deer, compelled to spend the daylight hours immobile in dense cover (they are noisy and clumsy browsers) can only emerge to graze at dusk and dawn. It would be hard for them to survive in winter without a full belly of coarse herbage to ruminate on; the internal 'compost heap' effect of rapid bacterial activity and fermentation must be very comforting in these circumstances. Two activities originating under these conditions seem peculiar to the Lake District. Yew is a favourite food of all deer (invaluably it flowers in midwinter) and in some woods the browse-line has been pushed out of reach; here the stags have acquired the knack of snapping off large branches with a twist of their antlers. (The same technique has developed in the Eland of Central Africa.) The other habit resembles the 'yarding' of North American deer. In areas selected for shelter and freedom from the drip of overhanging trees groups of Red Deer of either sex will pack together on winter nights. It is suspected that a morale-boosting effect is involved here.

Whatever the circumstances Red Deer groups always employ wallows —peaty or muddy baths situated on lines of travel—which, if conditions permit, are kept open on the same sites for generations. Both sexes use them at all seasons and many explanations have been offered for this habit. In spring it certainly discourages parasites and the irritation of loosening hair; in autumn it is a typical 'displacement-activity' of the sex-crazed stags—one of those apparently inappropriate actions that serve as a release for a thwarted impulse. Occasionally the observer is fortunate enough to witness a startling upsurge of excitement within a staid party of hinds on reaching a wallow; chasing activity, aimless prancing and numerous fights with battling forelegs break out—indeed the order of dominance manifests itself most clearly on these occasions. Here the ancient predator-prey relationship between wolf and deer provides the probable explanation. Wallowing is an excellent method of breaking scent and in a crisis precedence would be vital.

A similar purpose presumably underlies the hedgehog's well-authenticated habit of inuncting itself with saliva or evil-smelling material such as faeces. A similar foible has disgusted every dog-owner, suggesting that the predator also employed olfactory camouflage before hunting.

Once clearly seen, the antlers of a mature stag are as recognisable as the human face. This is unique in Nature, enabling the experienced observer to follow the fortunes of individuals for many years. Although cast annually the new antlers will closely resemble the old, with the appropriate changes for age and illness: notably, a limb-injury produces a distortion on the opposite side. Indeed the 'velvet' which protects and nourishes the growing antler is richly innervated and the completed antlers represent a basic expression of the deer's personality.

To secure a memento it is unnecessary to kill a particular animal; with patience and knowledge of the beast's habits the cast antlers can be found in many cases. The writer has picked up over seventy Roe antlers during the past twenty years and many more from Red Deer. The ultimate objective is to secure a series from the same individual and also its photograph.

Fundamentally, antlers are a cervine status symbol, not weapons, and their use in impressive rituals to overawe rivals constitutes a fascinating complex of 'superiority comportments' (the ugly term of the animal psychologists). The physiological strain of growing huge and complex antlers (the woodland deer of course greatly excel the under-privileged hill stags) is compensated by easy success in the rut. The converse occurs with a 'switch' stag. This beast has merely a brow tine and a bare upright, the perfect sword-like fighting weapon: had combat been decisive, evolution would by now have secured the preponderance of this mutation. Instead it is rare, and Highland stalkers call the switch quarrelsome—the old *post hoc propter hoc* fallacy. The unlucky beast merely becomes involved in repeated battles because his contemporaries misread him as an upstart youngster.

At least four species of deer seek to enhance their status by carrying tangles of vegetation in their antlers. Only last summer the writer observed a rutting Roebuck bearing aloft a tangle of shredded bracken that seriously impeded his forward vision, and twelve years earlier found the remains of a Martindale stag that had fallen panic-stricken to his death in a gully with scores of yards of abandoned field telephone-cable entwined about his head.

When cast, antlers are destroyed in a few years by deer, sheep and rodents hungry for calcium and phosphorus, but if preserved are almost indestructible. Macpherson records a complaint of the Countess of Pembroke that, in 1648, roving soldiers had removed from the 'Hartshorn tree' on Whinfell some antlers placed there by her ancestor in 1333.

Roe Deer

The Roe (Plate 31) is our second-largest native mammal and, until recently, the most neglected. In any other sphere a 'come-back' such as this resilient little beauty has made over the past fifty years would have been cheered and charted; instead it took place almost unaided and unrecognised; symptomatically, no tolerable photograph of a wild British Roe was in existence before 1952.

Roe were not highly regarded as beasts of the chase, and, being closely attached to their own small territories, were easily poached by hungry peasants. The species had almost vanished from England by the seventeenth century.

Lakeland has been repopulated in two ways. The native stock always survived in the Solway mosses. Seventy years ago Macpherson believed that a few might have reoccupied some woods near Armathwaite in the Eden Valley, which are still a stronghold of theirs. With the respite of World War I they were able to spread widely up the Eden and its tributaries, and, with World War II established themselves securely in the north-west of the Lake District. In the woods near Keswick they have now linked up with even more widespread descendants of a few Austrian Roe liberated near Windermere about seventy years ago. The latter have occupied all suitable habitats as far west as the industrial coastline and southward to the shore of Morecambe Bay; indeed their southerly thrust has carried them well beyond our area.

The Roe is a true forest dweller and distinctly asocial. Each spring the young of the previous year leave the parental territory and wander haphazardly until they find a suitable niche—a dangerous period, until with the upsurge of the bracken they vanish for the summer like bronze dolphins into a green sea.

A pair of Roe will occupy the same area, of perhaps thirty acres, for many years. The buck clears his new-grown antlers of velvet in the spring and marks the periphery of his territory with frayed saplings and hoof-scrapes, 'setting' scent in the process. The rut is in late July and his intense jealousy wanes with the autumn. Refugees from areas rendered uninhabitable by the nakedness of winter are permitted to assemble in the more secluded hideouts, but there is no social cohesion within the parties of six or eight sometimes seen at this season. Unfortunately such groups are often reported as fabulous general increases in numbers.

Even if given total protection Roe do not usually eat out their habitat, being browsers rather than grazers, and rather choosy; when vital winter foods such as bramble, honeysuckle and dormant fern-shoots have become scarce the population thins out. Unfortunately man often nullifies their natural control-methods. In Lakeland the ruthless infiltration of lorry-borne wintering sheep has ruined most of our native broad-leaved woodlands since World War II. The greed of the few has presented us with an ecological disaster, a minor effect of which has been to push the browse-line beyond the reach of the Roe. Too much grazing instead of browsing leads to heavy infestation with parasites, and population 'crashes' have occurred. Although Roe continue to appear in new areas, their total population in the Lake District has certainly fallen over the past ten years.

The modern forestry-technique of planting large conifer-blocks carries its own hazard; such an area is ideal for Roe until the canopy closes over, when it becomes rapidly sterile. Unless further suitable sites are available near by, drastic culling is necessary. This problem was first clearly propounded by Mr Jack Chard of the Forestry Commission. Thanks to his guidance and enthusiasm and that of a few enlightened colleagues, the

Commission has done much to reconcile forestry, sport and conservation throughout England.

Roe have certainly demonstrated their capacity to coexist with man, notably by their survival on Leith Hill, twenty-five miles (40 kilometres) from Charing Cross, and eighty years after their escape from a Victorian paddock. In our area they survive not only in many niches alongside heavy traffic, but also close to a main railway-line and a large quarry-cum-stone-crushing plant. Indeed they are pathetically vulnerable to the fascination of regular human activity. The writer remembers one family party that invariably spent the day watching the loading of rockery-stone; and a woodman found six or eight Roe most reluctant to leave his lop-and-top bonfire when he arrived at work throughout a recent frosty fortnight—they were breakfasting on the tangle of warm twigs around the still smoking centre.

As a result of current treatment a Roe population is like an iceberg, only one seventh appearing on the surface—the inexperienced and the displaced. But these innocent outlaws are infinitely forgiving; under strict protection the old buck whose photograph appears on Plate 31 suddenly reversed his implacable shyness in what was probably his eighth summer and regularly at twilight allowed his admirers to walk past within thirty yards (27 metres).

Other Deer

Fallow have been unlucky in the area. They were formerly kept in several parks, of which but two remain—Holker near Cartmel and Dalemain near Penrith. A few outliers from the former used to be seen occasionally in the neighbouring mosses. Wild Fallow are precariously established just outside our district in dense limestone woodlands near Arnside and stragglers have occasionally reached Whitbarrow Scar (Plate 16). Both these stocks are of the beautiful Mesnil type, a very light-brown coat, white-spotted throughout the year, and lethally visible in the winter woods.

After two centuries the deer of Gowbarrow Park were allowed to become extinct quite recently. The National Trust can hardly be proud of this loss.

Sika Deer are thinly established on the Forest of Bowland, and, being great travellers, one or two stags have appeared in our area.

One of these succeeded in breeding with a Red hind on Cartmel Fell and at least eight hybrids were produced. These animals were fertile and, as the offspring tended to resemble the Sika, they have had to be eliminated to avoid deterioration of the native Red Deer.

List of Lakeland Mammals

Hedgehog (*Erinaceus europaeus*) Common, except on open mountains and moorland. Numbers appear unchecked by road traffic casualties.

Common Shrew (*Sorex araneus*) Very widespread.

Pygmy Shrew (*Sorex minutus*) Very widespread.

Water Shrew (*Neomys fodiens*) Well established in suitable habitats.

Mole (*Talpa europea*) Common in all habitats up to 1500 feet (450 metres). Reported from 2000 feet (610 metres).

Rabbit (*Oryctolagus cuniculus*) See page 176.

Brown Hare (*Lepus europaeus*) See page 178.

Blue or Mountain Hare (*Lepus timidus*) Successfully established near Ulverston 1903–11. No records since World War II. Probably exterminated long before. See page 179.

Bank Vole (*Clethyrionomys glareolus*) Well established in suitable habitats. Needs deeper cover than Field Vole.

Short-tailed or Field Vole (*Microtus agrestis*) Our commonest and most widespread mammal. See page 180.

Water Vole (*Arvicola amphibius*) Well established in suitable habitats.

Long-tailed Field Mouse (*Apodemus sylvaticus*) Well established in suitable habitats. Preference for older deciduous woods.

Harvest Mouse (*Micromys minutus*) A very few Victorian records from near Silloth. Possibly imported with fodder.

Dormouse (*Muscardinus avellanarius*) No post-war records from area. Established in the seaward valleys in Macpherson's time (1892). Losing ground in the face of modern husbandry.

House Mouse (*Mus musculus*) Common. Distribution normally coincides with man's.

Brown Rat (*Rattus norvegicus*) Common. Losing ground in countryside as stackyards vanish.

Red Squirrel (*Sciurus vulgaris*) Present in most suitable woodlands. See page 181.

Grey Squirrel (*Sciurus carolinensis*)   Stragglers reported since World War II. Profoundly hoped not yet breeding. See page 181.

Fox, Common (*Vulpes vulpes*)   See page 182.

Badger (*Meles meles*)   Well established in some areas. See page 183.

Otter (*Lutra lutra*)   See page 184.

Pine Marten (*Martes martes*)   On verge of extermination for seventy years. Possible slight recent improvement. See page 185.

Stoat (*Mustela erminea*)   Widespread. Less common since myxomatosis. Ermines often reported in winter.

Weasel (*Mustela nivalis*)   Widespread.

Polecat (*Mustela putorius*)   Extinct in area for nearly a century. Polecat-ferret escapes may cause confusion. Also the next species. Habitat low-lying marshy areas.

Mink (*Mustela vison*)   Escapes from fur-farm probably now established in Eskdale. Riparian habitat similar to Polecat.

Red Deer (*Cervus elaphus*)   See page 186.

Roe deer (*Capreolus capreolus*)   See page 189.

Fallow Deer (*Dama dama*)   Rare straggler only. See page 191.

Sika Deer (*Cervus nippon*)   Very rare straggler. See page 191.

Coypu (*Mycaster copyus*)   Four killed near Hawkshead 1960–61. Ill-conceived attempt of introduction believed terminated by this.

Bats   Six species believed resident in the area: Pipistrelle (*Pipistrella pipistrellus*); Whiskered (*Myotis mystacinsu*); Natterer's (*Myotis nattereri*); Noctule (*Nyctalus noctula*); Daubenton's (*Myotis daubentoni*); and Long-eared (*Plecotus auritus*). Barbastelle (*Barbastella barbastellus*) has not been recorded for over a century. Observation in this field is badly needed.

EPILOGUE

The writing of this book has been, we believe, a source of great joy to all the contributors. This is partly because we are all writing from our own personal experience, and each creature or piece of landscape described brings back to memory some particular scramble or walk; but also because, like all enthusiasts, we have a strong desire to share with others something of what we ourselves have found.

Our chief concern is how the richness can be passed on to our descendants without too great a loss. Some loss is inevitable. From all sides the wild country of the Lake District is being threatened, as it is in other parts of this overcrowded island.

As we have seen in the preceding sections nature never stands still; the face of the Lake District is changing all the time under the influence of wind, snow, ice and rain, and through the action of its countless inhabitants large and small. A rapid increase in the number of rabbits or deer (or its sudden decrease), the spread of some vigorous plant, or the predations of some insect, can quickly alter the face of the countryside; but the tempo of change was greatly accelerated by the coming of man, and has been reaching a crescendo during the past fifty years or so.

Threats to existing habitats and communities may come from many quarters. In the first instance, draining, tree-felling, clearing the land and the process of agriculture altered the mountain slopes and the valley floors. We have already discussed the immense changes brought about by sheep rearing. The woodlands were further altered by coppicing for charcoal in order to smelt the iron ore of the Furness area. Quarrying for slate and mining for lead, barytes and copper all left their scars—some very big ones such as the copper mines at Coniston.

Changes in land use of this kind need not necessarily have any great effect either on Natural History or amenities if only a relatively small part of a vast total area is involved, as in the U.S.A.; or where the scale is immense, as in Switzerland. In the Lake District it is very different. Here the total area is very small and a great variety of scenery and habitats is packed into it with such delicate adjustments between parts that only a small disturbance of one part can seriously upset the balance of the whole.

During the past century more serious alterations to the appearance and general ecology of the Lake District have arisen through considerable re-afforestation to produce timber for commercial purposes. Large areas of the fellside have been planted with conifers—planted so densely that after the first few years all undergrowth disappears except in the rides. It is encouraging that in recent years the foresters have shown a much greater desire to blend forests into the landscape, and there has been most welcome co-operation with the naturalists in leaving certain areas unplanted and by introducing a judicious mixture of hardwood.

Also during the past century, there has been a vastly increased demand for water both for domestic consumption and for industry, and it is only natural that the water engineers should turn to districts of heavy rainfall and deep valleys such as the Lake District. Thirlmere, Haweswater and Wet Sleddale are already reservoirs, other lakes are having water drawn from them, and thirsty eyes are already upon most of the others. This is only to be expected, but the flooding of a valley may well destroy a unique natural community, and increasing the surface area of water can alter the climate of a whole district, thereby substantially altering the communities that inhabit it. Alternative methods of obtaining water are being vigorously sought and there is little doubt that ultimately other and more economic methods will be found than flooding valleys and impounding the water in reservoirs, but for the moment that still remains by far the cheapest method.

More recent still, and no less drastic in its results, has been the introduction of mechanised farming and the new methods associated with it. These are developing all the time to produce better crops, heavier yields and quicker returns, so that the livestock tends to be regarded solely as a means to production, like the parts of a great machine, rather than as living entities with rights of their own; and the intensive cultivation of the land is based on a very different policy from that adopted by our eighteenth-century ancestors, which has given us the English countryside of which we are so proud. Under the present system hedgerows disappear to give larger fields to the machines and with them go a rich habitat for birds, plants and insects; wire fencing replaces the old walls and with them goes yet another rich habitat for ferns, mosses, lichens, spiders and a host of other small creatures.

Yet another recent threat comes from the increasing popularity of the beauty-spots made easily accessible by new roads, more leisure and an affluent society. This applies with particular force to the Lake District. Not only does sheer weight of numbers in a small area tend to destroy or drive out wild life (we have already mentioned that the trample of feet on a once secluded bay has destroyed one rare plant) but with the development of tourism, promoters wish to put up amusement halls, lidos, ice-cream stalls, tea rooms, car parks and so forth to entertain and refresh them, all of which militate against wild life. With these many threats coming from so many and such diverse sources, some system of recognised 'watch dogs' becomes essential if genuinely wild life is to continue in this country at all except in the most inaccessible places.

Fortunately the danger is being faced by various organisations at all levels—national, regional and local, some statutory and many voluntary. Their powers are limited and all of them, national and local alike, are desperately short of the necessary finance. All of them, however, help to build up the strongest bulwark of all, which is an informed, deeply con-cerned and vocal public opinion. In this each of us has a part, and an impor-tant part, to play.

The chief national body is the Nature Conservancy. This is a statutory body now a component of the Natural Environment Research Council, dependent on the Treasury for its funds and therefore naturally account-able to the Treasury for all its expenditure. The Lake District is included in its northern region which has its headquarters at Merlewood Research Station, Grange-over-Sands. As its name suggests, the function of the Nature Conservancy is to conserve; and here a word of explantaion is often necessary. To 'conserve' is not the same thing as to 'preserve' though the two may overlap. To preserve something is to keep it as it is for an indefinite period; conservation only rightly applies to some living and developing organism, whether it be a single entity or a corporate body such as a plant community. To conserve it means to help it to go on developing unchecked along its natural lines of development. One can preserve a ruined castle, one cannot conserve it. To conserve an area of downland does not mean to leave it to itself—nature left to itself would quickly become a jungle—and characteristic downland plants would be exterminated by their unchecked hardier competitors. To conserve, there-fore, implies deliberate human control which must be to some extent arbitrary according to the particular end which the controller has in mind.

An example perhaps may make this clearer. In order to conserve the Lake District deer we must control them. We have already disturbed the balance of nature by eliminating their only serious predator, the wolf, some six centuries ago. Now their only serious enemy is man. If we left them to themselves they would rapidly multiply, and not only would they become a pest to neighbouring farmers but the herd itself would deteriorate owing to their being more in number than the area could support. Hence, in order to conserve, the herd has to be thinned out regularly by shooting. It is essential that the shooting be done with careful discrimination and not just haphazardly, still less for the sake of gaining trophies. In this way man is controlling the actual development and health of the herd.

Some of the most important areas of scientific interest have been designated as Nature Reserves and are administered by the Nature Conservancy. Other areas of importance have at the request of the Nature Conservancy been designated as Sites of Special Scientific Interest (S.S.S.I.). This designation gives little actual power to the Nature Conservancy but it does at least ensure consultation with the Nature Conservancy before any development can be undertaken, though even this is waived in the case of forestry or agriculture.

There are two national bodies, which are voluntary, whose principal aim is conservation. The Council for Nature is an association of field natural history societies, museums and other scientific bodies. This is able to deal with conservation problems at top level and exerts considerable influence. The other, and older, body is the Society for the Promotion of Nature Reserves (S.P.N.R.). This has come into much greater prominence during the last few years since the formation of the County Naturalists' Trusts of which it is the co-ordinating body. Norfolk and Yorkshire were the first counties to form Trusts and this was before World War II, but it was not until the late 1950s that many other counties followed suit; then, in the 1960s, there was a great burst of activity and by the middle of the decade there was hardly any part of Great Britain which was not included in some County Trust. Sometimes two or three counties are grouped together. The Lake District Naturalists' Trust (L.D.N.T.), covering Cumberland, Westmorland and the detached northern part of Lancashire, was founded in 1962.

There is no doubt about the great value of these local Trusts. Just because they are local they are able, by the vigilance of their members, to keep a close watch on the countryside and can often save a valuable site too small for the Nature Conservancy to deal with. The aims of the L.D.N.T. as set out in the prospectus are two-fold. Its first task is to find out and protect as far as possible such sites of scientific importance as are threatened, or likely to be threatened, by any of the forms of development already mentioned. Sometimes it may be one particular animal or plant we wish to safeguard, more often it will be a typical example of some particular habitat and the community it supports. The methods of protection will vary according to circumstances. It is not often that a County Trust has the funds to purchase a site outright, but various agreements can be entered into with the owner, either by lease, or permission to put in a full- or part-time warden, or by a gentleman's agreement to leave certain areas undisturbed. This applies equally to large firms or private individuals.

The second aim is educational—to build up for the future, mostly through children, an informed public opinion to appreciate, to reverence and to enjoy the riches of the countryside. The two aims are complementary, for there would be little use in educating an appreciative public if no more sites of interest were left. Much is being done in the Lake District by way of lectures throughout the year for residents and in summer for visitors; well-attended residential courses are run each year by the Extra-Mural Board of Newcastle University and other bodies. Several nature trails are in existence, some with guides at certain times of the year, all with a leaflet to enable them to be followed alone. In these ways interest is kindled and fostered in both adults and children. The children are the most important of all for it is on them that the preservation of our rapidly decreasing wild life must depend in the future.

With the widespread and rapid development of mechanisation in all departments of life, so that we can even talk of an electronic brain, reverence for life itself tends to be crushed out. Even if he so wished, the modern farmer can no longer lavish the devoted care on his stock that his grandfather did. With loss of reverence for life goes one of the most vital factors in living. It is our hope that this book, in giving some fuller knowledge of this very lovely part of our country, may help to stimulate a deeper reverence for that life with which it teems.

G. A. K. HERVEY

ORGANISATIONS WITH NATURAL HISTORY INTERESTS IN THE LAKE DISTRICT

The Brathay Hall Trust

In 1947 Brathay Hall, near Ambleside, was opened as a centre for adventurous holidays for boys in industry, and a few years later a separate Exploration Group was formed which has undertaken geographical and biological field studies in Britain and overseas.

In 1967 a Field Study Centre with a well-equipped laboratory and a rapidly expanding library was opened on the Brathay Estate. One-week courses of field study in geography and biology for Sixth Form boys and girls are organised by a well-qualified academic staff with the help of visiting teachers. Long-term field research projects in the Lake District are being carried out. The biology course is essentially ecological, and the main aim is to introduce students to the concept of environmental variation and habitat differences and to the techniques used to study their effect on plant and animal populations. There is close co-operation with the Nature Conservancy and the Lake District Naturalists' Trust, especially in the important matter of recording and indexing the data collected in various surveys.

The Council for the Preservation of Rural England

The national organisation of the Council for the Preservation of Rural England is centred in London, and the Lancashire Branch is located at Samlesbury Hall on the A677 between Preston and Blackburn. This branch has a full-time secretary, assistant secretary and staff to deal with the many queries and problems concerning the wise use of our rural areas.

Always the C.P.R.E. has been concerned about threats to habitats, in particular quarrying extraction, tree-felling activities and pollution of rivers, all of which directly affect wild life.

The Forestry Commission

Grizedale Forest, 7600 acres (3075 hectares) in extent, lies in the Furness Fells district between Windermere and Coniston Water. The underlying rock is Silurian slate and shale. Soils are generally thin, of a light clay nature, well mixed with grit and stones.

At Grizedale the Forestry Commission have provided many educational and recreational facilities aimed mainly at integrating wildlife management, forest management and public recreation. The main facilities are as follows: *Wildlife Centre*, which covers the three main species of deer and most of the other larger animals and birds of the district. A tape commentary also includes the sounds of the wild life.

Observation Hides where wild life may be viewed in natural surroundings.

Ridding Wood Nature Trail, a self-conducted trail illustrating wild life and forest management.

Research Nursery which concentrates mainly on tree genetics.

Forest Walks, colour marked and of varying distances, offering panoramic views of the Forest.

All displays and walks demonstrate the nature of a forest and the task of the forester, who has to balance the needs not only of timber production but of wildlife conservation and public recreation as well.

The Freshwater Biological Association

The Freshwater Biological Association is an independent body, grant-aided by the Government under the auspices of the Natural Environment Research Council. It is also supported by individual subscriptions, angling clubs, water authorities and industry.

The Association was set up to undertake fundamental research into a whole range of problems connected with water and aquatic animals and plants. It runs two laboratories, one at The Ferry House on the shore of Windermere (Plate 2) and the other on the River Frome in Dorset. The work done at these laboratories is published in journals that go all over the world.

Large numbers of visitors come to the Windermere Laboratory from Britain and overseas to consult the staff and use the library, which contains an extensive and unique collection of books and periodicals. Students come to be trained for work elsewhere and others come for shorter courses on freshwater biology.

The inexpensive scientific publications of the Freshwater Biological Association include a number that are keys for the identification of freshwater invertebrates, including crustaceans, mayflies, stoneflies, water-bugs, leeches and other worms, flatworms, etc. A detailed list may be obtained from the Librarian, The Ferry House, Far Sawrey, Ambleside.

The Friends of the Lake District

The Friends of the Lake District is a society founded thirty-five years ago to protect and cherish the landscape and natural beauty of the Lake District and the neighbouring countryside; to unite those who share these aims; and to take common action with other societies when need arises.

The society has opposed water abstraction schemes, the flooding of valleys, the general widening of dale roads, large-scale afforestation of the central fells and many other proposed developments which would have endangered the scenery and character of the Lake District. Much work has been done on the protection of rights of way, the registration of commons, and in the field of education, in the proper use of the National Park.

The Lake District Naturalists' Trust

The Lake District Naturalists' Trust manages, wholly or in part, more than a dozen Nature Reserves, is conducting long-term studies of ecological changes on land and in water, has arranged Nature Trails and produced pamphlets on aspects of Lakeland Natural History for free distribution to the public, and maintains a large number of well-used nesting-boxes spread over a wide area in differing habitats. Through the vigilance of its members and the co-operation of local authorities it has been able to save roadside verges from spraying and premature cutting, ponds and quarries with rich floras being used for tipping, birds and animals from undue disturbance.

In short the Trust tries to keep in close contact with all aspects of natural history over a large area in which pressures are increasing at an alarming rate and where, therefore, planned conservation is essential if many forms of plant and animal life are not be to irretrievably lost. The Trust welcomes the support of all who care for our native flora and fauna and for this beautiful but greatly threatened region.

Museums

The Museums at Carlisle, Kendal and Penrith have useful geological and natural history collections and exhibits with special reference to the Lake District.

National Park Centre

The Lake District National Park Centre at Brockhole, Windermere, opened in the summer of 1969. The Centre consists of a small country mansion set in thirty-two acres (13 hectares) of grounds and gardens and there is access to the lake shore. The object of the Centre is to encourage visitors' appreciation and understanding of the area. To further this end there is a modern exhibition tracing the development of the Lake District; material of interest to naturalists is included, but it is intended to have more detailed displays elsewhere in the house. The grounds include attractive formal gardens and a wooded area which is rich in bird life.

The National Trust

In the Lake District the Trust now protects 87,000 acres (35,200 hectares) and owns 73,000 acres (29,500 hectares) of them, much of it the most beautiful countryside in the British Isles. It allows as much public access to its properties as is consistent with the conservation of the features which prompted their acquisition and subject to the needs of agriculture and forestry, and the preservation of plant and animal life. Not surprisingly, several of its properties have been designated Sites of Special Scientific Interest; notable among them are Glencoyne Wood and Johnny's Wood in Borrowdale.

Nature Trails have been established in several properties in collaboration with the Lake District Naturalists' Trust, the Ambleside Field Society and the Freshwater Biological Association.

Natural History Societies

The following societies operate wholly or partly within the Lake District: Ambleside Field Society, Arnside and District Natural History Society,

Carlisle Natural History Society, Cumberland Geological Society, Eden Field Club, Grange-over-Sands Natural History Society, Kendal Natural History Society, Keswick Natural History Society, Lancaster and District Bird-watching Society, Penrith Natural History Society, West Cumberland Field Society.

These societies hold winter meetings and arrange summer excursions, and some, especially the Lancaster and District Bird-watching Society, take part in national enquiries or organise local ones. The Association of Lake Counties Natural History Societies co-ordinates the work of the societies and produces annual reports on the natural history of the region.

Regional or county representatives of national organisations such as the Botanical Society of the British Isles and the British Trust for Ornithology are resident in the area and can be contacted through the headquarters of the organisation.

The Nature Conservancy

The Nature Conservancy, a component body of the Natural Environment Research Council, is the national body responsible for the establishment of National Nature Reserves, provision of advice on the conservation and control of the flora and fauna of Britain, and for the research related to these objectives.

The Conservancy's aims in the Lake District are to protect and rehabilitate examples of the wide range of semi-natural habitats present, and, in a farming and forestry area strongly influenced by tourism and amenity considerations, to bring about the integration of conservation measures in the general planning of a policy for land use. Work towards these ends is carried out by the North Regional Office and Merlewood Research Station from Grange-over-Sands.

National Nature Reserves so far established (May 1969) include Roudsea Wood, a Reserve of remarkable diversity with acid oakwood, limestone mixed woodland, and also areas of peat and alluvium; and three small peat Reserves, North Fen, Blelham Bog and Rusland Moss, representing stages in the characteristic succession from fen to bog. A local Nature Reserve on Drigg Dunes has, notably, Black-headed Gull and Tern breeding colonies. Some sixty-eight Sites of Special Scientific Interest have been notified to the Lake District Planning Board. These are the focal points of conservation activity, and survey continues.

The contribution made by the Research Station has included the study of characteristic woodland nutrient cycles, but is now more directed towards woodland classification, between site and within site comparisons, and woodland management studies, to form the basis of conservation treatment and advice.

Nature Trails

Several trails, with explanatory leaflets, through different types of Lakeland habitat have been established by such bodies as the Forestry Commission, Manchester Corporation, National Trust, Lake District Naturalists' Trust and local Natural History Societies, and new ones are steadily being added to the list. Among the best known are those at The Swirls and Launchy Ghyll on Thirlmere, Grizedale Forest, Penny Rock between Rydal Water and Grasmere, Skelghyll Wood near Ambleside, Claife Heights on the west side of Windermere, and Brantwood near Coniston. Further information can be obtained from the caravans of the National Park Information Service.

Talks on the Lake District National Park

During the summer months illustrated talks on geology, natural history and some aspects of human activity are provided by the University of Newcastle-upon-Tyne and the Lake District Planning Board as a service for visitors. The talks are held on Monday to Friday evenings at Keswick and Ambleside and are designed to form a linked series, repeated weekly, although each talk is complete in itself. Excursions are run in connection with the geological talks.

This provision began at Keswick in 1961 and later the Ambleside venue was added. Organisation and the bulk of the cost are met by the Department of Adult Education, University of Newcastle, to whom any enquiries should be directed. There is a small charge for admission.

Youth Hostels Association: Field Study Facilities

The Lakeland region of the Youth Hostels Association has hostels equipped for field studies at Hawkshead and at High Close, near Elterwater. Both hostels offer simple laboratory and library facilities, and can accommodate about thirty-five students at any one time. They are particularly suitable for senior school or university groups with their own teaching staff; no instruction is provided by the Y.H.A. Hawkshead field study centre is in an area especially suitable for the study of freshwater ecology; High Close is in Langdale, an interesting geological and hill-farming area. A nominal extra charge over and above the normal bed-night fee is made for the use of the centres, but there is no restriction on access to the laboratory facilities during the normal closed hours of the hostels.

BIBLIOGRAPHY

Alvin, K. L. and Kershaw, K. A. (1963). *The Observer's Book of Lichens* London, Warne.

Angus, R. B. (1964). Some Coleoptera from Cumberland, Westmorland and the northern part of Lancashire. *Entomologists' mon. Mag.* **100**: 61–69.

Armitt, M. L. (1897–1901). *Studies of Lakeland Birds.* Ambleside.

Baker, J. G. (1885). *A Flora of the English Lake District.* London, Bell.

Blezard, E. (1943). *The Birds of Lakeland.* Trans. Carlisle nat. Hist. Soc. vi.

Blezard, E. (1954). *Lakeland Ornithology.* Trans. Carlisle nat. Hist. Soc. viii.

Boycott, A. E. (1929). The Mollusca of Great Langdale, Westmorland. *N.West Nat.* **4**: 10–13, 50–53.

Boycott, A. E. (1934). The habitats of land Mollusca in Britain. *J. Ecol.* **22**: 1–38.

Boycott, A. E. (1936). The habitats of fresh-water Mollusca in Britain. *J. Anim. Ecol.* **5**: 116–86.

Brightman, F. H. (1966). *The Oxford Book of Flowerless Plants.* London, O.U.P.

Brinkhurst, R. O. (1959). The habitats and distribution of British *Gerris* and *Velia* species. *J. Soc. Br. Ent.* **6**: 37–44.

Bristowe, W. S. (1949). The distribution of Harvestmen in Great Britain and Ireland. *J. Anim. Ecol.* **18**: 1.

Bristowe, W. S. (1958). *The World of Spiders.* London, Collins.

Britten, H. (1912). *The Arachnida of Cumberland.* Trans. Carlisle nat. Hist. Soc. ii.

Campbell, B. (1954–55). The breeding distribution and habitats of the Pied Flycatcher (*Muscicapa hypoleuca*) in Britain. *Bird Study* **1**: 81–101, **2**: 24–32, 179–91.

Clapham, A. R., Tutin, T. G. and Warburg, E. F. (1962). *Flora of the British Isles.* C.U.P.

Corbet, G. B. (1966). *The Terrestrial Mammals of Western Europe.* London, Foulis.

Davidson, W. F. (1959). Some insects (mainly Coleoptera) of the Caldbeck Fells in Cumberland. *Entomologist's Rec. J. Var.* **71**: 83–86.

Davidson, W. F. (1961). Notes on Cumberland and Westmorland Coleoptera. *Entomologist's mon. Mag.* **97**: 15–21.

Darling, F. F. (1937). *A herd of Red Deer.* O.U.P.

Ellis, A. E. (1969 edition). *British Snails.* O.U.P.

Farrer, W. J. (1896). Notes on the land and freshwater Mollusca of the English Lake District. *J. Conch., Lond.* **8**: 152–61.

Findlay, W. P. K. (1967). *Wayside and Woodland Fungi.* London, Warne.

Frazer, J. F. D. (1954). The breeding habits of toads (*Bufo bufo*) in Lake Windermere. *Br. J. Herpet.* **1**(9): 153–9.

Frost, W. E. (1965). Breeding habits of Windermere charr (*Salvelinus willughbii* (Günther)) and their bearing on speciation of these fish. *Proc. R. Soc.* (B) **163**: 232–84.

Garnett, Marjory (1946). Winter birds on Windermere—a retrospect. In *Lakeland Natural History.* Trans. Carlisle nat. Hist. Soc. vii.

Golley, J. and Davis, R. (1964). *Principles in Mammalogy.* London, Chapman and Hall (Reinhart).

Gresswell, R. K. (1952). The glacial geomorphology of the south-eastern part of the Lake District. *Lpool. Manchr. geol. J.* **1**: 57–70.

Gresswell, R. K. (1958), The post-glacial raised beach of Furness and Lyth, north Morecambe Bay. *Trans. Inst. Br. Geogr.* **25**: 79–103.

Gresswell, R. K. (1962). The glaciology of the Coniston basin. *Lpool. Manchr. geol. J.* **3**: 83–96.

Harris, J. R. (1952). *An Angler's Entomology.* London, Collins.

Heath, J. (1959). The autecology of *Eustroma reticulata* Schiff. (Lep. Geometridae) in the Lake District. *J. Soc. Br. Ent.* **6**: 45–51.

Hering, T. F. (1966). The terricolous higher fungi of four Lake District woodlands. *Trans. Br. mycol. Soc.* **49** (3): 369–83.

Hodgson, W. (1898). *Flora of Cumberland.* Carlisle, Meals.

Holden, A. E. (1952). *Plant Life in the Scottish Highlands.* Edinburgh, Oliver and Boyd.

Hollingworth, S. E. (1954). The geology of the Lake District—a review, *Proc. Geol. Ass.* **65**: 385–402.

Kloet, G. S. and Hincks, W. D. (1945). *A check list of British insects.* Arbroath, Buncle.

Kok, Annette (1966). A short history of the Orchil dyes. *Lichenologist* **3**(2): 248–72.

Lange, M. and Hora, F. B. (1963). *Collins' Pocket Guide to Mushrooms and Toadstools*. London, Collins.

Leckie, J. D. (1951). The food of pine martens. *Mammal Society Bulletin No. 8*.

Lewis, W. V. (1960). The problem of cirque erosion (in) Investigations on Norwegian cirque glaciers. *R.G.S. Res. Ser.* **4**: 97–100.

Linton, D. L. (1957). Radiating valleys in glaciated lands. *Tijdschr. K. ned. Aardrijksk. Genoot.* **74**: 297–312.

Locket, G. H. and Millidge, A. F. (1951–53). *British Spiders* Vols. I and II. London, Ray Society.

Macan, T. T. (1950). Ecology of fresh-water Mollusca in the English Lake District. *J. Anim. Ecol.* **19**: 124–46.

Macan, T. T. and Worthington, E. B. (1969). *Life in Lakes and Rivers*. London, Collins.

Macpherson, H. A. (1892). *A Vertebrate Fauna of Lakeland*. Edinburgh, Douglas.

Mammal Society (1969). The otter in Britain. *Oryx* **10**(**1**): 16–22.

Manley, G. (1959). The late glacial climate of north-west England. *Lpool. Manchr. geol. J.* **2**: 188–215.

Marr, J. E. (1916). *The geology of the Lake District*. C.U.P.

Matthews, J. R. (1955). *Origin and distribution of British flora*. London, Hutchinson.

Mitchell, G. H. (1956). The geological history of the Lake District. *Proc. Yorks. geol. Soc.* **30**: 407–63.

Monkhouse, F. J. (1960). *The English Lake District*. The British Landscape through Maps, No. 1, Sheffield, The Geographical Association.

Moon, H. P. (1957). The distribution of *Asellus* in Windermere. *J. Anim. Ecol.* **26**: 113–23.

Moon, H. P. (1968). The colonisation of Esthwaite Water and Ullswater, English Lake District, by *Asellus* (Crustacea, Isopoda). *J. Anim. Ecol.* **37**: 405–15.

Newman, E. (n.d.). *Illustrated Natural History of British Butterflies and Moths*. London, Hardwicke and Bogue.

Parker, J. R. (1962). British spiders: new species and records. *Ann. Mag. nat. Hist.* **13**: v.

Parker, J. R. and Duffey, E. (1963). Notes on the genus *Maro* (Araneae). *Ann. Mag. nat. Hist.* **13**: vi.

Pearsall, W. H. (1921). The development of vegetation in the English Lakes, considered in relation to the general evolution of glacial lakes and rock basins. *Proc. R. Soc. (B)* **93**: 259–84.

Pearsall, W. H. (1950). *Mountains and Moorlands*. London, Collins.

Pearson, W. (1863). *Papers, Letters and Journals*. London, Faithfull.

Ratcliffe, D. A. (1960). The mountain flora of Lakeland. *Proc. bot. Soc. Br. Isl.* **4**: 1–25.

Ratcliffe, D. A. (1963). The status of the Peregrine in Great Britain. *Bird Study* **10**: 56–90.

Ratcliffe, D. A. (1965). Organo-chlorine residues in some raptor and corvid eggs from Northern Britain. *Br. Birds* **58**: 65–81.

Raven, J. and Walters, M. (1956) *Mountain Flowers*. London, Collins.

Reynoldson, T. B. (1966). The distribution and abundance of lake-dwelling triclads: towards a hypothesis. *Adv. ecol. Res.* **3**: pp. 71.

Satchell, J. E. (1962) Resistance in oak (*Quercus* spp.) to defoliation by *Tortrix viridana* L. in Roudsea Wood National Nature Reserve. *Ann. appl. Biol.* **50**: 431–42.

Shackleton, E. H. (1966). *Lakeland geology—where to go: what to see*. Clapham, Dalesman Publishing Co.

Shorten, M. (1954). *Squirrels*. London, Collins.

Smith, M. (1951). *The British amphibians and reptiles*. London, Collins.

Southern, H. N. (1964). *Handbook of British Mammals*. Oxford, Blackwell.

Stokoe, R. (1962). *The Birds of the Lake Counties*. Trans. Carlisle nat. Hist. Soc. x.

Summerhayes, V. S. (1941). The effect of voles (*Microtus agrestis*) on vegetation. *J. Ecol.* **29**: 14–48.

Tansley, A. G. (1939). *The British Isles and their Vegetation*. C.U.P.

Taylor, R. H. R. (1948). The distribution of reptiles and Amphibia in the British Isles, with notes on species recently introduced. *Br. J. Herpet.* **1**: 1–38.

Williams, C. B. (1958). *Insect Migration*. London, Collins.

Wilson, A. (1938). *The Flora of Westmorland*. Arbroath, Buncle.

Wordsworth, W. (1835) *A Guide through the District of the Lakes in the North of England*. (5th edition). Kendal, Hudson.

Yapp, W. B. (1962). *Birds and Woods*. London, O.U.P.

INDEX

Scientific names of birds and mammals will be found in the lists on pages 173–5 and 192–3

THE LAKE DISTRICT

Lake District National Park Boundary — – – –
Roads ————
Railways ————
Land over 500 feet shown in brown tint

Scale

Miles